Penguin Books

D0038835

Style and Civilization / Edited by John Fleming and Hugh Honour

High Renaissance

Michael Levey has been interested in the Renaissance since he first read Browning and Pater on hot afternoons at school during the Second World War.

Among his books are several on aspects of eighteenth-century European art, a recently republished biography of Mozart, and three novels. He is also the author of *The World of Ottoman Art*. From 1951 to 1986 he worked at the National Gallery, becoming Director in 1973; he was knighted in 1981. He is married to Brigid Brophy and they have a daughter and three grandchildren.

High Renaissance is the sequel to his widely-praised *Early Renaissance* in the same series, published in 1967 and awarded the Hawthornden Prize – the first paperback to receive such an award.

Michael Levey

Style and Civilization

High Renaissance

Penguin Books

PENGUIN BOOKS

Published by the Penguin Group
Penguin Books Ltd, 27 Wrights Lane, London W8 5TZ, England
Penguin Books USA Inc., 375 Hudson Street, New York, New York 10014, USA
Penguin Books Australia Ltd, Ringwood, Victoria, Australia
Penguin Books Canada Ltd, 10 Alcorn Avenue, Toronto, Ontario, Canada M4V 3B2
Penguin Books (NZ) Ltd, 182–190 Wairau Road, Auckland 10, New Zealand

Penguin Books Ltd, Registered Offices: Harmondsworth, Middlesex, England

First published in Pelican Books 1975
Published in Penguin Books 1991
10 9 8 7 6 5 4 3 2 1

Printed in England by Clays Ltd, St Ives plc
Set in Monophoto Garamond

Designed by Gerald Cinamon

In memory of
TONY RICHARDSON
(1941–69)
one-time publishing editor at Penguin Books

Contents

Editorial Foreword

The series to which this book belongs is devoted to both the history and the problems of style in European art. It is expository rather than critical. The aim is to discuss each important style in relation to contemporary shifts in emphasis and direction both in the other, non-visual arts and in thought and civilization as a whole. By examining artistic styles in this wider context it is hoped that closer definitions and a deeper understanding of their fundamental character and motivation will be reached.

The series is intended for the general reader but it is written at a level which should interest the specialist as well. Beyond this there has been no attempt at uniformity. Each author has had complete liberty in his mode of treatment and has been free to be as selective as he wished – for selection and compression are inevitable in a series, such as this, whose scope extends beyond the history of art. Not all great artists or great works of art can be mentioned, far less discussed. Nor, more specifically, is it intended to provide anything in the nature of an historical survey, period by period, but rather a discussion of the artistic concepts dominant in each successive period. And, for this purpose, the detailed analysis of a few carefully chosen issues is more revealing than the bird's-eye view.

Acknowledgements

This book owes much to John Fleming and Hugh Honour who commissioned it and have waited patiently for it. The text has benefited from their comments and suggestions, just as the author has throughout benefited from their friendly encouragement. Great practical help was kindly given also by them in collecting many of the relevant photographs.

At Penguin Books Nikos Stangos has shown generous interest and has done much to foster the book's publication.

To all three people I am warmly grateful; and I hope they will accept this acknowledgement, while – I should like to think – joining with me in the dedication of the result.

M. L.

London, July 1973

High Renaissance

... these Arts, in their highest province, are not addressed to the gross senses, but to the desires of the mind, to that spark of divinity which we have within, impatient of being circumscribed and pent up by the world which is about us.

REYNOLDS: *Discourse XIII*

I

The 'Highest Province' and the High Renaissance

With his sight failing and his hearing gone, Sir Joshua Reynolds addressed the Royal Academy students for the last time in December 1790, aware that this was indeed likely to be his last opportunity to speak to them. Never before had he been so openly autobiographical and reminiscent. Never before, perhaps, had he been moved to such dramatic eloquence. He had travelled a good deal and studied, on the spot, art of many periods. He was a sensitive connoisseur, and a collector, as well as a painter. He had often surveyed art in his discourses and defended the power of the imagination, always coming back to that period of the great style, that 'highest province' exemplified by Titian's 'kind of magick', the 'exquisite grace' of Correggio and Parmigianino, Raphael's purity and correctness, and by Michelangelo's vast and sublime ideas.

Reynolds never used the term 'High Renaissance', but he had come close enough to it in referring to the *highest* province, for he boldly believed that there lay the supreme period of art; and his last discourse raises one final monument to the greatest genius of that great age, Michelangelo. Seldom rash in his pronouncements, Reynolds now levelled the ground so drastically both before and after Michelangelo that he declared him 'the exalted Founder and Father of modern art', whose divine energy had brought art to sudden maturity, while subsequently 'the Art has been in a gradual state of decline'. And so it was fitting as well as moving that the last word of Reynolds's last discourse should be in tribute to the sublimity and grandeur and perfection of a heroic artistic period, all summed up by his solemn farewell pronouncement of the name Michelangelo.

Whether or not sharing his esteem for Michelangelo, few people would nowadays turn to Reynolds for their art history. It is simply not true that from Michelangelo onwards art declined – any more than that he had been single-handedly responsible for bringing it to a 'sudden maturity'. Quite apart from his own role, it had long been mature and its development was the very opposite of sudden. Yet, nobody perhaps has ever better characterized the grandeur of the period now usually called the High Renaissance than Reynolds.

Reynolds's views were the result of a number of factors, but they notably accorded eventually with those of Vasari, surveying art from the standpoint of the mid sixteenth century. Vasari never travelled outside Italy but he too tried to appreciate widely, and he too was a collector as well as being painter, writer and architect. In publishing his *Lives* of the most famous painters, sculptors and architects in 1550, Vasari had divided art, like Gaul, into three parts: three periods he thought he could distinguish, comparable to childhood, youth and maturity in human life. A renaissance had begun with Giotto; it was followed by an improved age, youthful but greatly advanced, in which the arts came close to capturing Nature: 'the truth of Nature was exactly imitated'. And finally there had come the modern, mature age, Vasari's own: at once graceful, inventive, diverse and accomplished. A whole range of artistic Himalayas had been thrown up, but its Everest was undoubtedly Michelangelo whose work represented the most absolute perfection ('*una molto più assoluta perfezione*'). Beyond him Vasari saw virtually nothing, but he suspected a decline. No higher peak was visible; the path led only one way – down. After man's maturity comes old age; if art followed the cycle of human life, it was bound to decay. And Vasari would have been gratified to learn that approximately two and a half centuries later, Reynolds agreed that this is what had happened, as well as agreeing with his estimate of Michelangelo.

Vasari was, of course, a witness of much that he wrote about. To him Michelangelo was an artistic deity but also an actual living person whom one could meet and correspond with. Yet proximity can be a disadvantage to the historian, and hero-worship is always a hindrance. Vasari notoriously denigrated Tintoretto and largely misunderstood the aim of Venetian art. His art history has always a strong Tuscan accent. Increasing examination of the supposed break he saw between the rude 'Greek' manner and the miraculously improved style represented by Giotto has shown that this was not so much a simplification as positively misleading, because Byzantine influence on the evolution of Italian painting is demonstrable. The inferior plane on which he placed fifteenth-century art, until the arrival of Leonardo da Vinci, was a somewhat contrived depression, designed to throw into more effective relief the rocky eminence where modern giants sat enthroned. The very words he used to define the new style the latter practised – freedom (*licenzia*), diversity (*varietà*), charm (*vaghezza*) and grace (*grazia*) – require definition to make it plain why these qualities were not sufficiently embodied already in the work of, say, Agostino di Duccio or Botticelli. Vasari was a pioneer in writing about the story of art as well as artists (where his facts were often totally wrong), but he had a pioneer's faults.

Both he and Reynolds are guilty of claiming too sweeping and too ultimate a superiority for the artistic period represented very approximately by the lifetime of Michelangelo (1475–1564), which may be presumed to have seen the creation of any High Renaissance style that might exist. But when that objection has been made, there is an accord between the two men so striking as to suggest that some shift, shift rather than break, must have taken place in that period for them to believe that it was then that a new 'modern' or 'great' style came into existence. And it must be said that most scholars, critics and theorists who have looked at European art have inclined to agree with them, though not everyone has been able to respond with such eloquence, and some – like Ruskin – have been unable to respond with enthusiasm. Taking belated revenge for Vasari's slights on Tintoretto, one of his heroes, Ruskin thus introduced his own view of the High Renaissance: 'Then Raphael, Michael Angelo, and Titian, bring about the deadly change, playing into each other's hands – Michael Angelo being the chief captain in evil.'

There is something, indeed much, to be said for Ruskin's view. It was based on exactly the same observations as had been made by Reynolds and Vasari – different though their conclusions had been. Reynolds had frankly defended the great style as 'artificial in the highest degree, it presupposes in the spectator a cultivated and prepared artificial state of mind'. If Vasari had not put it quite in these words, he certainly recognized that consciously artful art was the achievement which separated his period from previous pursuit of truth to Nature in art.

This phrase itself ought possibly to receive definition, but it is one which the fifteenth century would largely have understood and accepted. Nature had been the century's goal, Nature ordered and regulated. It had tried to incorporate truth into art, curbing fantasy often in the interests of science, knowledge and experience. Lucidity had been, perhaps, its obsession:

lucid planning of buildings, coherently lucid proportions of the human form in sculpture, and liquid light caught in the glowing prisms of pictures by such painters as van Eyck, Piero della Francesca and Bellini. And in a positively Ruskinian sense, truth to Nature is conveyed by, for instance, the *Christ walking on the water* of Konrad Witz (one of many remarkable non-Italian painters unknown to Vasari), where the glassy, translucent element grows shallow towards the shore and through it is glimpsed the pebbly bed of the lake. Something of the civilization of the fifteenth century and the style it fostered – as well as some references to Witz – will be found in the *Early Renaissance* volume in this series, to which the present work is a sequel.

It would be wrong to imply that Vasari disapproved of the goal of fifteenth-century art. Although never quite clear whether 'Nature' was something the artist should follow or should outstrip, he believed it should be kept steadily in view. But the faults of the fifteenth century partly came from being too simply natural; he found its art lacking in those qualities which, by inference, were present in the best 'modern' work. Some of them have already been mentioned. Ease, softness of colour, subtlety of tone, and blend of light and shade are other comparable qualities. Instead of the bright, light, hard-edge effects of much fifteenth-century painting, he admired the smoky tonality of Giorgione (*'il quale sfumò le sue pitture'*). In sculpture he required finish and assurance. And constantly he laid stress on *'grazia'*, something stronger and more essential than the word 'grace' in ordinary English usage. Perfect ease and perfect accomplishment – not only in the control of art but in the very persons painted or sculpted – are the sort of graces he seems to have had in mind. In the work of Fra Bartolommeo [1], a key early protagonist of the High Renaissance style, there was – in addition to force and sweetness – *'grazia'*. The flying angels, with their wings of shot colour, the two suavely grouped trios of male figures and, especially, the effortlessly air-borne vision of the Virgin and Child, all exemplify grace to a quite novel degree. The altarpiece is rich in fresh solutions and combinations – despite or because of its deeply traditional subject-matter. The donor, prominent in bright-red gown, calmly joins the adoring saints and yet gazes out, enjoining us to share in the act of adoration. The setting is an interior, providing opportunities for majestic, soaring architecture, but

1. *The Carondelet altarpiece*, *c.* 1511. Fra Bartolommeo

2. *The Carondelet altarpiece* (detail of 1)

also opened up boldly at the back to allow a fully-realized landscape, virtually a picture in itself [2].

'*Grazia*' becomes the gift of totally refined invention, and one can understand Vasari feeling – as he did – that Parmigianino possessed even more of it than had Correggio. The perfect exponent of it, in his eyes, was Raphael, until surpassed by Michelangelo, in whose statues Vasari found the 'most graceful of all grace' (*una grazia più interamente graziosa*). And although Michelangelo must receive the highest award, particular commendation is bestowed on Leonardo, who 'began the modern style', because among his gifts was '*grazia divina*'.

This significant mention is enough to reveal Vasari's standards. It casts retrospective light on much typical fifteenth-century art – austere yet human, truthful, often mathematically plotted – which indeed quite fails to possess the almost disturbing invention and shadowy spell revealed as early as the *Virgin of the Rocks*, where graceful accomplishment and strangeness and un-natural beauty are everywhere. The heavy-lidded angel's head [3] is turned bewitchingly towards the spectator, seeking suavely to arrest and hold our gaze – and so it does, with ambiguously melting and yet secret expression. This pale face, framed by electrically crisp tendrils of curled hair, blooms

3. Angel's head, detail of the *Virgin of the Rocks*, *c*. 1483. Leonardo da Vinci

4. *Baldassare Castiglione, c.* 1515. Raphael

like a perfect, inaccessible flower, sprung from some soil on which we shall never tread: a symbol of art's new achievement, before which we remain in awe, but a little uneasy.

An angel's nature is not ours, the artist seems to remind us – and one may recollect the Florentine boys who pose as Botticelli's angels, Piero's grave peasant-angels or the often stolid features of angels in contemporary Northern pictures. It is with almost literally divine grace that Leonardo's angel turns its head slowly outwards and we are confronted not with some clearly-drawn, firmly-sculpted and untextured face but with an almost palpitating surface brushed by soft light and moulded as if from velvet, where the eyes sink into shadowy, flawless flesh and the lips curve with the pulpy vividness of fresh-opened fruit. Far from being forcefully recorded and ascertainable, this head seems to dissolve on inspection, as its features dissolve. Unlike anything previously seen in Nature, it seems rather to challenge Nature.

Even in its turning to fix, indeed transfix, the spectator, there can be sensed new confidence, if not positive challenge. In a new way, perhaps, the artist obtrudes his style and requires one to submit to his vision. How he creates is as important as what he creates, and when Leonardo undertook the *Mona Lisa*, a portrait which virtually parallels this turning angel's head, he evolved something far beyond mere likeness: the woman has become herself a work of art. Dürer was to do much the same, by his own methods, for his own face.

Raphael achieves it in the *Castiglione* [4], so elaborately constructed to give an impression of simplicity and so supremely confident that it can afford to throw an artful veil over confidence – just as the sitter can afford the subtle luxury of dressing in muted colours. Reality has been stringently revised and re-arranged. The accidents of costume are transmuted into soft, slightly generalized shapes which curve and flow into each other as if whorls of a perfect shell, all complementary to the big circular shape of the hat. Everything seems perfect but it is not placid, for the sitter's gaze is wistfully appealing – the unspoken hovering on the edge of speech – and, after the smooth, silvery beauty of the clothes, there is poignancy in the sense of the face as lived in, somewhat worn and not unweary. Conscious himself of the portrait's eloquence, Castiglione wrote a poem about it, supposedly written by his wife looking at this image in his absence and finding it virtually speaking: '. . . *dicere velle aliquid*'.

The *Mona Lisa* and the *Castiglione* between them begot a whole progeny of portraits. The century's sense of personality as eternally absorbing, combined with artistic accomplishment, resulted in a range of masterpieces, making almost a new category out of the portrait. Sometimes, sitters turn to question life like so many Hamlets, *dramatis personae* in settings of romantic landscape or, occasionally, complex urban association; and something of the *Mona Lisa*'s mysterious loneliness, as well as the conscious sobriety of the *Castiglione*, is still felt in the scholarly, artful, tensely elusive image which Bronzino evolved out of Ugolino Martelli [5], where the portrait is of a particular environment as well as of a man.

5. (*opposite*) *Ugolino Martelli*, *c.* 1535. Bronzino

6. *Andrea Odoni*, 1527. Lorenzo Lotto

Personality impresses itself forcibly in many of Lotto's portraits [6]. There too the environment may be highly personal but what is most arresting often is the challenging air of gaze or gesture, making it almost impossible not to stop before such a vivid image of life in art. The authority is sheerly art's – deriving not from the sitter's rank or necessarily even character – and

7. *Portrait of a Woman*, 1558. Frans Floris

few portraits of the period make the point more memorably than Floris's portrait of an unknown woman [7]. In the apparent simplicity of the frontal pose there is brilliant use of physical bulk and a suggestion of benevolent confidence. The austerity of the design makes tenderly effective the introduction of that staring, half-suspicious dog's head, a second, unexpected face in the portrait. Woman and dog – constant companions, the painter seems to suggest without sentimentality – confront us with a charge of vitality which is supernatural but utterly, over-whelmingly, convincing in art. A century before Frans Hals, one of his commonly praised effects is anticipated, without stridency.

What is achieved here is much more than mere record of a likeness, and that achievement is typical of a great deal of High Renaissance portraiture. If so much can be done with the like-ness, when this standard is irrelevant the image can become completely, wilfully, personal: an ideal of beauty or fascination entirely the artist's own creation, an improvement on the human species. Leonardo's angel represents if not beauty at least an ideal being, incarnated literally through the artist's power. Stripped of ambiguity and mystery, it is almost the face of Titian's Venus [8], painted some fifty years later and equally exemplifying *grazia divina*, in a woman who is worthy to be a goddess. This was Titian's ideal of beauty, and inevitably it is different from Leonardo's.

Yet it speaks much the same language, not least because of its astonishing display of art to rival nature: with rich, almost one might say hot, mesh of hair against which the flesh of the glowing cheek is faintly pressed – and flesh so palpable, though delicate, that a single jewel hangs gleaming like a drop of water, seeming to tremble between the areas of skin and hair. Posed as an invitation to love, this bland Venus hardly smiles, simply stretching along the crumpled bed, tautening the line of her breasts and offering for inspection not only her luxurious body with its sensuous suggestion of weight, but that perfect face of pleasure, open where Leonardo's was secret, warm where his was pale, its large eyes lustrously dark and the mouth, dark too, a ripe stain of promise. Leonardo's was a strange, waxen flower of patent, almost baleful artifice but Titian's makes one forget art in its blossoming, relaxing beauty. And all this is painted, not to instruct or edify, but to give – as indeed it does – pleasure. In the fifteenth century the picture might have seemed almost shocking in its pure hedonism.

Before such new accomplishment, it scarcely seems necessary to argue about the meaning of Vasari's *vaghezza* or *varietà* – qualities which might indeed be illustrated by other artists, like Correggio, but which it is useful to emphasize in Titian – for he is still somewhat edged out of the old-fashioned Roman-Florentine concept of the High Renaissance. (Something indeed is wrong with a book like Wölfflin's over-praised and deplorably influential *Classic Art*, the English edition of which provides nearly forty illustrations of Raphael's work and only four by Titian.) Vasari did at least praise the *Venus* reproduced here: '. . . delicate draperies, very beautiful and well finished'.

It will be one of the side-purposes of the present book to bring Titian back firmly into any concept or discussion of High Renaissance style, and to try and make it unmistakable that he is as much a great architect of it (for all he did nothing but paint) as Raphael.

The fact that Titian outlived Raphael by fifty-six years may cause difficulties for the tidy-minded type of art historian who has decided to close the High Renaissance style around the period of Raphael's death (1520) or at the Sack of Rome (1527), or even at the death of Correggio (1534), but Venetian sixteenth-century art altogether makes such a door-slamming attitude both silly and historically misleading. It should be noted straightaway that Vasari saw nothing of any such closure or subdivision, content with the three major periods already mentioned. Indeed, in the second edition of his *Lives* (1568), he included some account of a new and comparatively young artist, Veronese (born 1528), too young for the first edition, and praised his work in the highest of his usual terms, grandeur, design, varied costume and '*invenzione*'. In other words, he accepted this fresh talent as part of the tradition he had already defined – rightly, for Veronese was formed by study of Raphael, Correggio and other exponents of the 'modern' style. If Veronese is not a High Renaissance artist, it may well be asked, of what stylistic period is he? This question, along with some other related points which arise, will be touched on later in this chapter, because it is necessary to explain what 'High Renaissance' will mean in the rest of this book.

First, however, it is worth stressing some of the ways in which the achievements Vasari praised in his own period had actually come about. A technical ability underlay Leonardo's creative realization of the *Virgin of the Rocks* – a development of the medium of oil paint, which was to be experimented with

8. The '*Venus of Urbino*', *c.* 1538. Titian

and finally exploited by Titian in a manner quite unparalleled before or since. Gradations of light, variations of texture, the very *grazia* of smooth transitions by which one form flows into another: all such things can be beautifully conveyed in oil paint, itself so smooth-flowing, so luminous and so obedient – it seems – to the personality of the user that in its actual application he expresses himself. In Titian's late pictures – where we know he would use his fingers as well as brushes – every degree of working the paint, scratching, kneading, *frottage*, seems to have left the surfaces vibrant with energy, regardless of what is depicted. Handling and style can be discussed with new meaning, for a painter leaves his impress on the medium as individually as if it were a thumbprint.

With the typical fifteenth-century medium of egg tempera, drying quickly and somewhat dry in character, there tends to be a uniform effect, as if only thin skins of colour were laid over the basic bone structure of the drawing. By the time Titian was practising his dynamic late style, he was in fact destroying what he had once wonderfully exemplified: the glowing illusionistic power of oil paint. And painters like Tintoretto and El Greco were to find novel, even more highly personal uses of oil paint, tracing their individual calligraphy with brushes that almost seem dipped in some phosphorescent medium.

The development of oil paint was perhaps partly prompted by the wish to suggest subtle optical effects, truer to what is actually seen but deliberately less accurate in conveying what is known to be there. Jan van Eyck had certainly used, and used beautifully, the medium of oil paint, but his care had been to suppress all strokes, all 'expression' in the paint itself, so as to achieve a clarity which records impassively and minutely every object the eye encounters. But in fact we see much more impressionistically and less microscopically, have an 'idea' of objects rather than scrutinizing them – unless required specifically to do so – and do not need, perhaps, to anchor ourselves to reality by staring at it, content to let it ebb and flow, impinge on the sight or be remote. That way the eye is less fatigued, and what is seen inclines to fuse together harmoniously, even gracefully.

The High Renaissance painter aimed to achieve such effects, often following Leonardo in preference for muted light (where objects and edges may blur and soften) – what Vasari meant in praising the *sfumato* of Giorgione. Such an effect is more immediate and optically convincing; a suggestion seems more intriguing, maybe more ingenious, than patiently recorded fact. And a way is opened out of observed reality into a realm of artistically harmonious objects, where figures and drapery, and indeed everything, proclaim a perfection beyond our ordinary experience. One need only recollect a della Robbia child-angel, charming but solidly lifelike, and then look at an angel by Andrea del Sarto [9], a spirit in paint – almost an expression without substantiality – whose airiness is communicated to the ballooning drapery he holds, more graceful than any real fabric for all its silky texture. As for charm, he exudes a positive spell with an artfulness intolerable outside art.

9. Angel, detail of the *Marriage of S. Catherine*, *c.* 1512–13. Andrea del Sarto

10. *Adoration of the Shepherds, c.* 1530. Correggio

Perhaps no single picture better sums up the sheer virtuosity of new handling of the oil medium – absurd as it may be to try and select one example from a period of supreme virtuosity – than Correggio's *Nativity* [10]. Night scenes had certainly been painted during the fifteenth century, even in fresco. Nor was the idea of light emanating from the Child, illumining the night, altogether novel (compare, for example, a Netherlandish picture, pl. 103 in *Early Renaissance*). Yet oil paint here not only creates the penumbra of atmospheric darkness, through which we gradually descry further shapes and even the cool, faint glow of dawn in the distance, but the incandescent brightness from the Child is intensely conveyed by the graceful drama of light and shade (one forgets it is merely paint) which flickers across the fascinated peasant woman, half-fearfully shading her contracted features before the suddenly encountered blaze. *'Farsi scudo colle mani'* (making a shield with their hands) was how Leonardo recommended figures close to firelight at night should be shown. To combine grace with such a powerful physical sense of how a human being reacts to bright light, and to use this to contrast with the steady regard of the Virgin, effortlessly able to gaze at the God-head, is an extraordinary achievement not paralleled again perhaps in European painting.

When Caravaggio explored this type of sensation in the seventeenth century, he abandoned Correggio's essentially High Renaissance elegance. Although Caravaggio is usually described as daring, he would not have dared to paint shepherds in the ideal and almost affected poses which here make them brothers to the luminously graceful, entwined angel group above. Correggio's picture is far from being realistic. It is indeed quite openly artificial and either did, or should have, deeply upset such nineteenth-century critics as Ruskin. Lord Lindsay (the author of *Sketches of the History of Christian Art* [1846]) placed Correggio under 'Triumph of the Sensual Element', and passed on in silence. But in ease, harmony, invention, and charm – as the sixteenth century meant them – the *Nativity* is simply a masterpiece.

Vasari was not altogether favourable to Correggio intellectually, but he could not help being visually ravished; this picture in particular stirred his eloquence and while he found the woman shielding her eyes marvellously well observed, he thought the angels quite literally rained from heaven (*'piovuti dal cielo'*). A further aspect of achievement is represented by the picture's scale, which aids these effects. Although not huge by sixteenth-century standards, it is over eight feet high and its light-filled darkness when it was *in situ* as an altarpiece must have been tremendous. Like some visionary stage scene, it is – as Vasari hinted – at once convincingly life-like in impact and yet patently, flagrantly, remote from normal experience. And in that combination it is a quintessence of High Renaissance style.

From confidence in handling oil paint, there came perhaps, and paradoxically, a new freedom in drawing. The painter might approach his task of creating a picture by first sketching possible compositions, yet now leave himself free to make a final decision only when actually engaged in the painting. Oil paint encourages improvisation. Few pictures of the period, even highly wrought Florentine ones, seem without some such touches and occasionally last-minute alteration. Drawings cease to have to serve as specific blue-prints for a final composition, carefully executed with the intention of being transferred into paint. For frescoes, obviously, cartoons were still used, if not on every occasion. Vasari records the reaction of Girolamo da Treviso who questioned whether cartoons were necessary and proclaimed the inspirational nature of painting by declaring 'I, I have art at the point of my brush' (*'io, io ho l'arte su la punta del penello'*). Florentine linear obsessions probably meant that drawing continued to be treated as a more serious preparatory stage there than at Venice. But drawings themselves might record a whole series of unresolved thoughts towards the eventual picture – virtually inspired doodles, as with Veronese [11] who is often found still sketching, improvising, in passages of the paint of the final work.

The assurance of Veronese's finished pictures [137] – and few painters have displayed this quality so confidently – may seem in contrast to the almost worried, hurried scribbling of motifs in his drawings. The latter, however, not only exemplify *varietà* but display a bewilderingly fertile imagination, constantly trying out, rejecting, resuming – though never, one might guess, irrevocably selecting – ideas for the eventual picture. Drawing as an artistic activity in itself, not just as part of the preparatory process to painting, develops a quite new importance in the eyes of both artists and collectors. Vasari's connoisseurship is again typical, as he refers constantly to drawings collected 'in our book': not merely as records but as things beautiful in themselves. If Leonardo is the first example of an artist with a huge and wonderful drawing *œuvre*, much of

11. Studies for an *Adoration of the Kings, c.* 1573(?). Veronese

it unrelated to his paintings, Dürer may reasonably be cited as the first example of an artist whose true genius is in his drawings, leaving only talent for his pictures. And Dürer's very finest drawings are those which exist in their own right, as sure as they are spontaneous.

Drawing and painting were not the sole media to have developed, aesthetically and technically. Originating in the

very first years of the sixteenth century, almost contemporaneously as it happens, two works of art revealed in style,
invenzione, and sheer size, achievements in other media which
made them marvelled over for the rest of the period – never to
lose their fame. Michelangelo's *David* [12] has indeed been
debased by familiarity, replicas and, most perverse of all, miniature reproductions. Dürer's S.Eustace engraving [13] cannot
claim to have suffered exactly that fate, and its fame has perhaps

12. *David*, 1501–4. Michelangelo

dwindled merely to its size, while its achievement has been a little neglected in the light of Dürer's later engravings.

As the signed manifesto of a new artist, a Northern genius of whom Italy must take note (as it speedily did), the *S.Eustace* is important enough. At the same time, it transforms the medium of engraving into something which can rival painting: seen here to possess its own chiaroscuro, to be both grand in concept and detailed in execution, with *varietà* which ranges

13. *S. Eustace, c.* 1501. Albrecht Dürer

from thick-tufted grasses and rippling water to the minute specks of the wheeling flock of birds about the high castle tower. It is true that far from detail being suppressed, detail proliferates, but that is part of the medium. Gracefulness is not, at least to modern eyes, very apparent.

14. Head of David (detail of 12)

In some ways, the engraving may be seen as a culmination of fifteenth-century concerns (not unreasonably, since its creator was already twenty-nine in 1500). Yet, for those people who first saw and admired it, its accomplishment, its profusion of motifs, its triumphant handling of a difficult and previously somewhat humble medium, would have made the strongest effect of novelty. We have the testimony of Sabba da Castiglione, a sixteenth-century Italian connoisseur and collector, to the impression made on him as he sat in his arbour, marvelling over this very print arrived from Germany.

To have a career just as an engraver becomes possible, and Marcantonio Raimondi is merely the most famous example. And who before Dürer had achieved anything like the *S.Eustace* in engraving? The display of *invenzione* in the varied poses of the dogs, the carefully studied proportions of the horse (which almost distracts from the saint) and, above all perhaps, the sense of the whole natural world surveyed and recreated in art make it fit to belong with Vasari's modern style. It is easy to see that Dürer has created his own extensive cosmos, a steeply rising terrain of countryside and castle, and tree-fringed water where swans glide; nor is it too far-fetched to claim that the total result falls within the definition of artistic creation as 'an artificial imitation of Nature' which the mid-sixteenth-century theorist Benedetto Varchi proposed.

Several sorts of challenge were offered by the block of marble which became Michelangelo's *David* and all are successfully met. Its size (the statue is some fourteen feet high), had been unique when it was quarried in the fifteenth century. When executed the *David* was certainly the largest free-standing marble statue of modern times and a rival to such colossal antique statues as survived, like the *Horse Tamers* on the Quirinal. More than one fifteenth-century sculptor had been assigned the gigantic block, which was, as a result, badly mutilated and neglected. But the implicit challenge, the chance to excel and astonish, made a magnet out of a liability in the new climate of the sixteenth century.

Leonardo was at one point considered as a possible sculptor of it, but Michelangelo received, perhaps seized, the commis-

sion: 'confident that he could get something good out of it', (. . . *la confidenza ch'egli aveva di cavarne cosa buona*), as his pupil Condivi wrote in his biography. And confidence is certainly exemplified in the finished work, the traditional shepherd–boy–hero turned into an Apolline Goliath, giant and god, the first of Michelangelo's disturbingly, imperiously, sensual male nudes. There is no attempt to *illustrate* David; the statue is bare of all reference except for the scarcely noticeable sling, but it incarnates a spirit of timeless, heroic defiance expressed in the proud stance, the powerful torso and frowning idealized head [14].

Probably even in the first fifteenth-century plan for the statue it had been intended to represent David, though perhaps as prophet rather than in boyhood. Michelangelo may have shifted that concept, just as the location shifted from the original destination of the cathedral façade – where its scale would have been less striking – to the comparative accessibility of a pedestal in the Piazza della Signoria. And there, as can be judged from the copy on the site, its remoteness from human scale and human preoccupations is patently declared. It aims at nothing less than perfection: a perfect body, at a perfect age, stripped for admiration as much as for action, the athlete of God and himself god-like. It has broken with the life-like sculpture of the previous century but is a forerunner of the giant figures on the Sistine Chapel ceiling [52], especially the *ignudi*, and of the heroic Princes of the Medici tombs, Giuliano de' Medici in particular [45]. Such extremes are typical of Michelangelo, and of him alone; they mark a totally new type of personal achievement, almost arrogant beside the suavity of Raphael, daunting even to great contemporaries of his own period yet encouraging in showing the divine power of the imagination to create in superhuman terms. What he created would be hailed by Aretino as a 'new Nature'.

In architecture, a sense of new aims, and of their achievement too, was no less great than in other visual arts; but from Vasari onwards there has been a tendency to discuss them less fully. Few High Renaissance buildings are world-famous in the way that the *Mona Lisa*, for example, is – or the Michelangelo *David*. It is not merely that architecture exercises less widespread appeal and is always a difficult art to write about in any seriously appreciative vein. Several important High Renaissance buildings and architectural schemes are no longer as their designers intended them, or were worked on by a variety of architects over a considerable period of time. A building can rarely if ever bear the impress of personal achievement comparable to that felt in the carving of a statue or the handling of an oil painting. Inevitably, discussion of architecture is liable to lead to questions of a gap between design and execution. It is by no means a modern phenomenon whereby plans are prepared in collaboration, or even by a team, and the actual building put up without being supervised by the original designer.

Some of these difficulties are illustrated by the case of the staircase of Michelangelo's vestibule to the Biblioteca Laurenziana [15], claimed here as a High Renaissance work of art and

15. Staircase of the Biblioteca Laurenziana, Florence, 1524 onwards

undoubtedly unlike earlier staircases. The vestibule was designed and built by Michelangelo in Florence around 1524 but the staircase was not completed until the 1550s and then by the sculptor-cum-architect Ammanati (designer of the famous Ponte S.Trinita at Florence), with Vasari perhaps involved. Michelangelo sent a drawing for it from Rome, but he never saw the staircase as executed, and it seems unclear whether it represents his concept or was modified by Vasari and Ammanati. The vestibule is a small and reasonably coherent construction to appreciate. The history of the evolution of St Peter's, probably the one building which could claim High Renaissance origin and world-wide fame, is as huge as the final building, and more complicated. Inside and out, what we nowadays normally see is anyway hardly any longer a High Renaissance monument – and to appreciate something so diverse is certainly difficult, if not indeed impossible.

But the germ of St Peter's is a true spark of High Renaissance fire: daringly bold, colossal in size, a combination of antique example and modern style in temple portico and vast dominating dome. Such is the building [16], of which Julius II

16. St Peter's
Foundation Medal,
1506. Caradosso

laid the foundation stone in 1506, three years after his election as Pope. He dreamed of renovating or restoring the old basilica, until it would resemble what is shown in this commemoration medal. It was intended, Vasari says, to surpass any previous building in *bellezza, arte, invenzione ed ordine . . . grandezza . . . richezza e d'ornamento*.

At this stage Bramante was the architect, but the commission passed at his death to Raphael and eventually to Michelangelo. Under Bramante, as the medal design suggests, the idea was for a centrally planned, domed building, a favourite Renaissance theoretical concept which had attracted – among others – Leonardo. Thus, in different ways, a series of the greatest figures in creating the High Renaissance style can be said to be connected with St Peter's, and in this connection there is symbolic aptness. Like the giant altarpiece, the dome is the culmination of earlier, usually still tentative ambitions. United with a temple or temple-style façade, it became the very type of High Renaissance church, regardless of central planning; and something of Bramante's original grandiose concept can be sensed in Palladio's S.Giorgio Maggiore [17] of many years

17. S. Giorgio Maggiore, Venice, begun 1565. Palladio

later, with its huge scale and delight in dramatically dwarfing humanity.

'*Bellezza*', '*invenzione*', '*ordine*', '*richezza*': Vasari's vague-sounding words take on real meaning before the splendid achievement of S. Giorgio, and they help to define too what is aimed at in the apparently constricting space of the Biblioteca Laurenziana vestibule. The surfaces are richly wrought, carved with niches, hung with swags, culminating in the solemn, twin-pillared doorway to the library which is literally built

43

up to by the broad staircase which sweeps boldly out, virtually filling the room.

For a truly sweeping staircase, there is actually little space. It is invention which has given the effect of great grandeur to what in fact are only fifteen steps, and ingenuity which has contrived this without its becoming overpowering. If a fifteenth-century architect had received this task, we may guess that he would have tried to blend function with simplicity, gracefully proportioning his staircase to perform its essential task in the limited area available. Simplicity is eschewed by Michelangelo, or his continuators, providing much more than could possibly be expected. A quite narrow staircase, hemmed by balustrades of bulging balusters, begins the descent from the library and then dramatically opens out (spirals of stone coiled like ribbon seeming to increase the sense of movement) with a sudden hiatus, to divide into three staircases providing alternative approaches. The lines of balustrade resume, and mark off the central flight which ends with three curving slabs of steps, an almost musical flourish, contrasting with the straight flights of the side staircases, themselves more spatially vague because they lack any handrail or balustrade (necessarily, for further balustrades would prove oppressive). It is not enough to say that this staircase is a work of art (the fifteenth-century staircase in the Ducal Palace at Urbino, for example, had been that). It is a work of art which declares its artful nature and is quite as intentionally astonishing in its virtuosity as Correggio's *Nativity* or Michelangelo's *David*.

And at this point it must be admitted that while the *David* is usually agreed to be a High Renaissance work, as is Raphael's *Castiglione* and even Correggio's *Nativity*, and while Palladio and Veronese are seldom characterized at all, another stylistic adjective is often reserved for the Biblioteca Laurenziana staircase and vestibule: 'Mannerist'. What this style might be has been most ably defined by John Shearman in a companion volume, *Mannerism*, in this series. In recent years this phenomenon, much discussed and disagreed about even among its adherents, has been claimed as a distinct style which replaces that of the High Renaissance, being born – according to some – in Rome approximately about 1520. That it had its roots in the High Renaissance and was not some violent reaction *against* the High Renaissance is the view of its more intelligent and subtle students (e.g. Shearman). Instead of the neurotic piety and disturbed sensibility which used to be thought explanatory of certain 'Mannerist' artists, a majority of scholars would probably now agree with Shearman's emphasis that it was a consciously 'stylish style' which these artists were practising.

The number of meanings attached in the sixteenth century to the word *maniera*, something undoubtedly prized in art by Vasari, do not unfortunately take the matter very much further, because Vasari did *not* use this word to distinguish between the century's art before and after 1520 – or at any other date. And on this score it is hard to follow a statement in *Mannerism* (p. 16) which says that this 'label [Mannerism] did, in fact, come down to us firmly attached to something; we have inherited, not invented, it'. This inheritance cannot be traced back, certainly not 'firmly', much before 1900. Nowadays, when we are constantly told to use the evidence of the period we are discussing, that date must seem rather late for detection of a phenomenon.

Of course, it does not follow that Mannerism did not exist because Vasari and his contemporaries never noticed it. Equally, a modern historian is not bound to accept the existence of a style which, the closer it is defined, the more it seems second-generation High Renaissance rather than anything of a distinctly different nature. 'Poise, refinement and sophistication . . . works of art that are polished, rarefied and idealized away from the natural': such are some of the terms carefully selected by Shearman in speaking of Mannerism; and elsewhere in his book he names grace and elegance as other characteristics of the style.

These valuable definitions – especially 'idealized away from the natural' – may more easily and conveniently be applied to the figurative arts than to architecture. Further, the Laurenziana staircase can itself be reasonably described as such an original, abstruse creation – as well as such a late one of the sixteenth century – that it should not be cited as typical in any argument. Instead of beginning by clawing back a 'Mannerist' work into some High Renaissance concept, it may anyway be better to consider an earlier key masterpiece, traditionally assumed supremely typical of High Renaissance art, and see how far it accords with, or is distinct from, the Mannerist qualities of poise, refinement, grace and idealization.

Raphael's *Madonna della Sedia* [18] is a famous and highly popular painting, universally recognized as a virtuoso achievement of harmony, in composition and in its blend of naturalism with idealization. Vasari does not mention the picture. Nothing

18. The *Madonna della Sedia*, c. 1514–15. Raphael

is known of the circumstances of its commissioning, and its fame dates from long after Raphael's death. Its popularity is understandable, because it is patently appealing – just as it is patently accomplished. Its very calmness, confidence and (some people might possibly add) its charm make it perhaps not altogether easy to discuss, but it deserves its place in any discussion of the High Renaissance style and it inevitably appears in Wölfflin's *Classic Art*.

Some critics have laid most emphasis on its vein of naturalism, seeing here a Roman woman of the people nursing a shrinking Child; and presumably the picture's stress on the maternal – apparently intimate and apparently unmajestic – is a distinct part of its appeal. Even the Madonna's shawl has been interpreted as a 'popular' touch, although such richly fringed and patterned shawls are worn by the most sophisticated Madonnas of Botticelli's devising, and there is nothing popular or ordinary about the elaborately turned, polished upright of the chair from which the picture takes its name.

Such hints point the way to detecting how very consciously and unrealistically the picture is composed, though its artfulness is veiled and unassertive. In its way, it is the perfect complement to Raphael's *Castiglione* [4], even to the flowing, curving forms skilfully designed to fit within each other (and here finally into the circular frame) and the faces turned out towards us as if wishing to communicate. The tondo form was no novelty, having been used ingeniously by, above all, Botticelli, but Raphael suggests something quite new illusionistically in the sense of a mirror-like, convex surface on which arms, legs and draperies seem to swell and curve towards the spectator. What is mere suggestion here will blossom eventually into the full illusionism of Parmigianino's circular self-portrait. Only by some sense of planned distortion can one explain in Raphael's picture the swollen bulk of the Madonna's right arm, with its unrealistically smooth drapery, and the strong projection of the Child's left shoulder behind which his face is recessed. The chair itself is conveyed both economically and almost surrealistically: hard, prominent and vertical, the single foreground post thrusts up to anchor not only the Madonna but the whole series of softly floating, gracefully rippling shapes which might otherwise become too loose and vague.

Just how little Raphael was being naturalistic – even while being, of course, artistically convincing – is seen in detail in the area of the Madonna's raised left knee, where remarkable indentations of crumpled drapery possess a life of their own. (To appreciate the daring effect fully in a reproduction, it is necessary to cover the figure of St John.) Perhaps it is worth adding too that for all the swelling of the forms they are conceived as essentially weightless; the vast Child bears with no more pressure than a balloon on his Mother's uncreased thigh.

In that buoyancy there is not only a lack of naturalism but a concomitant, positive grace. The group is so clearly ideal that the thought of a real mother and real baby – not to mention them 'palpitating and breathing with the hot life of the Roman sun' (as one critic put it) – is irrelevant and ludicrous. This calm Madonna is still very much the queen of heaven, as well as – in terms of her Litany – *Mater amabilis, Mater admirabilis*; and her chair has virtually pontifical or royal richness, suitably for one who is also *Sedes sapientiae*.

Raphael and his contemporaries would be more likely to respond to such allusions than to wish to preserve in paint any domestic scene glimpsed in fact. How far the *Madonna della Sedia*, like so many of Raphael's Madonna pictures, has moved from anything resembling the observed and the actual can be appreciated by comparing it with one of his sheets of vivid studies [19]. Here we encounter the artist in the process of creating, coming at least closer to the reality of a mother with a strugglingly active baby. The intense repose and wide-eyed, intensely solemn gaze of the Child evolved for the *Madonna della Sedia* convey their own message (even if we miss the import of St John's adoration): this is the Son of God and the saviour of the world.

Certainly the picture's intention is to be refined and sophisticated, more than naturally graceful and rich, polished to an accomplished brilliance in concept and handling that should strike us as totally novel. Very likely it was a private commission; it is rather a pity it did not belong to Castiglione, for he might have produced a poem about it which would have better prepared us to understand it than Victorian and post-Victorian sentimentalities about an 'ordinary' mother and child in supposed intimacy. That does little justice to Raphael's serious study of Leonardo and Michelangelo, in a wish to fuse qualities from them both to make his own individual achievement. It is part of Raphael's manner not to insist on that achievement but to let it appear easy, gracefully assimilable and, to some extent, even obvious. Thus, paradoxically, in the ease of manner his sheer art can be missed. Yet, set against the

19. Studies of the Virgin and Child, *c.* 1508. Raphael

Madonna and Child groups of great Early Renaissance painters like Masaccio and Piero della Francesca, the *Madonna della Sedia* seems almost intolerably conscious and contrived, artificial, sophisticated and inhumanly suave. Raphael had indeed the gift, as Vasari says when speaking of another Virgin and Child by him, of making the style of his heads 'most sweet and most graceful' (*dolcissime e graziosissime*).

It is hard to see how pictures like the *Madonna della Sedia*, and the Castiglione portrait, can be excluded from the definitions of Mannerism already quoted here, even though they may not in themselves be extreme examples of the style. Raphael himself was deliberately creating art out of the art of Leonardo and Michelangelo (to name only two of the older artists he studied), and the challenging achievement represented by the Doni tondo [22] probably played its part in his thoughts about the *Madonna della Sedia*.

A true break comes not post-Raphael, though further degrees of refinement were then sought, but much earlier with the innovatory genius of Leonardo. The angel of the *Madonna of the Rocks* announces a new manner, to be developed – not altered – by Correggio. Grace, elegance, high sophistication and artifice cannot be denied to the art of Veronese (which is certainly not intended to pass as in any way naturalistic), himself positively influenced by Correggio.

Such standards are exactly those by which Vasari judged Michelangelo to be supremely great. '*Sveltezza . . . grazia . . . artificio*' are the words he used to praise the *David*, which is indeed 'idealized away from the natural'. Some modern critics have found the statue ugly, even calling it a hobbledehoy. Aesthetic judgements are their right, but these are in disaccord with Michelangelo's intentions and at variance with Vasari's near-contemporary standards.

Either Mannerism must be pushed right back to the beginning of the century and recognized as the century's basic style, created actively by Leonardo, Michelangelo and Raphael – to all of whom, by the way, the conventional 'Mannerists' were deeply, openly, indebted – or, if it is to be defined in such a limited way that it excludes the great trio (as well as Correggio, and Veronese – not to mention certain great Northern European artists), then it seems not so much a true style as a limited trend, hardly more than a Tuscan–Roman manifestation, with a few late camp-followers like Spranger.

As a result of the attempts to give a specific character to Mannerism as a widely dispersed, complete style of its own, the High Renaissance has undergone a process of fossilization and been allotted an arbitrary purpose for which the written evidence is meagre indeed and evidence in the works of art hardly more apparent. When Mannerism was seriously formulated as a stylistic entity in the early part of this century, it was connected with unease and uncertainty in the arts, in society and in religion. The death of Raphael, the Sack of Rome, the Reformation, all seemed to go to explain, for example, Pontormo's moody art. For this type of explanation to be effective, the previous artistic period had to appear notably calm, balanced, harmonious, what can still be described as 'the moment of equilibrium' (Shearman).

Such a view of the early years of the sixteenth century was consecrated by Wölfflin's *Classic Art* (first published in 1899), the very title of which is a trap, for by 'classic' the author implies serenity, repose, restraint and all the other qualities then associated with Greek art (by which that of the fifth century alone was meant). Beginning with Leonardo's *Last Supper*, the High Renaissance persuasively took shape as a period when everything reached maturity and became not merely measured but fixed (as Wölfflin says at one point, 'nothing can be moved or altered, even in thought'). From this concept there followed harmony, in a very special meaning of the word. Certain works of art, especially some by Raphael in his early years in Rome, will support these views – though Raphael's calmness and balance are, in fact, more explicable probably as an inheritance from fifteenth-century Umbrian art (e.g. Piero della Francesca and Perugino) than as pioneering a High Renaissance style. What is called typically balanced is the *School of Athens* [20], but it is significant that the Raphael of the later Vatican Stanze, and especially the 'Stanza dell' Incendio' [21], fits the argument much less well. Those frescoes have to receive much less emphasis, because their drama is quite patent and almost wild in places; rhetoric infuses the draperies and gestures, declaiming in a way that is forceful and exciting – as well as deliberately louder than the tone of ordinary life – once we understand its rules and intentions. The very figures of the suffering inhabitants of the Borgo have become heroic athletes, and the Borgo their gymnasium. Raphael then comes closer to Michelangelo, whose nature and art had long before revealed a

20. *The School of Athens*, 1508–11 (detail). Raphael

21. *The Fire in the Borgo*, 1514–17. Raphael

challenging Promethean power, unable to conceal its disturbing, restless nature.

Classic calm certainly left Wölfflin's own normally smug style, to be exchanged for Ruskin-like moral indignation, when he came to what he optimistically assumed could only be work from Raphael's studio: 'strident in colour, ignoble in conception, theatrical in gesture and, above all, lacking in proportion'. It might almost be said that he had defined, accidentally, a much criticized key monument of the true High Renaissance style, Michelangelo's *Holy Family* [22], painted in the first three or four years of the new century. For most of that century it was admired and influential. Only when the style it had fostered had fallen from favour did it too fall; later centuries did not hesitate to criticize it. Yet it is a fountainhead of the new manner in its heroic refinement, its polished surfaces and unexpected colour, its display of virtuosity and contrived grace.

Most of the phrases Wölfflin threw at Raphael's studio are criticisms really of something endemic in the High Renaissance style – especially his complaint about theatricality of gesture. The 'theatrical' (itself a somewhat naïve, puritanical and loaded term of pejorative criticism) is exactly what separates the lucid, human, fifteenth-century world from the new stage-like grand manner in which emotions are acted out by people who, like antique classical actors, seem masked, strangely robed and moving on *cothurni*, those high-soled boots which conveyed superhuman physical and emotional stature. It is easy to understand how Reynolds could be led from the grand style to comparisons with opera. 'I would not admit as sound criticism,' he wrote, 'the condemnation of such exhibitions on account of their being unnatural . . . Shall reason stand in the way . . . and prevent us from feeling the full effect of this complicated exertion of art?'

In those last few words he aptly summed up the effect too of Michelangelo's *Holy Family*. Reason would tell us that no mother ordinarily takes her child from its father with such an exercise in callisthenics as this Madonna performs –, and reasonable critics have often recorded this sort of objection. But we are confronting, once again, a rarefied, divine ethos and what the Madonna is receiving into her arms is the Creator of the World, an intensely solemn burden, to whom she turns in homage as well as love. Consciously or not, there seems in Michelangelo's concept an echo of the St Christopher story: the giant who took on his shoulders a child whose weight revealed

22. The 'Doni Tondo', c. 1505. Michelangelo

that he was God. In the *Holy Family*, the moment of transfer – perhaps intended as symbolic of Christ's divinity and destiny being revealed – is witnessed by the youthful Baptist: not as part of some playful family group but with visionary, rapt fervour. And the naked youths in the rocky distance, which opens out into a winding river-scene, stand perhaps for the sinners to be baptized in the Jordan, where St John is going also to baptize Christ, whose divine nature will thereupon be confirmed by a voice from heaven. Even if such an interpretation is not correct, it at least suggests an explanation for the youths often criticized as irrelevant, if not irreverent, and provides some way of comprehending that the composition is not a pointless exercise; if it is rhetorical, its rhetoric is seriously intended and imbued with meaning, as indeed might be expected of its creator.

That it is a completely new concept of the Holy Family (though possibly influenced by Leonardo's ideas of Christ's divinity revealed in infancy) is as obvious as the novelty of its style. No less novel and choice is its colour, especially the cold pink of the Madonna's dress, at once flowing and congealed, polished and yet translucent, the paint applied like some enamel of the period – and clasped at the breast by a brooch or border not conventional gold but pale blue.

In painting Michelangelo certainly aimed at strong relief-like effects, almost carving the surface, but to some extent so had Masaccio. What is new is not the sculptural effect as such but its combination with the swinging serpentine rhythms which cross back and forward from the Child's head to the Madonna's right foot and which dictate the disposition of anatomy and folds of drapery – in the interests of grace rather than truth. St Joseph's extraordinary pose is effective artistically, though doubtless agonizing in reality; but he must swell as a firm block of hard, polished drapery-forms, a bulwark of dark-coloured bronze from which the Madonna and Child sinuously twist out towards the spectator, almost like reflections in some vast convex mirror. The holy group is a perfect group: of rippling muscle and elegant strength, topped by the unsmiling, victorious Child, a miniature athlete (an effect increased by the band about his curls) who presses his hands on the Madonna's head in benediction and perhaps in anticipation of her coronation in heaven.

Whether or not concerned about such nuances, no sixteenth-century spectator could have failed to feel the accomplished

23. The 'Canning Jewel',
sixteenth-century Italian(?)

art of this picture. Of its style it is indeed perfect – and only
Bronzino proved able to emulate it without being eclipsed.
But its significance lies less in its actual style than in the sense
of its accomplishment; and that is the characteristic the High
Renaissance sought in civilization, and art, in jewellery [23] as
much as in painting or architecture, in a dish [24], a sonnet or
in behaviour. The so-called minor visual arts reached a sophisticated level of accomplishment and artfulness perhaps never
equalled, and these arts were closely involved with daily life: a
jewel was worn and superb tableware accompanied a banquet.

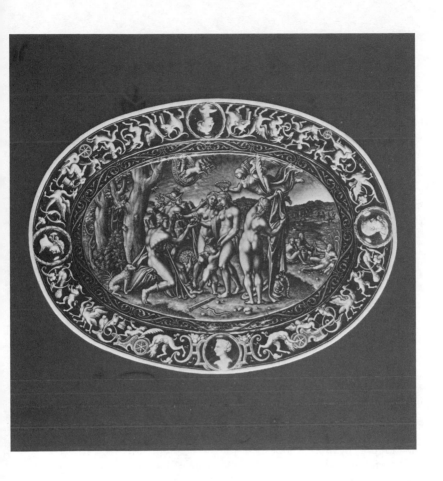

24. Enamel Dish, *c.* 1560. Pierre Reymond

Reymond's dish illustrates a Raphael composition; and Cellini himself might have envied the ingenuity of pearl, gems and enamel which has gone to make up the merman. Accomplishment is announced in Leonardo's famous letter of about 1482 to Ludovico il Moro, Duke of Milan, in which he calmly states his absolute assurance in his own powers: 'I believe I can give the fullest satisfaction . . .' (*credo di soddisfare benissimo*). He goes on to specify architecture, but he has already listed ten methods of warfare which he has perfected, and he claims equal competence in painting and sculpture.

Whether the results of such High Renaissance assurance themselves actually convey assurance through exuding calmness, balance and restraint is not only doubtful but largely irrelevant. Vasari nowhere characterizes the modern style in those terms and, as has already emerged, they are not particularly apt to describe much of the art. It is true that some theorists contrasted Raphael and Michelangelo, claiming that Raphael's ease and elegance was – reasonably enough – greater. Since Vasari praised Michelangelo's grace, he clearly allowed for tremendous force in his meaning of '*grazia*'. In writing about Leonardo, he laid emphasis on his curious, ingenious experiments and devices, with their power often to disturb. Calmness and restraint are not the qualities, as far as can now be judged, which either Michelangelo or Leonardo embodied in their proposed great battle pictures for the Palazzo Vecchio at Florence: two works over which their contemporaries marvelled.

A style in art is not something like a team shirt which must be adopted by those who want to join in. It comes into existence through the achievements of individual artists, who may be – as were Leonardo and Michelangelo – rivals in many ways. But neither man had a particularly 'classic' or serene personality (Goethe not having yet created that rather Teutonic touchstone of greatness) and Vasari in fact characterized with remarkable precision the tragic flaw in Leonardo's restless nature, the gap between idea and execution: '*la mano aggiungere non potesse alla perfezione del'arte nelle cose ch'egli s'immaginava*' (the hand not being able to realize the perfect art of what he imagined).

What Vasari defined as the achievement of art in his own century – perfection – was virtually everywhere accepted, with important results. If art can, as Reynolds was to claim in an echo of sixteenth-century belief, satisfy the desires of the mind, then its value is established on a level beyond religious instruction or imitation of the natural world. Perfection becomes intensely desirable in art once it is accepted that human life and conditions are appallingly imperfect. When knowledge was drastically changing established concepts, the physical earth enlarged by discoveries, and the solar system quite altered, when religion itself was splintering into violently different sects, it was in fact difficult for art to incorporate 'science' or faith in the old way.

If 'new philosophy calls all in doubt', in Donne's words, then the artist may confidently assert the validity of his own personal vision. There is a real, recognized power in the artist to create challenges to ordinary experience: statues like Michelangelo's *David*, night scenes like Correggio's *Nativity*, buildings as white and dazzling, and as gigantic, as Palladio's S.Giorgio, a temple built seemingly on the water. The message of such art to those who are, in Reynolds's words, 'impatient of being circumscribed', is that there is a rival world of existence – the artistic one – which defies the normal and the expected. It is to the 'spark of divinity' within us that art speaks, and Reynolds can still call the artist divine.

Acceptance had come with the High Renaissance and it profoundly affected not only the artist's status but attitudes to art. The rise in the artist's status is probably the better known, since the reputations of most of the sixteenth-century artists previously referred to in this chapter were great in their lifetimes and have never diminished. Highly as we may now estimate Brunelleschi or Giovanni Bellini, for example, and highly as they were thought of in their own day in their own cities, neither of them enjoyed international fame and no awe gathered about their lives or their work. They were not, and would not have expected to be, hailed as 'divine'. But when an aristocrat recommended Titian warmly to a Cardinal, he called the painter simply '*il primo huomo della Christianità*'.

Yet the individual artist's status is really less relevant for High Renaissance style than the rise in the prestige of art altogether, centred on Italy. The artistic achievements of fifteenth-century Italy had not amazed – had not altogether interested – the rest of Europe. One reason for this is that other European countries had their own artistic achievements and traditions, some of them earlier established. A discussion of the origins of the Early Renaissance need not restrict itself to Italy. But it is not a piece of bias in the present book to have laid so much stress so far on Italy, because it was there that the

High Renaissance style was nurtured – so publicly that soon all Europe was aware of new achievements and possibilities associated with that country.

Although historically the sixteenth century is represented as the age of individual nation states, its culture was remarkably uniform, being Italianate with only trimmings of national style. All Europe recognized in Titian, for instance, a supreme painter. England and France imported Italian artists in all media. The court of Cracow, where a Milanese princess was queen, employed Italian workmen. Places as far apart as Prague (Belvedere, *c.* 1535 half Early, half High Renaissance) and Evora, in Portugal, (Tomb of Dom Alfonso, 1537) soon felt repercussions of the modern Italian manner. One can illustrate the pure High Renaissance quality of, for example, a relief of 1518 in the Cathedral at Barcelona [25], but the sculptor, Ordóñez, had been active in Italy.

The publication of Italian treatises on architecture – beginning with Book IV of Serlio's projected series *Regole generali di architettura . . .* (1537) and culminating in Palladio's *Quattro libri dell'architettura* (1570) – disseminated ideas about the style of buildings that could now serve as inspiration for those who had never been in Italy. To read Serlio was also to learn something about certain modern Italian painters, among them Raphael, Peruzzi and Giulio Romano (the sole sixteenth-century artist Shakespeare mentions, mentioning him perhaps because his eye had caught Serlio's reference, available in English only in 1611, the year of the first performance of *The Winter's Tale*).

Indeed, one aspect of the new prestige of the visual arts was due to the growing literature about them – to which Vasari made the least theoretical but the most popular, perhaps most typical, contribution. He writes of the artists' lives. Art criticism – in the sense of what characterizes an individual artist's style – was also virtually an Italian invention. The increase in the sheer number of books printed encouraged the publishing, and often the translation, of works which dealt with what can only be called culture, as well as the customs of various countries. There too Italy led the way. The Italian influence on especially England is a familiar topic, but it should also be remembered that part of the *va-et-vient* of culture at the period included Italian visitors to England, though most of their written comments were probably not intended for publication.

25. *S. Eulalia before her Judge, c.* 1518. Bartolomé Ordóñez

What finally separates the High Renaissance from the periods of art which had preceded it is that, at last perhaps, an artistic style and a civilization fully accord. The arts – writing, fighting and gardening, as well as the visual arts and music – were not merely received in society but became part of its fabric. Patterns of *how* to sing, or build or write, were disseminated, because there was a demand. An educated man, whether Italian, French, Spanish, English or German, would wish to know something, in however vague a way, about such things. He would not necessarily be either a scholar or an aristocrat but that new exemplar of culture: a gentleman. Two Italian books in particular shaped the century's ideal of this figure (so often to be portrayed in paint), Castiglione's *Il libro del cortegiano* (1528) and Della Casa's *Galateo* (1558). Both books were translated into French and Spanish before appearing in English. And as pendant to the gentleman it is important to add the lady, someone perhaps never better drawn than in Shakespeare's Portia, so frank, free and grand, as well as witty, brave and wise. In real life, such a figure as François I's sister, Marguerite of Navarre, represents the type most attractively: herself a voluminous writer, patroness of Marot and Rabelais, enlightened, philosophic, religious and preoccupied by love. She certainly could have fitted into the court of Urbino as seen by Castiglione, and had something of the all-round interests which he stipulated the lady must have: 'a sight in letters, in music, in drawing or painting'.

It does not matter that such figures, whether female or male, probably tended to remain somewhat sporadic or ideal. The novelty lies in recognition of 'drawing or painting' as among the skills and arts which any cultivated person should acquire. 'That it is comendable in a gentyllman to paint and kerve exactly, if nature therto doth induce hym', was already the view of Sir Thomas Elyot in *The Boke named the Governour* (1531). Rabelais's Gargantua, when educated on new principles, studies 'the art of painting or carving . . . how the lapidaries did work; as also the goldsmiths and cutters of precious stones'. Enough contemporary visual artists had proved that art could reach a height not to be ignored. The artist becomes someone who can easily be referred to in literature as symbolic of all art's image-making power. The artist can build or sculpt with such vitality as to challenge death and oblivion. Art can catch with new subtlety facets of the natural world, itself being freshly explored, a cosmos recognized as bizarre, even alien, but with secrets to be discovered. More than ever, art pursues a quest for absolute beauty, rich, complex, ideal. And pulsing strongly under all these manifestations is the steady belief that art possesses divinely creative energy and in its perfection can conquer Nature.

Something of what these themes were to mean in the High Renaissance forms the substance of the chapters which follow.

2

'Mine Eye Hath Play'd the Painter'

It is always dangerous in affairs of art and culture to claim total novelty for any concept or even current of taste. What changes is more usually the emphasis placed on a concept. Shockingly new artistic creations like Picasso's *Demoiselles d'Avignon* are rare enough – and even here it is too easy to falsify history and suggest that all Paris reeled in front of a picture which the majority of Parisians remained quite unaware of (it not being exhibited publicly until thirty years after it was painted) and indifferent to.

Probably it is more salutary to remember this fact than to dream wistfully of a better, more cultured and enlightened milieu, with every man an eager aesthete, if not artist *manqué*, when one considers conditions during the Renaissance. Because much was then produced which we now go to look at specifically as art, it might be supposed that Renaissance men looked at artistic products in the same way. This is not so. Often they will not have seen the 'art' for the subject-matter or for the utilitarian-cum-didactic purpose which had led to the object being created in the first place. Statues of saints and heroes, churches and palaces, altarpieces and fresco cycles – all were executed for purposes quite separate from, and much more urgent than, providing merely agreeable sensations for the eye. There is remarkably little evidence about how people in the fifteenth century reacted to the *style* of individual works, and perhaps they scarcely had this concept, having in its place a vague general standard whereby work was good or bad. Up to the late nineteenth century (if not, indeed, beyond) the general public at any period probably judged painting and sculpture in terms of its subject-matter; and from the Renaissance onwards a vague criterion of life-like representation was applied. It is no accident that architecture has never greatly appealed to that public, for it lacks subject-matter and the criterion of realism is of course inapplicable.

It is hard to exaggerate the hypnotic power which subject-matter had exercised in art. A Florentine church requiring an altarpiece of, say, the Crucifixion would be more concerned basically with having this painted well (that is, competently and, doubtless, quickly) than with choosing between Botticelli, Leonardo and Ghirlandaio as exponents of different, highly personal styles. Much the same is true in the secular category of the portrait. A competent resemblance to the features of the person portrayed is likely to have been the main test of its artistic quality. 'Art' would be, at most, a bonus and, in any sense of being fanciful, might be a positive demerit. Proof is obviously lacking of what exactly a mid-fifteenth-century citizen of Florence, Venice or Bruges felt on encountering some newly displayed picture in his local church, but it must have been difficult, if not impossible, for him to look with the unengaged eye of the average spectator of the same picture exhibited today in a museum. Art as a purely pleasure-giving experience would have been found much more easily outside the visual arts, in listening to music or in dancing.

Such a situation did not, could not, change abruptly. The Renaissance itself, in any manifestation, had not arrived in Europe like a new disease or an exotic animal, with its first year of appearance to be tabulated. In making any distinctions between Early and High Renaissance – between two styles which were as organically linked as stem and flower – chronology must not be used like pruning shears. One of the first works of art mentioned (and partly illustrated) in this book as a seminal High Renaissance object is Leonardo's *Virgin of the Rocks*, painted probably around 1483, the year of Raphael's birth. Yet not only is that picture in many ways the culminating (though unforeseen) achievement of much Early Renaissance striving, but its creation did not create the High Renaissance like the Spirit moving upon the face of the waters. There was not henceforward a tide of victorious new style sweeping across Europe, drowning in neglect those who painted differently from Leonardo.

And yet, gradually, the situation changed. The work and the personalities of Leonardo, Raphael, Titian and Michelangelo – to name only the most obvious artists – affected, interested and attracted more people in Europe than had previously been concerned about any artist or his art. This was not entirely a matter of art, for part of the new interest arose from a more developed interest in personality as such, and in recording it. It was a novelty that a living artist should be the subject of a biography, as was Michelangelo in Condivi's authorized *Life*

26. *Self-Portrait naked, c.* 1503. Albrecht Dürer

of 1553. Biography in general was in no way new, but auto-biography – especially by artists – was certainly rare before the sixteenth century. And so was the self-portrait. Dürer is the earliest example in the period of the artist producing both painted and written self-portraiture, but though his fascination with his own personality may be unusual in its intensity, it is typical in its conviction that every artist has a core of interesting individuality. The metaphor of painting came to Montaigne when he declared that, had he lived in a simpler and more primitive country, he would very willingly have depicted himself for his readers 'full-length and quite naked'. Dürer actually did so [26]. He would certainly have understood Montaigne's calm claim, '*Je suis moi-même la matière de mon livre.*'

Cellini's famous *Autobiography* (intended for publication, though not published until the eighteenth century) is full of subtle strokes as well as braggadocio. In it he lives no less as an individual than as an artist. More memorable than all his self-praise, quarrels and quips is the brief passage where he speaks of daily rides alone along on the sea-shore near Civita Vecchia, picking up pebbles and shells whose beauty and rarity appealed to him. His eye for such things positively brings to mind some of the highly wrought and often more than faintly marine jewellery of the period [23], Cellinesque though not by him, sophisticated transmutations of nature like the buskins de-scribed by Marlowe in *Hero and Leander*: 'Buskins of shells all silvered usèd she'.

Biography and autobiography were one aspect of a general interest in recording personality, an interest bound to be encouraged by the growth of printing and a widening audience of people who could read and possess books. The idea of what might almost be called 'self-portrait sketches' is found in another innovation, the publication of one's own letters; Aretino is the prime example (a first volume of his letters was published in 1538) but other people soon followed suit. For this there was if not quite a precedent at least an encouragement in Cicero's letters (rediscovered by Petrarch), a doctored selection of which had originally been intended by Cicero for publication in his lifetime. Although no artist published his own letters, the letters of Michelangelo were carefully preserved and certain letters from artists (often doubtless intended for publication) were to be published on matters of artistic concern.

While learned treatises might be addressed by artists to fellow-practitioners, a literally popular step – and a new one –

lay in the more 'human interest' story of an artist's life, whether or not told by himself. Much of the impetus of any treatise was increasingly to proclaim the dignity and creativity of the visual arts (as opposed to earlier instructions on how to practise them), and biography and autobiography offered opportunities for proclaiming the same qualities, often in dramatic ways. Most treatises make some mention of the arts having been honoured in antiquity; and it would be rare to find one of these works omitting the example of Alexander's high estimate of, and generosity to, Apelles.

But the creative power of a living artist (so frequently to be called 'another Apelles') can be more pertinently testified to by an anecdote from his own career. Thus what might seem merely boastful in Cellini's account of his artistic achievements is really part of what may be called High Renaissance doctrine. When he showed François I the model of his famous salt-cellar [142], the king exclaimed, 'This is a hundred times more divine a thing than I had ever dreamed of. What a miracle of a man!' A modern monarch is heard paying tribute to a modern artist (one frank enough to have told us a few pages before how the king entered his house one day to find he had just sent sprawling an assistant with a kick in the crutch). There was no particular expectation that the god-like artist was in ordinary life a deity – at least not an especially calm and good-tempered one. Raphael's notorious urbanity was probably less typical than Michelangelo's *terribilità*; certainly Cellini came closer to the temperament of Michelangelo, and Vasari described him frankly as *'terribilissimo'*.

That the great artist has not only creative power but also intense individuality, which expresses itself in art by a highly personal style, may not strictly be a 'discovery' of the High Renaissance, yet it was then that it became widely recognized and appreciated. The exchange of work between Dürer and Raphael is perhaps too specialized an example, although it is significant that Dürer should annotate the drawing Raphael sent him [27] as dispatched 'to show him [Dürer] his hand'.

A great patron like Isabella d'Este was content to have any-thing which Leonardo da Vinci would execute for her: 'we will leave the invention and the time to his decision'. Indeed, when once she tried to tie Bellini down to painting some subject which her intermediary Bembo should assign him, it was Bembo who explained to her firmly that it was necessary to accept whatever the painter himself wished to depict; Bellini

27. Nude studies for the *Battle of Ostia*, 1515. Raphael (?)

disliked restrictions being put on him, for he was accustomed 'to wander at will in his paintings' (*sempre vagare a sua voglia nelle pitture*).

Nor was it enough, when a superior artist appeared, for a portrait to be a competent likeness. Holbein had hardly reached Brussels to portray Christina of Denmark for Henry VIII, when the English ambassador stopped dispatch of a quite official recent portrait of her; 'it was not so perfect as the cause required' and also, significantly, 'as the said Mr Hans could make it'. Once again, we hear the adjective 'perfect'. Most striking of all, because most public, was Castiglione's statement in the *Cortegiano* that while Leonardo, Mantegna, Raphael, Michelangelo and Giorgione are excellent artists, each is quite unlike the other and yet we recognize 'each is most perfect in his own style' (*ciascun nel suo stile . . . perfettissimo*). As it happens, this idea is directly borrowed from Cicero, but made topical of course by Castiglione's examples.

The instances quoted are enough to suggest that the personal style of the great artist was what was valued; one further instance is the excitement generated at Venice by the news that Titian was leaving for Augsburg, to paint Charles V, which led to people besieging his house to obtain something – it hardly mattered what – from his hand. Incidentally, patrons soon learnt, if they did not already know, that waiting for a great man's flash of inspiration could occupy many years. Leonardo may be the most familiar example, but Bellini, Raphael and Titian also led several princes to stand – with increasing impatience – in Canossa-like situations outside their studios. But genius could seldom be swayed, still less hurried, and for all the secret or not so secret annoyance the patron had felt, when the object eventually reached him he usually wrote in hectically fulsome gratitude to the artist, praising his genius and confessing himself the artist's servant.

Such phrases are doubtless not to be taken too literally, but even as a convention the sense of recognition is marked. It is summed up in the moment when François I put his hand on Cellini's shoulder and called him '*mon ami*', positively anticipating Pope Urban VIII's remark to Bernini on his accession when he declared that he did not know if the pleasure was greater for the prince who finds an artist after his own heart or for the artist who finds a prince willing to encourage execution of his great ideas. The final step is that the artist himself should document such explicit homage, as Cellini did. And one may also recall that moving occasion recorded by Dürer, when he went to a banquet in Antwerp and at his entry the whole company rose, as if for 'some great lord'.

Such demonstrations – courtly and civic – dramatically mark the impact that the artist could make as an artist. Much less dramatic but perhaps ultimately of greater significance was the dissemination to a wider public – a wider public than ever before in Western Europe – of ideas about living artists and contemporary art. These were not expressed in a learned language but in the accessible vernacular. They were not part of theoretical treatises, nor practical handbooks, but essentially conversations by or for cultured people who were now assumed to be as interested in the visual arts as in, say, literature. The discussions are often in the form of dialogues, sometimes with fictitious people and sometimes with people as actual as Aretino.

That this new type of literature – art criticism – originated in Venice was no accident, and nor was its social tone. It was there that very early in the sixteenth century had developed the social-group picture, a sort of non-sacred *conversazione* [28], in which two or three people are painted, often playing music, and clearly communicating with each other. Such pictures may be portraits but they are also genre: reflecting, even if idealizing, the tone of ordinary civilized life between equals. This was the society in which painters like Giorgione and Titian moved. Vasari described specifically Giorgione's musical abilities and his popularity at musical and comparable social gatherings. Aretino, on settling in Venice, became a close friend of Titian's. Along with the sculptor-cum-architect Sansovino, they formed what was called the 'triumvirate', and one of their festive evenings in Titian's beautiful garden was rapturously described by a visiting scholar who did not fail to mention that time was spent before supper looking at pictures, 'of which the house was full'.

One practical reason for the appearance at Venice of books of art criticism and discussion was the flourishing state of printing and publishing there. This tradition was established by 1500, by which date over half of the books printed in Italy, it has been estimated, had been printed at Venice. But there is a further, more subjective factor in the non-courtly atmosphere of the city. At Rome and Florence, as in France, England and Spain, High Renaissance culture revolved round the person of the ruler, while at Venice the personality of the reigning doge scarcely affected the tenor of life; its citizens were never the subjects of an absolute prince. All the more did the idea of Venice, the proud and most serene Republic, exercise a myth-like power. It was she who was absolute, but once this was granted – and left uncriticized – there existed a certain tolerance and independence which Aretino and several other non-Venetian literary figures were glad to enjoy.

28. *A Concert, c.* 1512(?). Titian

Yet, ultimately, the impetus at Venice for publication of discussions about art lay in art itself, and particularly in one artist. As the sixteenth century progressed, Titian's longevity and ceaseless activity must have come almost to symbolize the vitality of the Venetian state. Raphael had died prematurely. Michelangelo, for all his fame, raised something of a problem in patriotism. He lived and worked in Rome, never returning to Florence during the last thirty years of his own long life. Florence in the middle of the century did not lack a great painter (for it possessed Bronzino) but it did lack a truly international and widely celebrated figure working there. Titian, however, remained in and of Venice. He had become one of its monuments towards the end of a career which occupied over sixty years. When in 1574, two years before his death, he was visited by the new king of France, Henri III, that visit was like some last tribute by the European monarchy to the painter so many of them had patronized. And it was not merely a question of monarchs. After visiting him in 1566, Vasari recorded that every man of letters and every gentleman, as well as every prince, who went to Venice went to see Titian. The obvious exaggeration does not matter, for Titian's colossal fame was as beyond doubt as is Picasso's today. His pictures had gone to Spain, England, France, Flanders and Germany. In Italy he had portrayed innumerable rulers and popes, in addition to several doges, and had painted other pictures for many of the people who sat for him.

Age no doubt consecrated his fame, and his art rightly continued to astound the ever increasing total of his patrons. But even before any general discussions about the arts were published, Aretino was giving Titian's growing fame the support of his influential pen. Aretino's interest in the arts, proclaimed in letters which were frequently published, must itself have exercised an influence at Venice. His attachment to Titian was at once genuine and valuable, and is only the more effective because of his warm admiration for other painters like Giulio Romano and Parmigianino. No previous painter had had the benefit of a literary figure steadily at his side – and, additionally, such a very powerful, persuasive and amusing figure – ready to support his art with eloquent prose. Even the very kind of praise which a few literary figures had on occasion given to some painter was usually deplorably vague and unspecific: the artist painted well and his work was life-like. But Aretino, who certainly said such things about Titian, was able to say much more. He was well aware of style in the sense of an artist's personal 'handwriting'; he could distinguish between Andrea Schiavone's skilful compositions and his too sketchy technique of execution – as he kindly wrote and told Schiavone. Somewhat similarly, he quite early suggested that Tintoretto should modify *'la prestezza del fatto'* into *'la pazienza del fare'*.

In a famous letter to Titian, he allowed his eye to play the painter with sensitive precision. In no academic–humanist mood, but after a lonely meal simply gazing out of his window over the Grand Canal in Venice, he saw something worthy of Titian's brush: a picture of light and shadow made by the setting sun, with buildings changing into unreal substances, while muffled clouds half-caught the fiery brightness. Far from this being some over-literary piece of embroidery, the description positively suggests certain effects achieved by Titian [29], as Aretino indeed recognized. The sky receded behind the palaces, he wrote, as it does in the landscapes of Titian (*'con il*

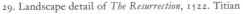

29. Landscape detail of *The Resurrection*, 1522. Titian

modo che la discosta il Vecellio . . .'). And he longed for Titian to be present to paint the scene, to catch in art what was gradually passing in Nature.

When in one of the best known of Venetian artistic discussions, Ludovico Dolce's *Dialogo della pittura* (1557), Aretino – to whom it is dedicated – is made the mouthpiece of praise for Titian, it is no contrived tribute. The painter and the man of letters had much in common: a sensuous, almost greedy grasp on life. In Dolce's *Dialogo*, Aretino praises the superiority of Raphael. His opponent, a Tuscan, argues for Michelangelo who is eventually allowed to stand supreme as a sculptor. As a painter Raphael becomes his superior, but Raphael is dead. Thus the way is cleared for the discussion with which the *Dialogo* ends, celebrating Titian as supreme among living painters. Aretino embarks on a quick outline of recent art – Giulio Romano, Parmigianino, Andrea del Sarto – but then concentrates on the one painter who sums up the varied qualities of lesser men: 'truly in him [Titian] alone can one see brought together in perfection all the excellent parts divided among others . . . he walks as Nature's equal' (*egli camina di pari con la Natura*). What in effect is a compressed biography follows, culminating in the final statement of Titian's unique genius. He is divine and unequalled: '*È adunque il nostro Titiano nella Pittura divino e senza pari*'.

That is a ringing, even challenging, declaration. When it appeared, by which time the real Aretino was dead, it represented something of an 'answer' from Venice to the Tuscan–Roman standards of Vasari, whose *Lives* in its first edition certainly had not treated Titian as other than one of several reasonably good painters. In the reserves and enthusiasms – whereby gradually Titian and Michelangelo became the leaders of rival factions – there was the exercise of taste, as well as local patriotism, and a keen consciousness of different styles, based in different cities.

By their very existence, the dialogues and discussions published testify to a new climate where literate people, as well as artists, can give their quite lively views about the art of their own day. Dolce, for example, was not at all an authority on art, any more than was another so-called polygraph, Anton Francesco Doni. But Doni dedicated his *Rime del Burchiello* (1553) to Tintoretto, calling him 'unique' and thanking him for having painted his portrait (lost) – one of the very earliest public mentions of a painter then probably little known outside Venice. Doni also wrote directly about art, in a rather dreary book *il Disegno* (highly praising the Florentine sculptor Bandinelli). But art more interestingly inspired him perhaps in his allegorical word-pictures called *le Pitture* (1564). These descriptions of love, fortune, chastity, etc., are not so far removed from the sort of descriptive programmes which might be drawn up for series of pictures to decorate rooms or serve at masques and triumphs, by littérateurs or by great poets such as Ronsard in France. Even in one of the more abstruse of these programmes incidentally – that devised for the Farnese villa at Caprarola – the freedom of the painter's imagination had to be recognized. 'Since he has obviously refused to adapt himself to you,' one of the scholarly planners of the Caprarola scheme wrote ruefully to another about the painter, 'we must of necessity adapt ourselves to him . . .'

No doubt a great artist's worth had always been appreciated by a sympathetic patron or in a select, often courtly, circle, though his obedience had also been necessary. But increasingly a wider and somewhat less restricted public became aware of art as an aspect of general culture – often stimulated perhaps by what it could now read on the subject. What was developing was 'taste' in the sense of personal preference for this or that artist's style, regardless of subject-matter. The artist's *art* is the essential thing to be appreciated. When in 1553 Mary of Hungary sent Titian's portrait of her nephew Philip to London to be seen by Queen Mary I, she explained that Titian's pictures must be seen at a fitting distance and were not to be looked at too closely. As for distaste, an early example seems to occur over Tintoretto at the Scuola di San Rocco, where one member of the Confraternity agreed to contribute to the cost of pictures for the Scuola only on condition that Tintoretto was not chosen as the painter.

It is probably not wrong to suggest too that more people were collecting art, forming small yet quite personal private collections. That activity certainly began to be documented for the first time, and an anonymous sixteenth-century writer in North Italy (possibly the Venetian Marcantonio Michiel) made interesting and detailed notes of the collections in private houses at Milan, Padua, Venice and other cities. A cultured person may be expected to own a few pictures and bronzes, just as he owns books. The artist's studio itself becomes a subject

30. (top) *The Studio of Bandinelli*. Enea Vico after Bandinelli
31. *An Artist's Studio*. Philippe Galle after Stradanus

for art [30 and 31]. In the engraving after Bandinelli's drawing, the evening occupations in a studio are impressive and varied. Books, antique casts and human skeletons all serve as reminders that the artist, especially the young aspiring artist, studies hard and seeks knowledge – no less than does the literary scholar or philosopher. Bandinelli himself is seen in profound thought. If in Stradanus's daylight scene there is less emphasis on the intellectual pursuit of art, there is evidence of the painter able both to follow nature competently, in the portrait-painting corner at the left, and to work from his imagination, as in the prominent central depiction of a painter finishing a large-scale canvas of St George and the Dragon.

Such factual scenes from the artist's life must have played their part in focusing attention freshly on art. In place of the story of Apelles painting Campaspe for Alexander, or St Luke painting the Virgin, we are given a depiction which is entirely contemporary and which illustrates no particular story. Instead, it answers the question of what goes on in an artist's studio. In Bandinelli's composition there is probably an explicit intention to stress intellectual, social and non-mechanical status for the artist. It is worth noting that his arms (he got himself knighted) appear above the fireplace. He – alone among Italian Renaissance artists of any rank – left both a painted self-portrait and also, perhaps encouraged by friendship with Doni, a *Memoriale* of his life.

In this document, which actually mentions his need to 'study at night', he displays an egregious insistence on his own ability and social success which is totally uncritical and much less attractive than Cellini's. The *Memoriale* is addressed to his sons, who are recommended to keep his outstanding drawings 'as so many jewels', and to have care especially of his self-portrait. They are also reminded of his poetic activities: '*ho composto da 200 sonnetti . . .*' Bandinelli was basically a sculptor and it was in sculpture finally that he decided to commemorate his existence, with a splendid tomb [32a] where egotism and piety mingle. The head of Nicodemus [32b] supporting Christ is an idealized portrait (executed by Bandinelli's son) and Bandinelli spent a long time 'going round the principal churches of Florence' – in Vasari's words – looking for a good place to set up a tomb planned to be more elaborate than it is.

Michelangelo, Titian, and Cellini are other artists of the period who intended work of their own to be incorporated in their tombs. Only Bandinelli managed to achieve this and raise

32a. *Dead Christ supported by Nicodemus*, 1559. Baccio Bandinelli
32b. (*opposite*) Detail of 32a

his own monument. This triumph, by an artist whom posterity ranks so much lower than the other three, would have been perhaps sufficient satisfaction for his ambitious sense of rivalry.

Although the ways seem, indeed were, disparate, and the motives mixed, the cumulative effect of discussion, advertisement and personal striving was that, culturally and socially, the artist had 'arrived'. No sooner, however, was the artist admitted to the family of the arts, than inter-sibling rivalry broke out. Among the visual arts, is painting superior or inferior to sculpture? This absurd question was quite seriously canvassed, being given a smart send-off by Leonardo da Vinci who claimed the superiority of painting. The Florentine littérateur Benedetto Varchi later ventilated the question among artists of the mid century at which time Michelangelo and Cellini predictably claimed the superiority of sculpture, while Bronzino argued for painting.

Hardly more useful a question, though one susceptible of more interesting discussion, was that of the relationship of painting to poetry; Leonardo again assumed the superiority of painting. But this discussion was not restricted to rivalry. There was a long tradition of supposing similarity and affinity between painting and poetry. It could be meaningfully revived at the very period when the painter had achieved an impact on contemporaries which forced them to take notice of his gifts. Instead of emulating Leonardo and claiming superiority for their own medium, poets joined with other literary figures (several of whom have already been mentioned here) in giving a generous new meaning to Horace's 'ut pictura poesis', and paying tribute to their artistic brothers, painters.

Probably more subtle – because individual artists had always drawn individual tributes – is the dissemination by metaphor and analogy, and sometimes by direct example, of the idea of painting as a great, skilled art. It is hardly excessive to see this following on the fact that it was painting, above all, which had impressed itself – almost abruptly – on contemporaries as the most evolved and perfect visual art. That it was truly an *art*, and can therefore rank with poetry, was recognized by, for example, a distinguished scholar of the period, Annibale Caro, who commissioned a picture from Vasari in a letter (written in 1548) more valuable perhaps than the commission. Caro willingly recognized that painting and poetry are akin in needing the stimulus of inspiration, and he declared that he would leave the subject of his picture to Vasari, 'remembering another similarity that painting has with poetry'. The similarity is that in both the tendency is to express better ideas of the artist's own rather than those allotted him by another person. (It must be admitted that having said all this, Caro goes on to give Vasari a subject and also to specify the passage in Theocritus which should provide his general inspiration.)

Facility, invention and inspiration were not of course lacking in the other visual arts, but the slower process of execution of sculpture and architecture seemed to offer less analogy than painting or drawing with poetic frenzy. Outside Italy even Michelangelo was perhaps more famous as a painter than as a sculptor; at least, the Elizabethan poet Constable's sonnet on a portrait by Hilliard begins by hailing him as 'Michael the arch painter' – a judgement with which Reynolds would have concurred.

33. *Candelabrum grotesque*, 1528. Lucas van Leyden

The existence of the painter alongside the poet, like the use of comparisons between their arts, could be traced back vaguely to Aristotle's *Poetics*; one reference occurs there to types of imitation in painting and one very cursory comparison introduces painting. The *Poetics* were first printed in the 1531 Venetian edition of Aristotle. Not particularly specific but much more familiar were the mentions by Horace in the *Art of Poetry*, where indeed the word *'pictor'* appears in the opening line. The license given to *'pictoribus atque poetis'* is something Horace admits, while setting un-Renaissance limits to the play of fancy – positively protesting against the absurdity of a picture attempting to marry a woman's form and a fish. What would he have said about Lucas van Leyden's controlled but richly fantastic design [33], which might seem to accept his challenge? In what has become the most famous of tags, *'ut pictura poesis'*, Horace appeared to equate a picture and a poem, though what he actually goes on to say in the context is merely that they are alike in needing to be assessed by the standards relevant to their individual achievement: some works of art love to be seen in a dim atmosphere; others show best in full light.

Not again until Petrarch perhaps does the supposed sisterhood of painting and poetry take on any real significance. In other words, a Renaissance impetus was needed. Petrarch certainly raised painting from being a mechanical art, not only by his praise of Simone Martini and Giotto, but by his praise of Homer as *'primo pintor delle memorie antiche'*. If the painter can be equated with Homer he need not complain of his status. In the fifteenth century Alberti had mentioned the community of interest between painters and poets. But by the sixteenth century references to painting have entered poetical language in several countries, and it was probably more common for the poet to claim he was playing the painter than, like Camoëns, to call painting 'silent poetry' (*muda poesia*). Struck by the art of a contemporary – as Ronsard was by that of Clouet – it was almost inevitable that a poet should let analogies from it creep into a poem such as Ronsard's elegy for Mary, Queen of Scots, whom Clouet and comparable artists had portrayed [34]:

> Bien que le trait de vostre belle face
> Peinte en mon cœur par le temps ne s'efface,
> Et que tousjours je le porte imprimé
> Comme un tableau vivement animé . . .

34. *Mary, Queen of Scots in white mourning.* After François Clouet
(Reproduced by permission of the Trustees of the Wallace Collection)

The very linear style in which she was depicted in thin white
mourning is brought to mind by Ronsard's lines about that
'*habit de deuil*' which the queen was wearing when he last saw
her:

> *Un crespe long, subtil et delié,*
> *Ply contre ply retors et replié,*

35. Nymphs from the *Fontaine des Innocents*, 1547–9. Jean Goujon

'*Ply contre ply*' seems to characterize other aspects too of contemporary French art, like the subtly entwined draperies of
Goujon's nymphs [35] or, perhaps closer still, the delicate,
alluring veils, covering without concealing the mysterious
Sabina-Poppaea [36]: '*Et la beauté de vostre gorge vive*'.

When Shakespeare began a sonnet with the words that are the title of this chapter, he was using a metaphor which plenty of people beyond the immediate circle of his 'private friends' would easily understand. What he says may not seem, and

36. *Sabina-Poppaea*. Mid-sixteenth-century French School

strictly speaking was not, new. Yet his recognition of a power in painting, combined with many other literary references of the period, suggests new awareness – come from painting itself – of what it can achieve. Like the painter, his eye has created 'Thy beauty's form in table of my heart'. It is a portrait –

that most popular category of picture not just in England but throughout High Renaissance Europe – and inevitably one thinks of it in terms of some sophisticated contemporary miniature by Hilliard [37].

The portrait of a gallant leaning immaculate against a tree-trunk amid curling briar-roses is itself no bad symbol of a perfect marriage between art and nature, nature here including real response to the texture of bark and the springing shoots of the wild rose that pattern, without scratching, his exquisite clothes. For all its small scale, it is a full-length portrait, painted with an accomplishment that has nothing small or cramped about it; and at the same time, it is beautifully finished, with the glowing precision of Renaissance jewellery and enamels. There was a European vogue for miniature portraits, though few, if any, can rival Hilliard's and more than one poet paid direct tribute by name to his art. Shakespeare certainly knew and elsewhere referred to such jewel-like miniatures, so often worn and exchanged as tokens by his contemporaries and by characters in his plays. 'Wear this jewel for me,' Olivia bids the disguised Viola in *Twelfth Night*, ''tis my picture'.

The sonnet references suggest something larger perhaps and less obviously portable: a 'table', framed and glazed, 'Which in my bosom's shop is hanging still'. One of the remarkable things about this sonnet is that the metaphors of painting continue throughout: 'For perspective it is best painter's art'. Although a picture may not be able to show more than the outward appearance of someone, its ability to do this in the hands of a talented master is yet something to prize:

> For through the painter must you see his skill,
> To find where your true image pictur'd lies.

The selection of the best painter, as opposed to a limited craftsman, is something referred to by, for instance, Ascham in *The Scholemaster* (1570), using this example as a simile of how the good teacher is chosen: 'And as in portraicture and paintyng wyse men chose not that workman that can onelie make a faire hand...' This is strikingly akin to an observation of Leonardo's which Ascham cannot have known. Much more explicit is the stress laid by Sir Philip Sidney in the *Apology for Poetry* (written *c*. 1583), making comparisons between two types of poet 'as betwixt the meaner sort of Painters (who counterfet onely such faces as are sette before them) and the more excellent, who,

37. *Young man standing amid briars*, *c.* 1590. Nicholas Hilliard

38. *The Duke of Alba*, 1571. Jacques Jonghelinck

having no law but wit, bestow that in cullors upon you which
is fittest for the eye to see'.

Hilliard's miniature may claim to be of this second sort, for
like so many other portraits of the century, sculpted and
painted [38 and 39], it suggests a mood as well as depicting a
person. The briars are more than naturalistic; they stand for
the lover's pains, themselves inflicted on him by his own
fidelity ('*Dat poenas laudata fides*' is written round the top of the
picture). Moroni's gentleman poses amid symbolic ruins, and
proclaims '*Impavidum ferient ruinae*'. Fearless to the point of
arrogance seems the character of Alba in Jonghelinck's bust.

39. *Portrait of a Man*, 1554. Giovanni Battista Moroni

40. *Venus and Adonis*, 1553. Titian

Sidney himself had been careful when in Venice to find the painters who held 'the highest place in the art' before selecting from them the one to whom he would sit for his portrait. Clearly, he discriminated with some care, because he found himself having to choose between Tintoretto and Veronese; it was finally the latter who painted him (in a now lost portrait). And several further references in his works confirm that he had a considerable interest in painting. The poet and the painter are admitted as equal in his eyes, probably more instinctively than in those of Shakespeare.

It is worth lingering over English attitudes, for if it was the last major European country to become aware of the achievements of Renaissance painting, it was also the one whose literature seems most impressed by the new art. Shakespeare and painting is a subject in itself, about which the last word has not yet been said because it is by no means clear what Italian pictures, for instance, he had or had not seen. But behind that 'first heir of his invention', *Venus and Adonis*, it would be tempting to think there might be somehow a faint recollection of Titian's composition [40], the prime version of which had indeed been sent to Philip II in London. Before Titian, it would seem, nobody in either painting or literature had conceived the idea of the reluctant Adonis who is the protagonist of Shakespeare's poem. Already there Shakespeare turns aside to praise the painter, in fully Renaissance terms:

> Look, when a painter would surpass the life
> In limning out a well-proportioned steed,
> His art with nature's workmanship at strife.

Few English painters of the period had attempted to paint horses of any kind, but the 'well-proportioned steed' seems a more than accidental echo of that interest which both Leonardo and Dürer had shown in the proportions of the horse, and which had been publicly crystallized in Sebald Beham's book (published in 1528) on that very subject. Art at strife with nature is not only in itself a major High Renaissance concern (dealt with here in Chapter 6), but it is the aspect of the visual arts Shakespeare stresses at greater length in his next narrative poem, again paralleled in subject by Titian's pictures, *The Rape of Lucrece*. The distressed Lucrece wanders to a piece of 'skilful painting' that depicts the fall of Troy: a wonderful, consciously impossible, work of art, a vast pageant-scene intensely affecting

in the passions it conveys and almost impressionistic in its
technique:

> For much imaginary work was there;
> Conceit deceitful, so compact, so kind,
> That for Achilles' image stood his spear,
> Grip'd in an armed hand; himself, behind,
> Was left unseen, save to the eye of mind:
> A hand, a foot, a face, a leg, a head,
> Stood for the whole to be imagined.

Art's power to suggest has seldom been more crisply summed
up. In such ways it becomes indeed more effective and com-
pelling than nature. Lucrece is a typical but highly sophisticated
spectator of this piece of contemporary art which can afford to
move fast, evoking the effect, rather than prosaically depicting
each figure of a crowd. What come to mind are the spears or
banners, heads and gesticulating hands in groups painted by
Venetian painters like Tintoretto and particularly Veronese
[41], so skilfully economical and artistically stimulating.
'Work, work your imaginations . . .' as the mature playwright
was to urge his audience.

It is not only in the sonnet (XXIV) already quoted that the
conceit of painting occurs, though in none of the others is it
worked out so elaborately. The eye literally picturing or
painting the loved one ('With my love's picture then my eye
doth feast') becomes a commonplace of Elizabethan poetry,
but such a commonplace is only possible when society responds
to it. Love paints 'thy heavenly shape' in another of Constable's
sonnets, and to espy 'how thou painted art' is mentioned in yet
another. Elsewhere the heart is 'the love-limned tablet' or
holds framed a 'faire counterfeit' – ideas perhaps suggested
simply because miniatures might be worn round the neck close
to the heart. Altogether, the poetry agrees to emphasize frames
and glasses and beautiful life-like portraiture. A rare reference
is to 'the label underneath', in a poem of Robert Southwell's,
Upon the Image of Death, which deals with a rather different yet
probably typical sort of picture, of a skull. A picture of 'carrion
Death' is what the Prince of Morocco finds in choosing the
golden casket when he seeks to marry Portia. The carved or
painted *memento mori* was hardly new. But perspective ('best
painter's art') can make a chilling effect out of the old device,
concealing it at first glance and then revealing it, as in Holbein's

41. Detail of *The Family of Darius before Alexander*. Veronese

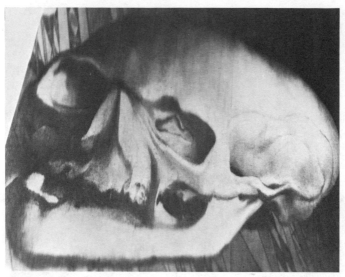

42. Detail of the skull (perspective corrected)
from '*The Ambassadors*', 1533. Hans Holbein

Ambassadors [42]. A quite early inventory records a 'cunning perspective of Death and a woman' – painted by Hilliard. Nor did the effect of such pictures pass unnoticed by Shakespeare. In *Richard II* are mentioned 'perspectives' which gazed at directly 'show nothing but confusion – ey'd awry/Distinguish form'.

In references to specific, if often imaginary, pictures and in the use of metaphors and similes drawn from painting, there is a constant sense of a new art discovered for literary purposes – not perhaps replacing music as the richest source of analogy but certainly offering the possibility of fresh affinities. The contemporary critic and friend of Spenser, 'E.K.', finds comparisons between his work and 'the most exquisite pictures'. No colours can depict Samuel Daniel's sorrows, nor are his passions 'limned for outward hue'. Worth and beauty are painted and portrayed in many poems. Ben Jonson refers specifically in one play to someone looking like a Venetian trumpeter 'in the battle of Lepanto', and again to a headdress being 'after the Italian print we look'd on t'other night'. At the end of *The White Devil* Flaminio boasts significantly of the horrible scene: 'I limned this night piece; and it was my best'. The Prince of Morocco is confronted with a painted skull, but the fortunate Bassanio discovers what is surely a Venetian portrait of Portia, with fine golden hair in which 'The painter plays the spider'. Drayton suggests a new breed of man, the connoisseur:

> When on those sundry pictures they devise
> And from one piece they to another run
> Commend that face, that arm, that hand, those eyes,
> Show how that bird, how well that flower was done.

Lyly naturally includes Apelles in his play of *Campaspe* (published 1584). Amid inevitable conceits around such words as 'colour' and 'shadow' there are also erotic mythological pictures – of Leda, Alcmene, Danaë – in Apelles' studio. And Alexander receives a lesson in art from his painter: at once moral as well as practical, for when he attempts to paint, he learns that even a successful king can fail as an artist. The task's difficulty is emphasized when Alexander asks how soon Apelles' portrait of Campaspe will be finished; Lyly makes Apelles reply: 'Never *finish*! for always in absolute beauty, there is somewhat above art'. Leonardo's *paragone* or comparison of painting and poetry is treated in dramatic terms in the opening scene of *Timon of Athens*, where a painter and poet each claim tenaciously, for all their surface politeness, the superiority of their own arts. When the Poet speaks of his concept of Fortune's hill, the painter expostulates that, 'more pregnantly than words', can painting convey such images. Most significant of all for High Renaissance aesthetics is the compliment that his piece of painting (perhaps a portrait of Timon) elicits from the Poet: 'It tutors nature'.

Probably no English poet of the period more seriously 'play'd the painter' than Sir Philip Sidney – less, however, in the imagery of his poetry than in specific references in the *Arcadia* and the *Apology for Poetry* which suggest a connoisseur's eye for pictures. Shakespeare can invent his own. Spenser may be pictorial, but Sidney is aware of painting as a distinct art, analogous to poetry yet with its particular achievements and effects. That Sidney should crystallize such new awareness seems no accident, because he crystallizes so well all the century's courtier-style aspirations. His life itself becomes a work of art, at least in Fulke Greville's account of him. His chivalry, his cultivated interests, his own literary gifts, his international reputation and, finally, the manner of his death – calling for music before passing into 'that everlasting harmony

43. *Hercules and Omphale*, 1537. Lucas Cranach

of angels whereof those concords were a kind of terrestial echo' – make him a European epitome of the cultured *gentiluomo*-cum-patron. 'His heart and capacity were so large,' Greville wrote, 'that there was not a cunning Painter, a skilful Engineer, an excellent Musician, or any other artificer of extraordinary fame that made not himself known to this famous spirit, and found him his true friend . . .'

Sidney's prose references to pictures seem quite spontaneous and uncontrived. When in the *Arcadia* Basilius falls down before Zelmane 'holding up his hands as the old governesse of Danae is painted, when she sodainly saw the golde[n] shoure', the effect is vivid to the point of making one wonder whether any of Titian's pictures of the subject had been seen by Sidney. He touches also on *sfumato* effects: 'as in a picture which receives greater life by the darknesse of shadows, than by more glittering colour'. In the *Apology* he speaks of the 'delight and laughter' which is bred by pictures of *Hercules and Omphale* [43]. The idea of art as pleasure-giving is something he always expresses eloquently: 'As the Painter, that should give to the eye eyther some excellent perspective, or some fine picture, fit for building or fortification . . .' Even what might otherwise seem a painful subject can become pleasurable through art: 'Oft cruel fights well pictured forth do please'.

'Well pictured forth' implies more than mere competence. Sidney was expressing once again, with fresh examples, the theory of art idealizing, and thus exceeding, nature. Minturno's *De Poeta* (1559), which Sidney had certainly read, had stated that painters idealize and so should poets. The true artist goes beyond nature, painting 'what is fittest for the eye to see'. Sidney instances the subject of Lucretia, and what he has to say illumines the way in which, for instance, Veronese's treatment of the subject [44] should be understood; the example is the more apt since the picture is contemporary with Sidney.

It is neither dramatic nor historical. Veronese does not paint the Roman wife of Livy's story – 'he painteth not *Lucrecia* whom he never sawe'. But the result is not merely decorative or just an excuse for a décolletée nude. It is at once rich and wonderfully tender, subtle in its tonal combination of blondeness and green drapery (green perhaps to symbolize fidelity), muted in feeling and deliberately decorous. There is not intended to be any violence or blood. Art is what should move us, and the expression of the story in patently artificial (yet not sterile) terms – somewhat equivalent to the conventions of later *opera seria*. The downcast face, the shadowed eyelids, even the blonde eyelashes, are painted with quiet feeling that catches what Sidney calls Lucretia's 'constant though lamenting looke'. The picture is an intimate meditation, as it were, on the subject. No bystanders witness the moment, and Lucretia makes no appeal – as she does in Livy's account and in Shakespeare's poem – for attention. A heroine, she yet remains withdrawn: a lonely martyr, seen only by the spectator – and even of him she appears unconscious. What is depicted is, in Sidney's words, 'the outwarde beauty of such a vertue'. By that standard, the picture's calm loveliness becomes entirely congruous.

There is one culminating, more general aspect of praise from poets to painters. Such praise is part of the arts' own steady message to the public that art, of all kinds, has great power. It lives, where human beings die. Sidney only half-jokingly curses the man who has no ear for poetry: 'when you die, your memory die from the earth for want of an epitaph'. Oblivion was perhaps the most fearful threat that the artist could wield, as fame the best boon he offered:

> So long as men can read and eyes can see
> So long lives this, and this gives life to thee.

The artist remembered, named, in art, does certainly live. Donne's praise of Hilliard, Barnfield's of Dowland, by introducing their names into the lines at once remind us of their contemporary fame and ensure that something of it survives. With brush and pen one can even kill death (*'De la mort mesme tuer'*), Ronsard wrote in a poem addressed to Nicolas Denisot, *'Toi qui est peintre et poète'*. Denisot probably now exists – in so far as he does – entirely through Ronsard's praise; the pen which has conquered death in this case being Ronsard's, as he would not have been surprised to learn. The same urge drove artists to self-portraiture and to written memorials of themselves. The life of a man like Sidney must be recorded if not in art at least by some account which posterity could read; and he too had greatly desired fame.

The power of art expressed in the works of a great artist must make his own death the more tragic. The first death to catch the imagination in this way was probably Raphael's. Giorgione had died earlier and no less prematurely, but Raphael's own position at Rome meant that his death became a

44. *Lucretia*, *c.* 1580. Veronese

public event. Foreign ambassadors sent reports of it back to their masters. In the Vatican palace Leo X wept. The body lay virtually in state in Raphael's studio. Castiglione was only one, though perhaps the most deeply affected, of the versifiers who mourned in poetry. The epitaph which Cardinal Bembo composed for Raphael's tomb not merely expressed grief but typically for the period brought art and Nature into rivalry:

> Nature, while Raphael lived, must fear defeat:
> He died; she too prepared her death to meet.

The death of Michelangelo was the occasion of uniquely elaborate obsequies at Florence. Not even Raphael had been honoured so greatly. In addressing the Duke of Tuscany, Cosimo I, the Florentine Academy of painters and sculptors stated their wish to pay tribute to 'the greatest artist of their profession who has perhaps ever lived'. The Duke's reply spoke of the consolation their wish had given him, 'after the loss of such a unique man', and he encouraged them to commemorate in every possible way 'la virtù di tanto huomo'. This exchange of letters, along with several poems, was published at the time in a detailed booklet describing the ceremonies, 'Esequie del divino Michelagnolo Buonarroti', so that when these were over a record still remained. Although Michelangelo's was no premature death, the sense of black loss suggested by the poems was intense. One of the more striking described how, deprived of him, even illustrious hands would necessarily 'paint on the waves and build in the air and sculpt in the wind'.

There is more than conventional sorrow or mere patriotism in such tributes, especially when they come from fellow-artists (in the widest sense). Titian's death in 1576 was planned to be publicly mourned by painters at Venice, but because of plague no ceremony took place. Art had been recognized as a miracle, a mystery, and a personal as well as a divine gift. The great artist's death might really seem, if only briefly, to mark extinction of art itself. Because of the realization that each artist is unique (a realization which had come about through appreciation of artists' styles), each death represented an irreplaceable loss. Cardinal Ercole Gonzaga wrote sadly to his brother on the death of Giulio Romano in 1546 that he had lost all taste for building or silverware or pictures, lacking Giulio's creative presence. Perhaps only in a work of art could death be assuaged. While poets played the painter, painters themselves increasingly turned to literature, and indeed to other arts, such as music.

Michelangelo is the supreme example of an artist doing more than merely play at poetry, but Bronzino – emulating him in this, as in so much – was certainly a competent versifier. The death of Pontormo, his adopted father, inspired him to several sad poems, though they mourn the loss of the man more than of the artist.

The most widely disseminated and probably most widely appreciated art remained that of music. And it is there that there occurs one of the best examples of High Renaissance art mourning a great artist – and in so doing helping to keep his fame alive. Byrd's tenor elegy on the death of Thomas Tallis (died 1585) is the more movingly beautiful since its words, as well as music, may well be by him. Viols announce a solemn, slow threnody, while the voice invokes the Muses to descend in mourning weeds. Like a cry of pain is the repeated phrase: 'Tallis is dead'. Tallis is dead 'and music' – a word illustrated musically with elaborate sweetness – 'dies'. With this scarcely breathed syllable, the elegy itself dies away as if the whole art of music had indeed ceased at the composer's death.

45. Tomb of Giuliano de' Medici. Michelangelo

3
Enduring Monuments

If time, which brings death and threatens oblivion, is the artist's enemy, how much more is it the enemy of those who are not artists. Night and Day were sculpted by Michelangelo [45] on the tomb of Giuliano de' Medici, symbolizing the remorseless action of time; in Michelangelo's own poem they speak of how with their 'swift passage' (*veloce chorso*) they brought death to the Duke. Time really is 'cormorant devouring', as the King declares in the opening speech of *Love's Labours Lost*: and Caraglio's engraving after Rosso's design [46] seizes horribly well the inevitable, voracious aspect of Saturn-Time.

46. *Saturn swallowing a child*, 1526. Caraglio after Rosso

47. Epitaph for Johannes Cuspinian, *c.* 1527

48. *Battle of Marignano* relief from the tomb of François I, 1551–2. Pierre Bontemps

The King's very first lines state and evoke a Renaissance preoccupation which needed the help of art:

> Let fame, that all hunt after in their lives,
> Live register'd upon our brazen tombs

Somebody must make those tombs. Without an adequate memorial even the most famous man will not survive posthumously, and Spenser is only one example of the artist found reminding patrons and public of how the memories of those who neglect art will be 'wipt out with a sponge'. The eternity promised is not heavenly but earthly; and it would probably have poorly consoled most great Renaissance figures planning not to be forgotten that, after all, the soul is supposed to be immortal.

The basic concern is the same, whether the monument be the comparatively modest one of the rector of Vienna University Dr Cuspinian [47], which yet contains the highest of claims, or the elaborate one of a King of France, François I, where the King's battles [48] are recreated in art. The bulky image of Dr Cuspinian (the subject of a beautiful early portrait by Cranach [100]) virtually adored by his hero-flanking wives, is accompanied by an epitaph in which he not merely speaks but, as it were, declaims: 'To boundless history I left eternal works. / In these Cuspinian will live for ever' (*Vivus in his semper Cuspinianus erit*). He does not clasp his hands in prayer but props his arms on those 'eternal works' which are today so seldom read. Indeed, Cuspinian largely survives as a name because of this epitaph and Cranach's picture.

Cuspinian relied a little too confidently perhaps on his own merits. The great patron should be shrewd enough to recognize that Spenser's advice was good; it is more likely to be in the artist's creation to his memory that he will live for ever. The greater the artist, it might be hoped, the greater the monument. When Pope Julius II, who battled against so many things, turned to battle against Time (for whom, in this context, a capital letter seems appropriate), he needed an ally of genius, and found one in Michelangelo. Between them they planned to raise a uniquely vast modern monument, a free-standing tomb for the Pope which should be designed and executed in his lifetime – itself something unusual enough to provoke comment and superstitious censure. Because what subsequently happened is now well-known – modification of the project, death of the Pope, fresh contracts and final completion of an unsatisfactory wall monument forty years later – it is easier to think of what became 'the tragedy of the tomb' than to realize the colossal challenge prepared in 1505 by the aspiring minds of the Pope and the artist.

For comparisons one must go back, significantly, to antiquity: to, above all, the mausoleum which the wife of Mausolus had raised at Halicarnassus after his death, one of the Seven Wonders of the ancient world, lying ruined and partly still buried in the early sixteenth century but glowingly described by Pliny and Vitruvius. That vast monument in the centre of Mausolus' own city had probably inspired two great Roman ones: the imperial mausoleum which Augustus began during his lifetime and which was surmounted by his statue in bronze; and, more importantly and relevantly, the *moles Hadriani*, the huge, dominating tomb of the Emperor Hadrian which had served for centuries as a fortress. Although familiar as the Castel Sant' Angelo, it was always known to have been begun by Hadrian and remained one of the most famous surviving monuments of classical Rome. Papal property and virtually part of the Vatican palace, it could also recall the grandeur and ambition of rulers in antiquity – as well as the enduring quality of what they built. As for Mausolus, though his tomb might not be standing, he had given his name in Greek and Latin (in English by 1546) to the very concept of such a large-scale, splendid monument.

The large-scale ideas of Julius II in aiming at power frankly temporal at least as much as spiritual impressed his not always unambitious or cloistered contemporaries. It seems significant that unlike his immediate predecessors, he had kept virtually his own, classical Roman name on becoming Pope (he was christened Giuliano) and he was to be hailed, inevitably perhaps, as another Julius Caesar. 'To be lord and master of the world's game' (*esser il dominus et maistro del jocho del mundo*) was how a Venetian ambassador of the period summed him up, and the Pope would undoubtedly have concurred. In planning his own tomb, he proved no less vigorous and global in outlook. Other Popes had chosen chapels of St Peter's in which to be buried; the tombs of two recent predecessors, Sixtus IV and Innocent VIII, probably provided some positive hints, to be developed and eclipsed in the collaboration of the fiery patron and equally fiery artist half the Pope's age.

The ambitions of Michelangelo at the time the tomb was first planned were scarcely less tremendous than the political

49. Design for lower part of Julius II tomb (detail). After Michelangelo

ones of Julius, and much more licit. With an echo of Julian grandeur, he told his friend, the architect Sangallo, that if the tomb were built 'it would have no equal in the world' (*non à la par cosa tutto el mondo*). That is the artist's boast – but it would have been proved true, one may reasonably suggest, if Julius had not faltered. Michelangelo stipulated five years in which to complete the tomb; Julius lived just so long, but by 1508 had diverted his artist's energies to another colossal task, the frescoing of the Sistine Chapel vault. The famous resulting frescoes are a gain to be weighed against the virtual failure of the tomb. Yet Julius II lost with posterity, because comparatively few people of the thousands who know the frescoes associate them with him.

Around his first project for a vast monument, destined for St Peter's but in height and sheer bulk truly a *moles Julii*, there hovered every personal association. To begin with, Julius selected the final design only after considering many proposed by Michelangelo ('*dopo molti disegni della sua sepultura*', Michelangelo himself later recollected). Those '*molti disegni*' would be fascinating to see, but all are hopelessly lost. What alone survives as some sort of record [49] may be poor in quality but is extraordinary and grandiose enough – and this is, in fact, a record of the tomb only in its considerably shrunken second stage. How completely the original monument was intended to commemorate Julius II personally is shown by Condivi's reference to bas reliefs in bronze which would show the achievements of the Pope ('*i fatti di tanto pontefice*'), possibly to be similar in style to the reliefs on antique triumphal arches. What certainly is notable, apart from scale, in all that Condivi says is the stress on Julius as ruler and as patron. Although St Paul and Moses were included in the scheme for more than forty statues on the tomb, the captive nude figures of the Liberal Arts (prisoners of death, because after the Pope's death they would never find a patron comparable to nourish them) and other statues perhaps of territories conquered (or to be conquered) by the Pope, would have most vividly characterized Julius's chief concerns.

And elsewhere, a few years later, tombs did not fail to be set up in churches without any Christian reference whatsoever. That for the poet Sannazaro [50a] in S. Maria del Parto at Naples is in every way one of the most remarkable: from its terse classical inscription ('*Da sacro cineri flores | Hic ille Maroni | Sincerus Musa proximus | ut tumulo*') to its prominent guardian

50a. Tomb of Sannazaro, c. 1537.
Giovanni Montorsoli and Bartolommeo Ammanati

figures of Apollo and Minerva, whom later piety identified as
David [50b] and Judith. A bust of the poet presides over a
sarcophagus raised above a central relief where Pan, Marsyas,
Euterpe and Neptune evoke an Olympian mythology ignorant
of the Resurrection and the Life, offering no promise that death
is not the end ('*Vix · An · LXXII · Obiit MDXXX*').

Neither Sannazaro nor Julius II was a pagan. Their tombs
were intended not as statements of their religious beliefs but

50b. Apollo (detail of 50a)

as memorials to characterize and praise them. The author of the pseudo-Virgilian *Arcadia* (1489), one of the most famous modern exercises in classical manner, was suitably commemorated by the imagery on his tomb – in the city where the tomb of Virgil had for long been venerated and in a church whose name recalled his own poem *De Partu Virginis* (1526) which reconciles Christianity and Paganism, sending to the Annunciation Mercury as well as the Archangel Gabriel.

Julius II was no poet but a great prince, and the scale of his projected monument was probably decided before its exact programme. It was to be itself a building, half chapel, half giant sarcophagus, more than twenty feet wide and over thirty long, occupying some 800 square feet of ground and being about fifty feet high. Old St Peter's was not sufficiently spacious for it; possibly, though the matter remains doubtful, one aspect of Julius's interest in planning the new church was in connection with his tomb. Wherever it stood, it would surely have dominated its surroundings. It was a shrine, with access through a doorway to a central chamber where the Pope's body was destined to lie. Its exterior would have shown statue-filled niches all the way round, with putti and herms; above this level at the corners were to be placed four large statues, of which the Moses alone was executed – a good evocation of the monument's grandeur of scale and style. Another storey, perhaps with the bronze reliefs, rose above, topped – according to Condivi, the source closest to Michelangelo – by two angels who held a bier.

It hardly matters to us whether these details, drawn here entirely from Condivi, though the scheme was also described somewhat differently by Vasari, are entirely correct. What is patent is the heaven-scaling ambition which thought up such a stupendous monument and dispatched Michelangelo to Carrara to spend most of 1505 procuring the necessary marble. Forty statues, four elaborately decorated façades, bronze reliefs, an interior room like a small temple (*'a guisa d'un tempietto'*): the project promised to be the greatest wonder of the modern world, the more wonderful in that one artist alone was to be its creator. When Condivi and Vasari published their accounts of it, the tomb had already passed into mythology and yet actual fragments from Michelangelo's first design existed in the so-called 'Slaves'. It was possible for a private collector to own a piece of it, for after the eventual monument was set up in S.Pietro in Vincoli (where Julius is not buried), Michelangelo

51. The Dying Slave, 1513-16. Michelangelo

gave the comparatively finished pair of these figures [51] to a Florentine acquaintance living at Lyons, who presented them to François I.

They too are important evidence for the language of the tomb: marble studies over six feet high of the male nude in action – but with a new sort of languorousness and sleepy sensuality, distinct indeed from the *vivacità* and *prontezza* so liked by the fifteenth century. Are they virtues or vices, one might ask, for – bound and yet quite flawlessly unmarked, struggling and yet indulging rather than resisting pain – they remain disturbingly ambiguous. Four walls of them to guard a ruler's sarcophagus might suggest the last days of Tiberius rather than anything to do with Christ's charge to St Peter.

But it is not merely their mood which is new. In simulating flesh in marble they go further than any modern sculptor had achieved or even attempted, conveying musculature of the torso, back and thighs with new delight in the expressive powers of the human body. They are more frankly ideal than the fifteenth century would have appreciated, yet are scarcely classical; the large, posed hand of the 'Dying' Slave recalls nothing except the hands of the *David* [12]. They are brothers to the athletes of the Sistine vault, where can be traced some-

52. The Prophet Joel, 1508–10. Michelangelo

thing of the intended idiom of the Julius tomb. Indeed, by taking and isolating, as in the reproduction here, a side area of the ceiling [52], one seems to get a remarkably good idea of how the upper portion of the main façade would have looked.

That may serve as a reminder that the tomb was not mere grandiose fantasy. It could have been built, though the fact it was not may seem to support Spenser inveighing against the tendency of rulers to utilize the visual arts in the very way that Julius II intended:

> In vaine doo earthly Princes then, in vaine
> Seeke with Pyramides, to heaven aspired . . .
> To make their memories for ever live.

> *(The Ruines of Time)*

Spenser is, in fact, an interested party, whose theme is not the perennial one of human vanity but the typically Renaissance one of fame – only, the fame he recommends is celebrated most suitably by a rival art, that of poetry. Time, according to him, will ruin the merely physical monument, whereas 'sweete Poets verse' can give the immortality which defeats time. Although literary not visual art is what, naturally enough, he champions, he certainly advises rulers to take steps, while they may, to enlist art on their behalf. He reminds them of its power, in a century which was perhaps more intensely conscious than any before had been of just how much art can achieve:

> Provide therefore (ye Princes) whilst ye live,
> That of the *Muses* ye may befriended bee,
> Which unto men eternitie do give;

> (ibid.)

It is a nice point whether the physical monument is necessarily doomed to decay in the way Spenser, and other poets, imply. The artist in words may like to boast that *his* work will stand when mere marble and bronze are fallen and melted; but from Horace onwards there was recognition that these substances have their enduring properties; at worst, they make worthy comparisons for the poet. For the patron they were perhaps more attractive than words as a medium in which to commemorate himself. Not everyone could yet read, but all except the blind could see.

Besides, it is possibly not too fanciful to suggest, in the very idea of building something or setting up a monument, there is an instinctive human satisfaction which goes back to childhood. And it is certainly easier for the patron to involve himself directly in the structure of something to be built than in that, say, of a sonnet. Julius II was not untypical when he so carefully selected a final design of his tomb from among many prepared by Michelangelo. The three famous tombs in the church at Brou commissioned by Margaret of Austria, Regent of the Netherlands, are very much governed by her wishes, even down to such apparent details as whether the material used for the images should be coloured (she preferred not). Several artists worked on the tombs but to the Regent's favourite sculptor, Conrad Meit, were reserved the figures of the commemorated and notably the tender pairs of winged putti who stand around the body of her husband on the central tomb [53] and who

53. Putto with helmet from tomb of Philibert of Savoy, c. 1526. Conrad Meit

remain perhaps the most memorable aspect of the whole scheme.

Obviously, sheer physical mass of a monument could be reassuring to the commissioner; and the life-sized image, whether sleeping or awake, is the simplest expression perhaps of defying death. The former at least would have been staggeringly conveyed if Michelangelo's earliest project for Julius II had been carried out; and it is hard to believe it was not intended that the Pope himself should appear in some guise or other on his own tomb. Nevertheless, it was not the mere scale proposed, and still less the presence or absence of any statue of the Pope, which would have made the monument so remarkable. Today we gaze at a wall-monument for Julius II which is assimilable from one position and at virtually one glance – being in that very like the average fifteenth-century Italian tomb. But Michelangelo had planned a complex experience for the spectator: the monument consisting of metaphorically encountering and entering the whole ethos of Julius II, as one would have walked around the four sides of the tomb and finally perhaps have entered the '*tempietto*' where the Pope's body lay. The effect would have been like a chapel turned inside out (almost a reverse therefore of Michelangelo's Medici chapel but with perhaps some anticipations of the appearance of the Holy House at Loreto [54]). Not only would it have taken time to appreciate but it would have required the spectator to move around it, only gradually experiencing a cumulative revelation – not totally removed from the experience of reading a biography of the subject. Thus time is cheated in a novel way, for the work of art unfolds at its creator's tempo; and since the reliefs and the statues all had a personal application (with unconventional, even unfamiliar iconography) the process of 'reading' the walls of them would have required particular attention.

It is this subtle cheating of time expressed in a different style for a very different patron that Raphael enshrined in the chapel for Agostino Chigi at S. Maria del Popolo [55]. Eternity is emphasized rather than glory; and time as ordinarily experienced is meant to stop as we step into an area which discloses a fresh dimension, beyond those which we are used to. When in 1507 Agostino Chigi received from his friend Julius II permission to acquire the chapel as a mausoleum, this transcendental aspect was recorded in the Papal Bull, where Chigi is

54. The 'Holy House', *c.* 1510. Designed by Bramante

55. The Chigi Chapel, S. Maria del Popolo, Rome,
c. 1513. Designed by Raphael

spoken of as 'longing to turn earthly things into heavenly
(*cupiens terrena in coelestia . . .*) and transitory ones into eternal'.

Although never completed in exactly the way planned, not
least because Raphael as well as Chigi died in 1520, the resulting
chapel is at once splendid yet austere, and richly luminous, a
temple of calm meditation where so many arts are fused – like
transitory things – to symbolize eternity. A description of its
marble statues, mosaic, bronze reliefs and paintings might
suggest a plethora of decoration but that is not at all the effect
it makes, or is intended to make, partly because everything is

56. Study for the tomb of the Medici Magnifici.
By Michelangelo (?)

accommodated within a harmonious architectural framework
of high-curving archways surmounted by a dome. To help
justify calling the result austere one may cite in contrast the
effect probably intended by Michelangelo on one wall alone
of the Medici chapel [56], a funerary scheme begun at Florence
in the year of Raphael's death. The drawing reproduced here is
connected with the tombs of the Magnifici, the famous fifteenth-
century Lorenzo de' Medici and his brother Giuliano, and this
double tomb scheme was planned as very much subordinate to
the familiar separate tombs of the Capitani, never fully com-

pleted on the flanking walls [45]. The elaborate sculptured array which Michelangelo intended to rise from the floor upwards around the visitor to the Medici chapel, clothing the walls, has to be created in part in the imagination; paradoxically, the chapel's present appearance of bareness is as misleading as some of the distracting ornament in the Chigi chapel is misleading, being baroque addition to, or interpretation of, Raphael's intentions.

But the real distinction between the two chapels is in their emphases. By symbolic mourning figures, and especially by the heroic statues of the Capitani themselves, Michelangelo created monuments of glory to the Medici involved: Night and Day, the Arno and the Tiber, the family's patron saints Cosmas and Damian, all were to emphasize the greatness of the commemorated dead. And death itself, or mourning at least, seems ever-present in this mortuary chapel.

Agostino Chigi was not a Capitano, and played no part in politics as such. Like the Medici in origin, he was a wealthy banker, pleasure-loving and a great artistic patron whose lifestyle is best conveyed by his Roman villa, the Farnesina, built for him by Peruzzi. After death it was not his deeds or his virtues, not his personality and scarcely even his appearance, for which he sought immortality. The emphasis of his chapel is on eternity; and from the centre of its bright dome there gestures down the commanding figure of God the Father, the *Padre eterno* [57] conceivably summoning the soul and certainly manifested in a vision of heaven, as if at the creation of the world, angels supporting his upraised arms. Just as in the Medici chapel, two similar tombs face each other on opposite walls, but their form is unexpected and discreetly impersonal; they are literally 'Pyramides, to heaven aspired', positively piercing the entablature, tall antique symbols, with suggestions of the obelisk mingling with the pyramid, of eternity.

Such are the monuments planned by Chigi for himself and his brother; gilt bronze (not, as now, marble) medallions with their profiles were the sole illustrative reference intended to identify the tombs, accompanied by lettering to have been arranged much more economically than in the present lay-out done in the seventeenth century by Bernini. The bronze reliefs to be placed on the tombs were of religious scenes. The four statues in niches around the chapel (two of them Bernini's) are of Old Testament prophets, God's witnesses not Chigi's patron saints. The altarpiece shows the *Birth of the Virgin*, on whose

57. Dome of Chigi Chapel, c. 1513. Raphael

feast-day annually Chigi had provided that a mass should be said in the chapel. What we know of the scheme suggests Chigi's personal involvement, but none of that was overtly displayed. Concerned with his salvation rather than his fame, he seems – almost ostentatiously – to have declined the easiest way of self-glorification, even while making the maximum use of art. Perhaps his own sculpted image whether active or sleeping on his own tomb seemed not merely unsubtle and even old-fashioned, but, to his sophisticated eye, in poor taste. How much more graceful, discreetly oblique and also classically antique would be a pyramid of marble and bronze: as tomb and as symbol of that immortality to which he aspired. Neither he nor Raphael can have forgotten the Pyramid tomb of Cestius; as for obelisks, one – reputedly containing Julius Caesar's ashes – had stood from Roman times on a site near St Peter's.

When we find another cultivated person from Raphael's circle, Baldassare Castiglione, commemorated by a vaguely

58. Tomb of Castiglione. Giulio Romano

similar, though stepped, pyramidal tomb [58], it is tempting to
think that the impetus for such comparatively novel use of this
form derived from Raphael himself. Although Castiglione died
in Spain, and his body was not brought back to Italy until 1530,
he had already stated in his will of seven years earlier that the
construction of his tomb was in the hands of Raphael's leading
assistant and pupil, an interesting artist in his own right, Giulio
Romano. It is certainly easy to feel that the sober, gentlemanly
figure of Raphael's artful portrait [4] would wish to be re-

corded in death, as in life, without stridency or display, preferring reticent dignity even if running some risk of being what Sir Thomas Browne was to call 'but Pyramidally extant'. Closer perhaps than Castiglione's to the discreet taste of Chigi's tomb is the monument (1563) of Bernardino Rota and his wife in S. Domenico Maggiore at Naples, where a tall, slim obelisk is flanked on either side by portrait-medallions of the couple. The effect of this probably unique variation is austerely antique, yet suggestive of an eternity to be shared; and marriage is commemorated in death.

Whatever Chigi's own ideas for his chapel, the creation of it is Raphael's. Had Raphael lived, the statues to be executed later by Bernini and, above all, the large altarpiece (actually painted by Sebastiano del Piombo and finished by Salviati) would have been designed by him; and the chapel's final coherence would have been achieved. A similar sense of a regular, faintly curved area of space, in the chapel on an intimate scale, is detectable in the painted background architecture of the *School of Athens* [20] where through the barrel-vault can be glimpsed a central area defined by statue-filled niches, with roundels in the pendentives (just as in the chapel) and a dome is to be presumed above. The Chigi chapel even has, as it were in miniature, a brief barrel-vault at its entrance. A germ of the chapel's design could exist in the fresco, for Raphael may well have still been painting the latter about 1510 and he is usually thought to have planned the chapel by 1513, if not earlier.

Where his part would have been at its most directly personal was on the altarpiece. Very likely the composition, had it been designed by him, would have encouraged the spectator to look upward, almost experiencing a flight from earth to heaven. Even as it is, admittedly in rather extraordinary fashion, the altarpiece presents two zones: Mary is born on earth, while God the Father is manifested above, thus appearing prominently twice in the same chapel (as well as in smaller compositions round the dome) and in some danger of overshadowing himself. The appearance of God the Father in a picture of the Virgin's birth is highly unusual, and it has been ingeniously suggested by one scholar that the altarpiece intended by Raphael would have been of the Assumption of the Virgin, borne up to the heaven of the dome as if summoned by Raphael's majestic *Padre eterno*.

Nevertheless, it was the feast of the Virgin's birth which Chigi required to be celebrated annually in his chapel; and there can be no doubt that Sebastiano del Piombo signed a contract with the Chigi family representatives for an altarpiece of that subject. It could well be, however, that Raphael would have linked dome and altarpiece by the presence of angels at the Virgin's birth (an angel is shown by Dürer in his woodcut treatment of the scene) and that something of what he intended had confusedly filtered into Sebastiano's mind. God the Father, half-brooding, half-conjuring, high over the moment on earth, would not merely connect the two areas artistically but would add resonance to the birth of the Virgin, immaculately conceived and herself an analogue of the Divine Wisdom. Far from being new, this idea was established and traditional. It is based on the passage in *Proverbs*, 'The Lord possessed me in the beginning of his way . . . I was set up from everlasting . . . or ever the earth was. When there were no depths, I was brought forth'. This very text, significantly, is used in the mass for the feast of the Immaculate Conception; and already in medieval times it had been part of the daily Office of the Virgin.

Thus it is quite possible that the common interpretation of God the Father's pose in the dome as Creator is the correct one, and that the subject of the altarpiece correctly follows Raphael's intentions, but that what remains unfulfilled is the relationship, both visual and spiritual, between them. Raphael's would certainly have been a fresh, yet entirely legitimate and devout treatment of a familiar theme. That he was not merely capable of, but positively sought, such fresh solutions is sufficiently proved by the much more revolutionary iconography of *The Transfiguration*, which is again a total re-thinking in visual and spiritual terms of a long-established subject. Since two of the four statues of Old Testament prophets in the Chigi chapel originate only in the seventeenth century it is not permissible to cite their existence as part of one coherent scheme, but together the four seem to mediate suitably between the Creator aloft and the birth of the Virgin, whom in various ways they prefigure. If Agostino Chigi and Raphael had chosen for the altarpiece that subject (and the commissioner's concern with it is a fact), it too could take its place, not as some charming, semi-genre scene but as one further expression of the whole chapel's preoccupation with eternity: 'I was set up from everlasting . . . or ever the earth was'. Chigi does not mourn, nor is he mourned. In the final, firm certitude of his lucid memorial the fear of death, and death itself, are somehow absorbed.

The chapel's message was perhaps better understood, artistically, in subsequent centuries when the pyramid itself became a popular form of monument. In the sixteenth century few people were to follow Chigi's subtle combination of personality suppressed and yet expressed, and a more typical funerary chapel – nearer to the concepts of Michelangelo's Medici tombs – is the mid-century one of the Caracciolo di Vico family in S.Giovanni a Carbonara at Naples [59]. Here in an

59. Caracciolo di Vico tomb, begun before 1544. Diego Ordóñez

imposing architectural setting, the full-length armoured figures of father and son stand like guards over their own high tombs (in which their effigies appear again). The context is fully religious, but the impact is secular. Glory and fame – which are of course not incompatible with piety – suggest triumph over death. There is a proud, human authority in the two men, felt in their stance and emphasized by the armour they wear. The physical detachment of them from the tombs increases the sense of still-living beings, and for the spectator they remain alive even while the occasion for their presence is death. In its accomplishment, art can thus come near to cheating experience.

Shakespeare's use of the supposed commemorative statue of Hermione in *The Winter's Tale* depends on art possessing this accomplishment. Twice in the scene the word 'mocked' occurs in connection with the statue's eye-deceiving effect: it is said to mock life as sleep mocks death, and Leontes speaks of how we are 'mock'd with art'. When he declares of the statue 'There's magic in thy majesty', he touches on a further requirement, beyond the mere life-like. Art not only fixes for posterity how a person looked when alive (itself a Renaissance achievement in the portrait, sculpted or painted) but can convey something of that person's fame and even the reasons for it.

A scene from the person's life, carved on a monument, is the most obvious way to suggest these, just as a portrait bust is there the simplest record of his or her appearance. Yet even when no fame as such required to be recorded, perhaps indeed *because* there was none, great art could create at the patron's wish such a vivid and elegant portrayal as Pilon's *Valentine Balbiani* [60a], so gracefully at ease on her tomb; and though below lies the grim reminder of her appearance in death [60b], it was not intended to be the dominant note of the tomb (though it may nowadays have become so through popularity in photographs). Her husband, the Chancellor René de Birague, planned a chapel where, in marble, she should for ever recline, not asleep but very much alert, piously reading propped on brocaded cushions: a great lady accompanied by her pet dog, real and yet a symbol also of fidelity. The dog itself was the subject of a touching elegy by a member of the Birague family, beginning '*Ce petit chien aima tellement sa maistresse*', for such was its sense of grief at Valentine Balbiani's death that it too had died after three days. It deserved its place on her tomb, and its presence is part of the monument's exactitude. When, in provincial England a very few years later (1582), a tomb was set up to a certain Thomas

60a and b. Valentine Balbiani tomb, before 1583 (details). Germain Pilon

Fermor and his wife, the contract laid down specifically how they should both be shown; and for Bridget Fermor there was to be '. . . portraicture of a fair gentlewoman with a French hood, edge and habiliment, with all other apparel, furniture, jewels, ornaments and things in all respects usual, decent and seemly for a gentlewoman'.

Pilon was a great sculptor, one of the very greatest ever produced by France, and part of the power of the *Balbiani* tomb comes from his subordination of proliferating detail, exquisite though it is, to the personality itself which invests the costume.

Personality is more than just observation of the face, but it is felt in the cool, pensive elegance of the pose, with only the lightest of glances given to the prayer book kept at arm's length, so that the lively, devoted dog seems to gain, as it obviously intends, her attention. Perfect fingers touch without disarranging the crisp headdress, and the uppermost cushion slightly dips under the elbow's pressure. There is magic in such grace – the artist's of course, but something too is felt, given by him, of the presence of a distinct individual. Perhaps Valentine Balbiani's hands had been as fluid and slender – nearly – as Pilon makes them, for even in her *transi* they retain in skeletal form their linear beauty. And Birague (who took orders and became a Cardinal after his wife's death) might go to gaze on her as she had once lived. When he died, his heirs had executed, also by Pilon, his kneeling statue – in bronze, not marble – for the same chapel.

Lack of fame again proved no handicap when, in much more restricted form – virtually bust-length – a Roman lady, Elena Savelli, was to be commemorated in St John Lateran. She died in 1570 and her monument [61] by a not very celebrated sculptor, Jacopo del Duca, is probably from about the same date, nearly contemporary therefore with Pilon's *Valentine Balbiani*. Much more keenly engaged, indeed transfixed, in prayer, Elena Savelli's image breathes a memorable intensity, as if straining from her setting as she turns ardently towards the altar – the type of projection, with its natural effect of involving the spectator, which Raphael had probably in some grander way intended in the Chigi chapel. Both chapel and monument anticipate – if that is the word – Baroque developments, and the *Elena Savelli* is recognized as the Roman prototype of Bernini's *Gabriele Fonseca* of just about a century later.

In fact, this essential flame of artistic vitality, much more living than life yet combined with observation of it, springs up in the Renaissance; to eternize, art must arrest, amaze, positively create the wondering sensations of a Leontes. Elena Savelli is first of all a portrait, to which life is imparted by activating it; and such a convincing image in prayer is already seen in the late fifteenth-century tomb of Donato Medici (cf. *Early Renaissance*, pl. 99). Yet, in comparison with del Duca's woman, Donato Medici is quiet and unastonishing. He does not, either literally or metaphorically, project from his monument, and quite fails (not, of course, that the sculptor makes him attempt) to act out – as if on stage – his piety. Thus his

61. Elena Savelli monument, *c.* 1570 (detail). Jacopo del Duca

monument seems scarcely to need spectators, while the *Elena Savelli*, small though it is, evokes an audience and might even be said to encourage applause.

As a result, we are more likely to remember the mimetic prayerfulness of Elena Savelli, the memorable effect of whose monument partly comes from the drama of mingled materials: herself in bronze within a setting of marble – a contrast much favoured in the sixteenth century, combining in a bronze figure against or amid marble suggestions of both vitality and eternity. For Elena Savelli no accompanying allegories or personifications are needed because the subject herself expresses and as it

62. *Leo X as Clement I*, 1520–24. Giulio Romano

were enshrines religion. There perhaps lies the heart of the
distinction between her monument and Donato Medici's: his
presents a pious image, hers an image of piety.

But for more public persons, especially those who in life had
been surrounded by a train of courtiers or servants, and borne
forward on the breath of praise, it was thought fitting that they
should in death be accompanied, celebrated, by their virtues or
other indications of their character and achievements. In Italy
this was a well-established concept long before the High
Renaissance; in Northern Europe it begins only around the

beginning of the sixteenth century. Probably nowhere, however, had such virtues and personifications previously assumed the prominence they possess in the monuments of the enthroned Popes [62] in the Sala di Costantino at the Vatican. Although only painted, these gigantic monuments are in effect planned as architectural units, massive interruptions to the expanses of feigned tapestry which occupy the central portion of the walls. The execution is Giulio Romano's but the general design may well have been originated by Raphael shortly before his death.

If distinctions between Early and High Renaissance are reasonably to be pressed, a real break can be felt between the simple rows of standing Popes which quattrocento artists

63a and b. *SS. Stephen and Sixtus II*, 1481–2. Studio of Botticelli

frescoed in the Sistine Chapel [63a and b] and this fresh breed of heroic Pontiffs, each presented and indeed revealed by attendant angels under a draped baldacchino set within a vast marble niche, itself part of a simulated architectural framework adorned with caryatids and flanked by Virtues. Once again, the Baroque tomb – this time, specifically, the Papal tomb – is anticipated; and once again, this anticipation is of less significance than the actual High Renaissance achievement.

In comparing the Popes of the Sistine chapel walls with their artistic successors in the Sala di Costantino, it is as well to remember that both series stress Papal continuity under divine origin. In the chapel, the Popes form a respectful frieze above parallel scenes from the lives of Moses and Christ. In the Vatican palace hall we move into virtually modern history: Constantine is commemorated for official recognition of Christianity, whose human representatives are not merely present but glorified. On either side of the *Allocution of Constantine*, the vast architectural-cum-sculptural settings exalt the chronological extremes of the Papacy: St Peter and the Pope under whom the decoration began, Leo X (called, perhaps tactfully, Clement I, but openly portrayed). Leo's baldacchino conveniently features the lion of the zodiac, while focusing adoringly on him are the personifications of Moderation and Affability, two non-cardinal but attractive virtues which Leo indeed possessed and which had perhaps not appeared in this guise before. All the more frankly

64. Tomb of Paul III, completed 1575. Guglielmo della Porta

do they hint at the humane qualities of the Pope in comparison with the lofty concepts of The Church and Eternity accompanying St Peter.

Such painted praise was to be transformed into massive physical substance in an actual tomb when some twenty-five years later Guglielmo della Porta was commissioned by Pope Paul III to work on what was destined to be his monument. What is seen today in St Peter's [64] lacks a good deal of the sculpture which was actually executed for it. When the tomb was set up, after some vicissitudes, the marble allegories of Justice and Prudence still present were paired by comparable statues of Peace and Abundance. Even in its shorn state the monument celebrates Paul III as a ruler, magnanimous perhaps rather than imperious, but noticeably not at prayer. Della Porta had executed portrait busts of the Pope in his lifetime and the

65. Designs for
monument
to Paul IV,
c. 1556–8.
Guglielmo della Porta

bronze image is now the most striking, convincing aspect of the tomb: the heavy, carved cope serves as impressive carapace for an aged body, quiescent yet felt to have by no means lost its force. Paul III is still very much master of his own monument. And in designs for a monument to a subsequent Pope, Paul IV, [65] della Porta showed the ruler beneath a splendid baldacchino, positively engaged in ruling.

With the image of the deceased shown alive and active, his virtues or attributes too might become activated, engaging the spectator by gestures, admiring the person commemorated or mourning their loss as Michelangelo had intended the Arts should mourn Julius II (and as Sculpture was to mourn prominently on his own tomb). On the tomb of Paul III Justice and Prudence exchange glances and, as it were, converse. It is only too easy to grow tired of the conventions of praise, whatever the medium, but again and again art was able to devise a fresh presentation of the somewhat limited range of virtues, just as it thought up new ways to represent the subject of the monument.

The French Renaissance concept of a group of Virtues or goddesses to guard the monument containing a heart resulted in several beautiful and novel works of art whose mood has tender, almost wistful grace – the more effective when the monument is to a great soldier. Prieur's nymph-like figures of Peace, Justice and, especially, Abundance seem to proffer flowers and make one pause before the monument containing the heart of the famous field-marshal, Anne de Montmorency [66]. Beneficence and prosperity, not victory or war, is the message of these tutelary spirits disposed suitably about the Constable's heart; in them what he had given to France is shown to live on.

67. Monument of the Marquess of Marignano, 1563. Leone Leoni

66. *Peace, Abundance and Justice* from Montmorency monument, 1573–8. Barthélemy Prieur

68. Jacob Fugger tomb, 1511-18. Sebastian Loscher

In Italy the death of another military leader, the Marquess of Marignano, was commemorated very differently in a splendid tomb of bronze and coloured marbles by Leone Leoni [67]; there Peace and Military Virtue are seated with sombre dignity, mourning the powerful brooding figure of the standing Marquess, raised somewhat above them but sharing the same subdued yet stoic mood. This seems some great hero's tomb, and its heroic tone is established by the severe temple-style façade on which, like a Roman emperor, in antique armour, the commanding Marquess grasps his sword, ready to return and fight again. So subtle is the tomb's rhetoric (and the sculptor was a great rhetorician) that we are at once persuaded of its subject's grandeur, bravery and fame; he might be, he ought to be, Don John of Austria instead of merely an admittedly able though scarcely any longer familiar historical personage who owes a monument to the fact that after his death his brother became a Pope.

Although the tomb includes in its upper part a relief of the *Adoration of the Magi*, its imagery (which extends to statues of Prudence and Fame) is otherwise resolutely secular and unconditioned by its place in Milan Cathedral. A certain irony attaches to the fact that St Charles Borromeo (the Marquess's nephew) apparently removed the sarcophagus, that was once part of the monument, in obedience to an edict of the Council of Trent that bodies should be buried not in such things but under the church pavement; 'those receptacles and vain trophies' (*quei depositi e vani trofei*) he ordered everywhere to be taken away. Yet it may be felt that he left the vainest, while removing the most harmless, of such trophies when he came to his uncle's tomb. Trophies and weapons, standards and captives might glorify even a banker's tomb [68], though it must be said that in this case the banker was the famous Jacob Fugger of Augsburg.

The splendour and drama of Fugger's tomb relief may appear at first glance tame beside the fully sculpted bronze and marble people who animate Italian and French monuments, but its language is certainly no less grandiose and its sense of triumph even in death perhaps still more remarkable. To Agostino Chigi, another banker of the same generation, it might indeed have seemed too assertive. Though skulls loom out above and below Fugger's coat-of-arms, they are hardly more than just two elements amid the upsurging, euphoric design. Warriors raise high the Fugger shield, at whose base are tied captive

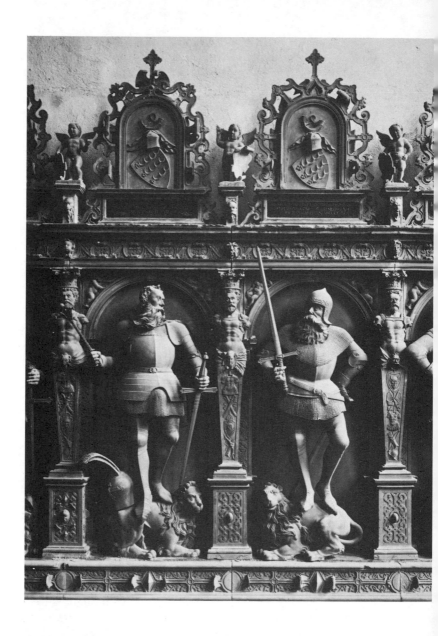

69. Monuments to the Counts of Würtemburg, begun 1578. Simon Schlör

figures of the type so familiar later on Baroque monuments to rulers and generals; armoured putti brandish the tall shafts of torches with fringed banners waving from them; and all this apparent defiance of mortality is celebrated within a spacious, soaring temple, under a coffered dome, with an oculus at its centre, recalling the Pantheon. In that perspective, with its hint perhaps of eternity, death scarcely needs to be mourned. Grieving putti, it is true, rest on the cartouche at the base of the relief, but the words of the epitaph addressed to Fugger tell of his long life and how death, 'envious to others, was to you alone favourable and fair'; and even the exactness with which his span is recorded – sixty-seven years two months – suggests achievement.

Rank, age and virtue can all be depicted, factually or allegorically. Imaginatively presented by art, they will stir suitable emotions in the spectator. Yet even while making claims on posterity in his own right, a patron might – where he could – stress the claims of lineage, as the Popes had invoked the most distinguished one of all. The Lord Lumley who collected, and had sculpted, towards the end of the sixteenth century, a series of fourteen effigies of his ancestors, 'in a continued line of succession even from Liulph unto these our days', was not unique. In the Stiftskirche at Stuttgart, the lineage of the Counts of Würtemburg comes to life along the choir [69]: so many highly animated suits of armour, each framed within the rich Renaissance arcade, the whole scheme designed by a single sculptor, Simon Schlör.

These figures remain tied to the wall, but in the most celebrated and accomplished example, the Emperor Maximilian's tomb in the Hofkirche at Innsbruck, it is the fact that the figures are free-standing which aids the moving, muted effect. The Emperor's actual and mythical ancestors are assembled about his kneeling image on his tomb, gathered from history as if to be mourners on the day of the funeral. Well before his death in 1519, Maximilian was having these bronze figures executed and they possess greater life and individuality than his own statue. Out of the distant past was conjured the Emperor's great-great-great grandmother, Elizabeth [70]. The result is a memorable portrait, so entirely free from fantasy that it might almost have been taken directly from the life. Far from attempting the Gothic style (which one often reads of as permeating Northern European art throughout the sixteenth century) or pastiching medieval costume, the sculptor works in a deliberately contemporary idiom. A Habsburg ancestor is, as it were, recovered from misty history and set vividly before us with no less outer detail and inner assurance than Valentine Balbiani as sculpted by Pilon.

If visual art can do so much to celebrate the dead – and marvellously much it did over the years from Michelangelo and Raphael to Pilon and Prieur – it may also be invoked to celebrate and commemorate the living. To have oneself celebrated and commemorated in one's own lifetime was no new idea, but new possibilities, especially in sculpture, were opened up by advances in handling the difficult but durable medium of bronze (in the fifteenth century few statues had followed the precedent of Donatello's free-standing bronze *David*). And then new heroic artistic ambitions – like the vast new St Peter's or Michelangelo's huge *David* – could coincide with a patron's. Already Leonardo's proposed equestrian monument to Ludovico Sforza's father was planned to be twice the scale of Donatello's *Gattamelata*: passing deliberately therefore out of any canon of realism, to astound by its colossal proportions, as if only on such a great scale could the great man be commemorated.

A tradition existed for commemoration and praise while still alive in the *tableaux vivants* and temporary decorations set up so often for the accession or marriage of a ruler, and for his or her triumphant entry into a city. The pageantry of these festivities was itself close to that utilized for funeral occasions. A triumphal car, bearing trophies of battle and naked figures (intended as prisoners perhaps), was designed in 1516 by Gossaert for the ceremonies in Brussels on the death of Ferdinand of Spain; and no doubt it would have served well enough to celebrate Ferdinand's *'joyeuse entrée'*, had he been making one. In the typical *tableau vivant*, there might appear allegorical or mythological personages (often nude) or distant distinguished namesakes of the person being fêted. At Foligno in 1502 when Lucrezia Borgia was travelling to Ferrara for her marriage to Alfonso d'Este, she was met at the city gate by a float bearing the Roman Lucretia who recited verses about her own inferiority to the modern holder of the name. When the future Philip II of Spain made a *'joyeuse entrée'* into Antwerp in 1549, being introduced to his people as their future ruler, he was greeted variously by both Philip of Macedon and St Philip. Twenty-nine years earlier, Dürer (who had previously examined the decorations before they were set up) bought at Antwerp

70. *Elizabeth of Görz*, 1516. Gilg Sesselschreiber

Aegidius' printed description of the celebrations on a similar occasion for Philip's father, the young Charles V.

Ephemeral though such festivities were, the devices used in them – devices often enough designed, after all, by leading artists – might well influence the design of less ephemeral monuments, where pyramids and obelisks and statues were made of more solid, lasting materials but their significance was virtually the same. The Virtues or other personifications who in human guise, perhaps of co-opted local girls, had hailed some prince on his entering their city might later be eternized in bronze on his tomb. Thus the Rivers of Arno and Tiber which Michelangelo planned for the Medici tombs may well have been suggested by the presence of these gods in the ceremonies at Rome in 1513 when the two Medici dukes had been made Roman citizens.

Fantasy could be freer and more exuberant in festive decorations – trophies, arches and so on – which were to be executed in light materials like wood and canvas, and which had to be prepared comparatively quickly. Vasari is an obvious example of the artist speedy in this sort of way, and proud of his speed;

71. Triumphal car of Fame for Henri II, 1550. French

but he is only one example. Entirely decorative painters like Polidoro da Caravaggio were also able to devise such schemes successfully, as Polidoro did at Messina in 1535 when the Emperor Charles V passed through the city in triumph. Equally, an architect like Bramante was expected to produce – without delay – *'qualche digna fantasia da mettere in spettaculo'*, in the words used in 1492 when he was involved in celebrating the birth of an heir to the Duke of Milan.

Whether the commemoration was meant for a day, or hopefully for all time, the visual arts were serving to make visible and palpable the common coin of literary praise: where every prince was a hero, a victor over envy, endowed with the virtues or accompanied by the graces, and destined for immortal fame. A great poet could always transmute such base metal into gold, and so could a great visual artist, whose creation might suffer through not being disseminable but would gain just because it was so sheerly visual, requiring no literacy to be 'read'. Justice might be seen greeting the ruler or seated for ever on his tomb. Winged Fame, poised perhaps as if about to soar to heaven, took on actual bodily shape, raising its trumpet aloft with such vivid gesture that its blast of praise could almost be heard.

With the development of printing and the increasing availability of books for ordinary people to buy – if only to look at the illustrations – there came into existence a medium to arrest the ephemerality of the pageant occasion. The splendour of comparable medieval ceremonies has to be gleaned from chronicles, but Renaissance fêtes and triumphal and mournful celebrations were constantly recorded in souvenir booklets, similar to that Dürer bought. When these books were illustrated, the very design of the decorations was made available for those who had not been present and, more important, the homage to a living person could itself be kept alive. Thus, for example, the processional cars which celebrated the entry of Henri II into Rouen in 1550 are positively documented [71]. On the car of Fame, the king sits forever being crowned. On another car Fame holds Death captive, in the sequence described by Petrarch in his *Trionfi*. But Petrarch had been concerned with a cosmic cycle: Time in turn triumphs over Fame and is itself conquered by Eternity. At Rouen in 1550, Fame was harnessed to service of the French monarchy; and death is what needs to be kept in hand when a living person is the centre of celebrations.

It was inevitable that love of fame, combined with the proved ability of artists, would tempt some important patrons to dream of the most ambitious perhaps of all monuments: one set up in their own lifetime. Commemorated or not in writing, the '*joyeuse entrée*' and other such acts of induced homage were essentially occasional; to plan, or actually to build, one's tomb during one's life might be melancholy and even perhaps unlucky (according to Condivi's 'authorized' life of Michelangelo, it was this belief which Bramante deliberately implanted in Julius II so as to interrupt Michelangelo's project of his tomb). Besides, some great personages thought they were entitled to solid, permanent manifestations of, say, a city's gratitude which should be set up while they lived to enjoy it. It is not surprising that Julius II was among those who planned such commemorative monuments to themselves and their exploits. Michelangelo was the sculptor of an over-lifesize bronze statue of the Pope, commissioned and begun at Bologna at the end of 1506, set up on the façade of the church of San Petronio two years later but pulled down by the Bolognese and smashed to pieces well before the Pope's death.

The problems of casting this work are agonizingly related in Michelangelo's own letters at the time, but more significant is the story Condivi tells of the sculptor's discussion with the Pope about how he wished to be represented. To Michelangelo's question whether he would like to be shown holding a book in one hand, Julius replied, 'Not a book. A sword'. In fact, the image was not executed in such a frankly menacing and martial way; perhaps on reflection even this Vicar of Christ felt there might be some incongruity in so appearing on a church façade. But his comment at least makes clear the role that Julius saw the statue performing: as an incarnation of his power, a permanent reminder not so much of what he looked like as of what he stood for.

Another ambitious, unpopular effort, much later in the century, was that commanded by the Duke of Alba (whose rather arrogant appearance has been seen in pl.38) at Antwerp. He conceived a larger-than-life statue of himself as a Christian Hercules, celebrating his conquest of the Netherlands, and it was indeed dutifully put up. But the egotism of such a monument was frowned on in his native Spain nearly as much as in the Flanders he ruled. For him to celebrate his achievements in this way seemed a sin of pride, and a very few years later the offensive statue was taken down. Too flagrant a monumental display of one's own conquering abilities, whether by a Pope or a Spanish grandee, was shown to be not necessarily the way to immortality.

Pride in actual power was elsewhere expressed, more patriotically and agreeably, by another large-scale monument, also destined to be overthrown. At Genoa the dominant figure of Andrea Doria, a great admiral and virtual dictator of the city, utilized the arts in a notable variety of ways which should have made him prominent in histories of Renaissance culture (from which, however, he is usually quite absent). In the palace which he had built, the modern hero commissioned Pierino del Vaga to decorate a loggia where the heroes of antiquity mingle with the great men of the house of Doria.

For a piazza at Genoa, the grateful citizens decided on a colossal statue of Doria himself and the sculptor Bandinelli was chosen to execute it. The story told by Vasari (no lover of Bandinelli) about this statue is muddled and factually inaccurate, yet revealing. Vasari believed that Prince Doria (as the admiral had become, ennobled by Charles V) kept a daily watch on the sculptor's work and was furious when it seemed it was not turning out well; according to him, Bandinelli left it unfinished because he feared his patron's wrath. Such documents as there are show, however, that the Genoese were remarkably patient about Bandinelli's undoubted delays, and that the statue was probably never seen by Doria, since it remained only roughly blocked-out in the marble quarries at Carrara. Its design cannot be certainly established but possibly Bandinelli intended to depict Doria in the highly suitable allegorical guise of Neptune (and perhaps some echo of this project is to be traced in Bronzino's portrait of Doria as Neptune).

Something no less grandiose and large-scale was later to be created when the commission passed to another sculptor, Montorsoli, who certainly seems to have pleased the Prince because he was also commissioned to design his tomb. The tomb has largely survived but only the headless trunk of Andrea Doria [72] now exists to convey some idea of Montorsoli's concept of the statue. Mutilated though it is, its robust and heroic air is a reminder that the sculptor had been associated with Michelangelo. Shown in armour, like a Medici Capitano, Doria must have appeared in non-allegorical form, recognizably a person but one elevated in art, as in life, by exceptional qualities, a god in comparison with ordinary men, the guardian and saviour of Genoa, and a symbol of its greatness.

Only a real-life hero could successfully assume such status.
And only some real-life heroes, as has emerged, would find a
city eager to pay them such homage in their lifetime. For most
of mid-sixteenth-century Europe the greatest international
figure – if not a hero, patently the most powerful ruler – was
the Emperor Charles V. He was indeed to be a subject for
monuments even while he lived, but an ordinary individual's
pertinacity could also be rewarded rather similarly. In the mid-
century at Venice, a city notoriously jealous of individuals'
claims to prominence (had not the Republic refused to permit
the statue of Colleoni to be placed in Piazza San Marco?), a
private citizen Tommaso Rangone sought 'to put and for ever
fix a figure of himself from the life . . . an image of bronze'
(*mettere et eternamente stare una sua figura dal vivo . . . imagine di
bronzo*) on a church façade.

72. *Doria monuments, c.* 1540–45. Giovanni Montorsoli

73. *Tommaso Rangone*, 1557. Jacopo Sansovino (?)

His first choice, that of San Geminiano in the Piazza, was judged much too exalted for a mere individual, but after he had offered to repair the façade of a more obscure church, San Giuliano, his wish was granted. There, designed in bronze by Sansovino, he sits *'eternamente'*, a weathered yet still striking likeness [73], a rare testimony on a Venetian church exterior to a private person's urge for immortality in art. That Rangone really did have some such compulsion seems evident from the way he had himself introduced into each of a series of pictures commissioned by him about the same time from Tintoretto. On the façade of San Giuliano, Rangone sits as simply as if in his own study, unsupported by the Virtues or the Graces, modest, studious and very much alive.

Around Charles V more grandiose ideas might naturally accumulate, though they were not always to be realized. Probably no living person had had an equestrian statue put up to him in post-antique times; and this way of paying tribute to the Emperor appealed to artists as well as patrons, if not necessarily to the subject himself. At Siena, Beccafumi executed a huge equestrian statue of Charles, made of cardboard, the horse rearing up and three conquered provinces helping to take the weight; this was planned to greet the Emperor on his proposed visit to the city, which never took place. Another project was for an elaborate equestrian monument of Charles to be set up permanently and prominently in Rome, to be sculpted by della Porta, creator of the Paul III monument. Nothing came of this, but ideas for it included the typical Baroque triumphal programme for such statues: conquered provinces would decorate the plinth. Another sculptor, Leone Leoni, author of the Marquess of Marignano monument, was eager to execute

74. *Charles V restraining Fury*, 1549 onwards. Leone Leoni

an equestrian statue of Charles in armour, on a Doric pedestal with reliefs showing his victories. This too came to nothing, but Leoni produced the frankly rhetorical gilded bronze group of *Charles V restraining Fury* [74]. '*È tenuta per cosa singolare*' Leoni's closest patron assured the Emperor in 1553, and it represents a visually unrelated combination of fulsome allegory, rather fussily designed, with a convincing image of the Emperor in imperial Roman pose. Its conscious virtuosity probably appealed enormously. Vasari mentions admiringly how Charles's armour could be removed to reveal the sculpted body beneath; and effects like the chains which loop around Fury doubtless seemed novel and ingenious. There is something perhaps too showy in the group's surface accomplishment, but in its flattering view of a conquering monarch, its deliberate display and intention to astonish, as well as to endure, it is typical of the period – yet as an object nearer in the last analysis to jewellery perhaps than to sculpture.

Other bronzes by Leoni of the Spanish royal family were often more straightforward, vigorous as well as strongly characterized. The subjects were living and had been studied by Leoni, but the artistic inspiration seems to come from the full-length figures on Maximilian's tomb at Innsbruck [70]. Certainly the precedent of that earlier Habsburg monument hangs heavy over the bronze groups of Charles V and his immediate family, and Philip II with his [75], which were to be

75. *Philip II and his family*, completed 1598. Pompeo Leoni

sculpted by Leoni's son, Pompeo, for the chapel of the Escorial. In these solemn kneeling figures perpetually at prayer facing the high altar, pride and piety, heroicization and realism, immortality and mortality, all seem strangely blended. A chilly splendour informs what is at once a monument to glory in this world and a graveside plea for consideration in the next.

Superstition swayed rather than discouraged Philip in turning the monastery of the Escorial [85] into one great royal mortuary where he, as well as his father, should be buried. He wished Pompeo Leoni's groups to be worked on at Madrid where he could watch the sculptor's progress; and shortly

76. *'Col Tempo'*. Giorgione

before the king's death both sets of figures were finished and had been placed in position. Unlike most of the other patrons referred to in this chapter, Philip II could thus die in the assurance that his tomb, in exactly the form he wished, was ready. And nothing has altered it. Bronze has proved enduring. Emperor and King, father and son, are forever on their knees before God; and the action of time seems halted.

That was what so many patrons had striven for, striving the more successfully perhaps as time itself was gradually being better comprehended. Yet the progress of man's life itself was unstoppable. The regrets for lost youth which Villon

77. *Nine Ages of Man*, 1540. Jörg Breu

had put into the mouth of La Belle Heaulmière could only be echoed in a variety of ways: from Giorgione's *Col Tempo* [76] to Ronsard's poignant lines:

> *Le temps s'en va, le temps s'en va, madame.*
> *Las, le temps non, mais nous nous allons.*

The Nine Ages of Man were made into virtually a triumphal arch by Jörg Breu [77], except that at the end there is nothing so very triumphal about what it is celebrating. Death is prominent at the top, though the perspective below shows a hope of heaven. Death had not in some mysterious way been exorcized by the Renaissance, and the idea that a concern with it is typically 'Gothic', instead of being, as it is, typically human, is poor history and worse psychology. Like eternity, death remained – remains, indeed – hard to grasp.

Time was also a vague concept to most people in periods when it was not in their power to measure it other than broadly. Large public clocks which struck the hours were no novelty by the fifteenth century, but portable clocks were still rare; the Marquis of Mantua in the 1470s could find no one competent in Florence to repair his own portable clock, nor could he find a

78. *Temperance*, 1499–1507. Michel Colombe

new one on sale anywhere in the city. But by the mid sixteenth century, portable clocks were comparatively common. On the tomb of Francis II of Brittany, begun in 1499, Temperance holds a neat-looking table clock [78] of the kind which usually in smaller format soon began to appear in portraits. Augsburg and Nuremburg became famous for their clocks and watches, increasingly works of art as well as of ingenuity [143]. Florimond Robertet, the French minister who commissioned pictures from Leonardo, eventually owned twelve clocks. Charles V also had a famous collection of them.

79. *Time*, 1509. English

Time-keepers like those were partly ornaments, and any fascination in them was probably connected with delight in mechanisms and automata rather than profound theories about time and its passage. And yet the development of the clock, allied to the development of other precision instruments, indicated an advance in knowledge. Perhaps it is not too far-fetched to suggest that the new possibility of possessing a pocket watch, or clock, gave the owner a new sense of awareness of time: he knew it, at least, in a way not previously feasible.

Ultimately, time must waste everyone, as it has eaten away at the face of the woman painted by Giorgione. On the Medici tombs, Michelangelo had meant (according to Condivi) to carve a mouse, signifying time, and he even left a small piece of marble for it; as the mouse always gnaws and consumes, so 'Time devours everything' (. . . 'l Tempo ogni cosa divora). To illustrate Stephen Hawes's *Pastime of Pleasure* (1509), Time himself appears like a figure from a masque, holding in one hand a clock and in the other a fire in which ultimately everything burns [79]. *'Tous les jours vont à la mort,'* Montaigne makes Nature say, quoting Lucretius, *'le dernier y arrive'.*

Against such strong awareness of time's inevitable course, the most macabre of all Renaissance monuments is seen to be neither inexplicable nor just a return to medieval concepts. On the tomb of the young Prince of Orange, René de Châlons, a sculptor who was probably Ligier Richier displayed his dreadfully decaying skeleton – activated beyond the grave [80]. The starkness of the corpse, but its earthly rank also, are emphasized by the sweep of the ermine-lined cloak painted behind it and by the shield it clutches against its torn and perishing skin. The prince was a *preux chevalier* of the period, an admired general of Charles V's, who had been mortally wounded at the siege of Saint Dizier in 1544, and much mourned. He engaged in warfare, the Venetian ambassador had written, 'through love of glory . . . His affability, liberality, noble bearing and valour caused him to be admired by all. He was only twenty-six years old'.

Most remarkable on his tomb is the assertion of immortality amid such vivid corruption of the flesh; even in this state René de Châlons stretches up his hand, holding out his heart to God, and on its withered neck his skull too gazes intently upwards. Thus the monument's message is far from being that all is vanity. Rather, it proclaims – with the greatest virtuosity of idea and execution, down to the skeletal marble hand originally clasping a heart of gold – that a part of us is unquenchable, enduring and eternal. Affirmation is its stirring, literally renascent note: 'And though . . . worms destroy this body, yet in my flesh shall I see God'.

80. Figure from the tomb of René de Châlons, after 1544.
Attributed to Ligier Richier

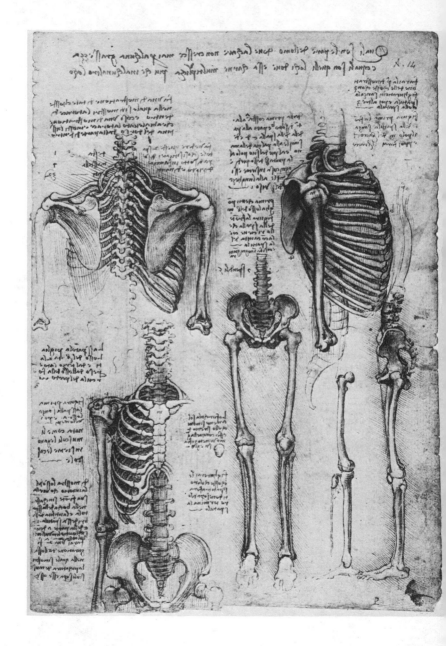

81. Studies of a skeleton, *c.* 1510. Leonardo da Vinci

4
Natural Magic

The sculptor who made the image on the tomb of the Prince of Orange was concerned primarily with an effective, rather than anatomically exact, corpse. Yet what he produced was perhaps better-observed, as it was certainly better-articulated, than it would have been a hundred years earlier. Undoubtedly, the opportunity existed by the mid sixteenth century for any artist to be more knowledgeable than ever before about the structure of the human body, and he could be so by studying illustrated books, without having positively to conduct his own dissections.

Various writers had helped the progress of such knowledge. Few had observed as penetratingly as Leonardo da Vinci (though even he was sometimes misled by traditional assumptions into wrong interpretation of the evidence), and none possessed anything like his power to draw what he observed [81]. But Leonardo's books of anatomical studies remained unpublished. Only those who entered his studio, like the Cardinal of Aragon who went to visit him outside Amboise in the October of 1517, saw these studies; and the Cardinal's secretary recorded that he told them he had dissected 'more than thirty bodies, both of men and women . . .'

For a non-professional person that was a remarkable number. Bodies of women particularly were not easy to acquire or examine, as even the greatest and most famous anatomist, Andreas Vesalius, was to discover. Vesalius was a child of five when Leonardo died. It was his treatises, published and notably well-illustrated [82] which were to represent the triumph of the new knowledge and research, disseminated and indeed plagiarized all over Europe; Vesalius complained particularly of a clumsy English plagiarization. The activated skeletons and 'muscle-men' in the plates which he had had carefully drawn to follow his own posing of the suspended cadaver were probably executed by several different artists, possibly from Titian's studio (as one early reference seems to suggest).

Of the illustrations to his *Fabrica* (1543), Vesalius wrote that they would greatly please those who had no supply of bodies for dissection, and though he sighed over the tiresomeness of artists, he valued the effectiveness of their contribution. The plates have a touch or two of macabre fancy and an almost surreal effect through being set often in front of minutely delineated Venetian countryside – backgrounds more suitable to some Giorgionesque pastoral conceit, it might be thought, than to bodies stripped of skin, revealing tabulated muscles. 'The first . . . to provide our contemporaries with an unusual opportunity for searching out the truth', was Vesalius's own description of himself and his achievement. Although he was not strictly the first, any more than he was always entirely accurate, his boast has a good deal of validity.

Vesalius held important, sometimes difficult posts, as a medical adviser. He was for a period in the service of Charles V (to whom he dedicated his *De humani corporis fabrica*, remarking in the dedication that he hoped the Emperor, whom he knew to delight in knowledge of the universe, also delighted sometimes in 'the most perfectly constructed of all creatures'). It was as a result of such service that he was present at the siege of Saint Dizier, though he seems not to have been called on to help the wounded Prince of Orange; nevertheless, that actual corpse came under his eye, and he later noted tersely 'I inspected the viscera of the Prince of Orange'. It would have been a neat piece of history had he actually advised the sculptor of the Prince's tomb at Bar-le-Duc.

Although Vesalius may rightly stand as one symbol of Renaissance advance in knowledge, it is useful to remember that not all advances were necessarily beneficial. Medicine itself had by no means learnt how to deal with natural ills, while men devised new ones to inflict on each other. It had been an advance when gunpowder was invented, but its use in cannon and other guns for warfare produced a new method of killing. A new patron saint was also required. St Barbara (whose cruel father had been destroyed by thunder and lightning) became patron of the *bombardieri*, and an instruction of Charles V's required each gunner to make the sign of the cross over the muzzle of the gun he loaded, calling on St Barbara's aid. Gunshot wounds proved complicated and horribly hard to cure, and the Prince of Orange, who had been shot, was a victim whom a later age would probably have been able to save. Vesalius was no omniscient wizard – indeed, it was from others

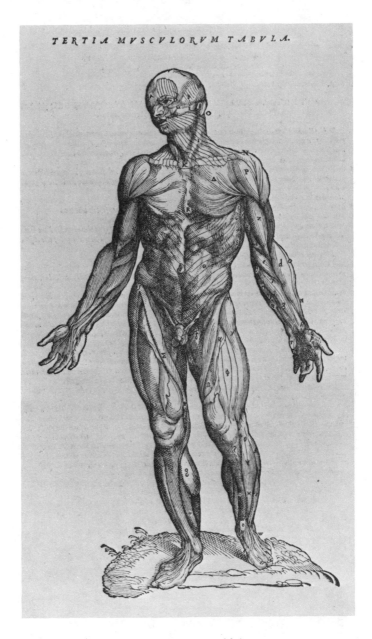

82. Plate from Vesalius's *De humani corporis fabrica*, 1543

that he learnt about the best methods of treating war-wounds – and on occasion his reputation perhaps dangerously increased expectation, as well as his responsibilities.

The period tended to invest the knowledgeable man, the seer, the proto-scientist, the philosopher, the physician, and the artist, with magical or semi-divine powers, and was ever-ready to admire their skills. All such people took on an aspect of magus. Having seen Leonardo's pictures, his anatomical drawings and studies of water, machines and so on, the Cardinal of Aragon's secretary described him simply as 'the most eminent painter of our time' (though Raphael was then at the height of his fame, and after the Sistine chapel ceiling Michelangelo might have been supposed a not negligible candidate). Leonardo's was one of the two names of Italian artists (Mantegna's was the other) which occurred to the Spanish explorer Fernàndez de Oviedo when he encountered a strange tree in the new land of America: only such a hand could have depicted what he could not describe. 'Virtue and cunning' (i.e. skill), says the wise medical man Cerimon, in *Pericles*, the very type of beneficent magus, can give immortality, 'making a man a god'.

Vesalius has probably achieved the immortality of fame, but he had no miracle of immortality to work on others – as became

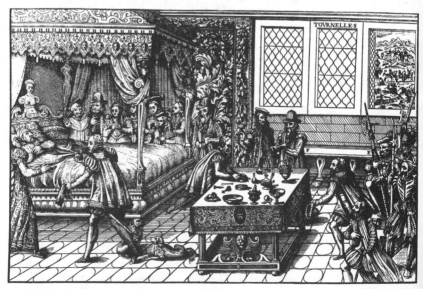

83. Deathbed of Henri II of France, 1559

clear when he was hastily dispatched from Brussels to take charge of the hopeless case of Henri II of France, fatally wounded in a tournament. At this deathbed, itself the subject of contemporary illustration [83], Vesalius met a great French surgeon, who also wrote of his cases and cures, Ambroise Paré – both men are portrayed in consultation at the central table in the print – but it was on the foreigner that the onus fell. His knowledge told him that the King's wound was incurable, and he apparently declared as much; seven days after his arrival, Henri II died. All that was left was for Vesalius to perform a post-mortem.

Vesalius seems not to have been blamed or criticized, and in that – as in other things – he was probably more fortunate than many other savants of the century, especially those who dabbled in magic or seemed in some way to upset established views of society or the cosmos, and thus, inevitably, challenge religion. Like Vesalius, these men were eager to be leaders in providing their fellow-men with special opportunities 'for searching out the truth'. Unlike Leonardo, they were usually active authors who sought publication of their work – even though this often proved contentious and dangerous. If printing had not existed, it would certainly have been necessary to invent it for an age which delighted in instructing, as well as in astounding, and which was constantly being fed with fresh information about the world.

An obvious physical enlargement had been provided by the discovery of 'this America, which we call New Lands', as a Parisian lawyer Etienne Pasquier wrote in the 1560s, remarking that it was a striking fact that classical authors had had no knowledge of that continent. This discovery is a complete topic in itself, but what seems notable is that interest seems to have increased throughout the sixteenth century. When Christopher Columbus died at Valladolid in 1506, the city chronicle failed to record the fact at all. In 1552 the author of a *General History of the Indies* (dedicated to Charles V) could declare that the discovery of 1492 had been the 'greatest event since the creation of the world', excluding only the Incarnation and death of Christ. And many other tributes might be cited, both to Columbus personally, though posthumously, and to the century's sense of 'the globe . . . opened up to the human race' (Vives, *De Disciplinis* [1531]).

The strangeness of what as a result was found made a great appeal – not just the gold but the flora and fauna, the people, the wonderful tints of their feathered costumes and their exotic artifacts. The people, who had struck some early observers as mere beasts, were solemnly declared by Pope Paul III to be 'true men'. They and some of the bizarre creatures who inhabited the land were to be drawn [84] before the century closed by such on-the-spot artists as John White, who sailed with Grenville to Virginia; and White's drawings were used to illustrate the second edition of Hariot's *Briefe and True Report of the New Found Land of Virginia*. Spenser speaks of 'painted plumes' comparable to those worn by the 'sunburnt *Indians*', and the shot colours of the Aztec feathered headdresses and fans brought back to Europe naturally appealed in a period in which painters like Grünewald and Pontormo exploited such novel colour effects for drapery. When the Venetian ambassador saw Montezuma's treasure, which had been given to Charles V, he compared the changing, shot effect of the feathered objects to a dove's neck. Most significant of all was Dürer's emotion, when he too gazed at these treasures, which included a moon of silver and a huge sun of gold. As a connoisseur of curiosities, he felt their exoticness, but was moved positively by what he called 'the subtle *ingenia* of men in foreign lands'. A whole world – unknown to all previous generations – existed far away, where the inhabitants proved no less capable than Western people of art in their own sophisticated idiom. The implications were considerable and it is not surprising that Dürer added that he did not know what he felt.

'The news of such great and unexpected things' was the Florentine historian Guicciardini's phrase for what had been carried back to Europe through Columbus's discovery. The aspect of the unexpected is an important one. Maps and navigational charts were not the only things that had to be re-thought, and vested interest in accepted creeds seldom welcomed mental changes. Guicciardini noted also that 'some anxiety to interpreters of the Holy Scriptures' had been caused, but any anxiety arising from the discovery of America was nothing to the emotions aroused by explorers of the apparently known world, those surveyors of the solar system or the laws of the physical earth who in a variety of ways pursued, and proclaimed, the right to know. It is this right which united Vesalius and Leonardo to Copernicus and Tycho Brahe, and to Galileo, which animated natural magicians like Paracelsus and Dr John Dee, and which was so confidently expressed by Marlowe's words, put into the mouth not of Dr Faustus but of Tambur-

The manner of their fishing.

84. Indians of Virginia fishing, 1585-7. John White

laine, a Scythian conqueror who pauses after battle to praise the human soul which can comprehend,

> The wondrous architecture of the world,
> And measure every wandering planet's course,

This might seem scarcely evidence, interesting though it is; yet in its way, it is no more than poetic expansion of what Cortés had written to an oriental potentate, that it is 'a universal condition of men to want to know'. Cortés himself well exemplified such curiosity, investigating volcanoes and Indian customs, and trying all the time to inquire into what he called the 'secrets of these parts'. And it is also worth remembering the tribute Vesalius paid Charles V for his knowledge of the science of the universe and the stars.

The 'secrets' of the universe were closely associated with magic of all kinds. Magic was partly the possession of knowledge which others did not have; it was the power to control things, and possibly to control spirits, to read the stars or foretell the future, or – on another level – to counterfeit precious stones and attract iron with a magnet. From one point of view it was a superior form of conjuring. From another it was spiritualism. From yet another, perhaps the most significant, it was a serious exploration of natural forces and the laws of physics. However it is defined, its ubiquitousness is unmistakable. On the subject in the Renaissance an outstanding authority has written, 'Magic was always on the point of turning into art, science, practical psychology, or, above all, religion' (D.P.Walker, *Spiritual and Demonic Magic from Ficino to Campanella*). Indeed, what the lure of antiquity had been in earlier years, the combined magical-scientific urge seems to become for the later period. And if sometimes too much stress has been laid on the effect of classical antiquity on the arts, not enough probably has yet been made of the affinities between magic and the arts. The artist, even when quite lacking Leonardo's intellectual gifts, could still be a sort of magician, deceiving the eye, creating marvels and showing himself no less skilful than other magus-figures in probing nature's mysteries. The visual artist too deals in images as the magician may; a picture is not exactly a talisman, though perhaps something of mysterious sympathy, transferred from living person to object, is felt in a portrait.

Even alchemy could have its utilitarian value, its white magic of investigating the property of metals and minerals; an Italian treatise on these aspects, Biringuccio's *Pirotechnia* (1540), speaks of the useful results of such responsible research, including colours for painting. Cellini too mentions in his *Trattato* how a new red enamel had been discovered by an alchemist who was actually seeking to make gold. In his autobiography he also, more frivolously, tells of his experiences when dabbling in necromancy, in a typical mixture of the comic and the bizarre. Few artists, probably, were actively involved with magic as such, though Jean Perréal was a friend or acquaintance of Agrippa of Nettesheim, a leading exponent, and Parmigianino notoriously studied alchemy, to the detriment, Vasari lamented, of not only his art but his life. Jacopo de' Barbari and Beccafumi are the other artists who have, more vaguely, been instanced in recent times as showing awareness of magic symbols and meanings. Some Renaissance buildings are susceptible to explanation as expressive of hermetic significance [85], though

85. The Escorial, 1563-84.
Juan Bautista de Toledo and Francisco de Herrera

the degree of this is sometimes not clear and such examples are anyway likely to have been rare. The cloudiness of the whole subject originates in the hermetic, magic, though not always coherent, texts themselves, but that does not alter the attractiveness it undoubtedly had – evidenced not least in pictures of philosophers and astrologers [105 and 106].

Something broader and less recondite unites artists and practitioners of true natural magic. 'Nature,' Leonardo wrote, 'is full of infinite causes which were never found in experience' (. . . *infinite ragioni che non furono mai in esperienza*), experience here perhaps meaning accepted beliefs. To reveal Nature's mysteries can be the artist's task, as well as the astronomer's, the botanist's, the physicist's, though the artist's revelation is inevitably different from theirs. Leonardo's studies – after all, intended eventually for publication – seem to bring him close to the sentiments of the arch-figure of wandering, often vilified, Renaissance magician-savant-physician, Paracelsus. 'It behoves me,' Paracelsus wrote 'to describe natural things, and thus when set down, much shall be known which until now has been supposed hidden' (. . . *so werden viel erkennt, die sich bissher verborgen behalten haben*). The Nature which Paracelsus saw was essentially arcane, even mystic, very much a World in a Grain of Sand, but it had positively to be observed and experienced, with as it were new eyes, not through book-learning. To explore Nature, he said, one must tread her books with one's feet (*mit den Füssen ihre Bücher treten*) – a phrase which brings to mind Leonardo's ascent of Monte Rosa, or Dürer's travels and constant depiction of what he saw when travelling.

Natural magic was to be defined by Bacon as 'the science which applies the knowledge of hidden forms to the production of wonderful operations'. How far this might extend in practice is conveyed in the extraordinary, encyclopaedic and popular *Magia Naturalis* (first published in 1558) by Giambattista della Porta, who organized at Naples an Academy typical of the period, concerned specifically with 'Natural Curiosities'. Other writers, like Girolamo Cardano, a wandering Milanese scholar whose life was a series of controversies, had produced books on such matters; Cardano's *De Subtilitate* (1551) was full of ingenious, illustrated suggestions for cipher locks, raising sunken ships [86] and improving chimney drafts, all ways of mastering Nature. Something else has also been mastered, though it is easily overlooked by modern readers, in the very concept of diffusing scientific and technical knowledge through illustra-

86. Illustration from
Cardano's *De Subtilitate*, 1551

tions accompanying the text in a book. The first book of this
kind had been printed in 1472. The *De re militari*, by Roberto
Valturio, was essentially practical in a matter of general Renaissance interest – how to wage war effectively – and had covered
naval as well as land equipment.

If Porta became more popular than Cardano, it was probably
because he was concerned less with fundamental principles than
with, in effect, party tricks. Yet these too can be related to
things which art can do – making a wall disappear, for instance,
and be replaced apparently by a view over Rome, as in Peruzzi's
Sala delle Prospettive in the Farnesina [87]. Porta would surely
have enjoyed this eye-deceiving, and still highly convincing,
defiance of solid fact. While he discusses the generation of
animals, and gives hints about new plants, he seems more
interested in offering advice on how to counterfeit precious
stones, how to remove pimples, and how to detect whether

women are using cosmetics. When he tells of how to produce grapes in the springtime, it seems almost an anticipation of the incident when Marlowe's Faustus conjures up grapes in mid

87. Sala delle Prospettive, Villa Farnesina, Rome, *c*. 1517-18. Baldassare Peruzzi

winter for the Duchess of Vanholt. Faustus needs the black art of Mephistopheles to aid him, it is true, whereas Porta states that he will have nothing to do with sorcery – a prudent disclaimer.

Few artists could seriously claim a scientific knowledge of the hidden forms of Nature, but in study of Nature and 'The wondrous architecture of the world', they might well consider themselves pioneers. To depicting phenomena, and in being inspired to create virtually rival phenomena, they too now brought new ways of scientific precision, responding to the sense of a universe enlarged, enlarging and, in certain ways, being surveyed as if for the first time. The intensity of Dürer's gaze in the so-called *'Great Piece of Turf'* [88] makes one feel positively down on the oozy ground, close to the hair-like roots, with grass-stalks brushing one's face – almost a pigmy

88. The *'Great Piece of Turf'*,
1503. Albrecht Dürer

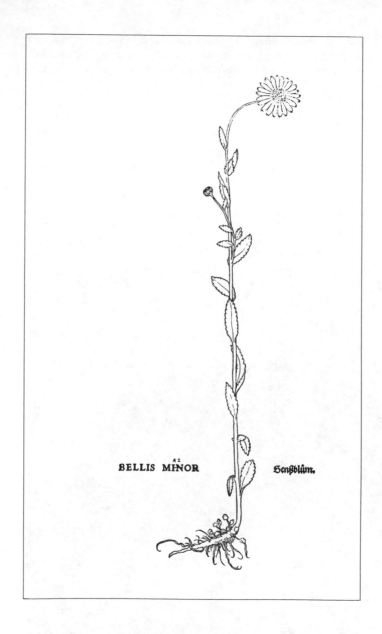

BELLIS MINOR Senßblům.

89. Illustration from Fuchs' *De historia stirpium commentarii*, 1542

in this thick jungle of tall sprouting plants, the form and foliage of each of which is so carefully delineated. Dürer's care is such that the study may be fixed as executed probably in May, when plantain, yarrow and dandelion – all apparent – are blooming. In accuracy the *'Great Piece of Turf'* can be compared with one of the finest and most famous herbals of the century, Leonhard Fuchs' *De historia stirpium commentarii* (1542), in whose woodcuts [89] the plants are so skilfully positioned on the page: specimens and yet still invested with vitality. Fuchs would doubtless have been delighted had Dürer been alive and available to collaborate on his work; as it was, more generous than Vesalius, he went out of his way to praise in his preface those artists involved in drawing the plants, copying the drawings and preparing the blocks. Herbals were no new idea, and Fuchs was only one of the many contemporary figures in Germany, France, Italy and England who published work of this kind. But his attitude was outstandingly botanical rather than medical. His range of plants took in those of the new land of America and for each specimen he gave some account of its root, habitat and characteristics.

Turning the pages of Fuchs' book would in itself have opened the eyes of anyone to Nature's own book, and Fuchs wrote of how pleasant it was to wander gazing at plants and flowers, whereas Dürer's study was for his own private use (probably with a view to incorporating something of it in a religious print or painting). Yet the empathy, as much as the accuracy, of Dürer's drawing is remarkable and, though they can be paralleled in other fine plant studies by him, the unique aspect of the *'Great Piece of Turf'* is that the plants are growing, not plucked from the soil. Scarcely less unusual is the fact that no one species is singled out for observation. Nor could anything be more ordinary than the plants themselves. The commonest grasses and a few dandelions are subject enough, and Dürer's response to them is the more intense for this restriction, so that every shift of pattern is keenly felt among the broad or spear-sharp or fretted leaves, with their varying tones of green, and it is with almost triumphant effect that there rise from the exquisitely contrived tangle a few feathery heads of the thinnest grasses. An apparently humble corner of the world's architecture, never previously scrutinized with such affectionate penetration (not even by Leonardo), has suddenly become most marvellous, and artistically rewarding.

Greater areas of Nature remained to be surveyed and captured by artists – none perhaps more challenging than the atmospheric envelope of sky, seen to be poorly conveyed by mere flat expanses of blue paint. Blueness itself in pictures gives place to more crystalline and colourless tones and aerial perspective, as if following some of Leonardo's observations on the subject: '. . . the blue which is seen in the atmosphere is not its own colour, but is caused by the heated moisture having evaporated into the most minute imperceptible particles, which the beams of the solar rays attract'. The sky was a subtle challenge, especially in its moods of changing and fading light (in which already some fifteenth-century artists had shown some interest) and burning there was the most exciting visual challenge of the sun.

It was to be something of a challenge in other ways too before the sixteenth century had reached its halfway mark. Its life-giving qualities had always been recognized, but as long as the earth was supposed static the sun was earth's satellite, revolving with the planets around the fixed centre of mankind's own territory. But supposing the earth moved, was itself a subordinate, even small, planetary body, merely one of several revolving in orbits around the great centre of the cosmos, which was the sun? Such was the idea which occurred to the Polish astronomer known in the latinized form of his name as Copernicus; but his own concept of the moving earth struck him as likely to appear absurd, as indeed most people thought it was when, gradually, awareness of his views became general. Galileo himself, when he first became a Copernican, said that fear of ridicule prevented him declaring his belief. The arguments which arose from Copernicus's theories have often enough been traced and belong in other books. But even among those who refuted him popularly there was awareness of the implications of what he believed.

> Making the Sun the Centre of this All,
> Moon, Earth, and Water, in one only Ball.

That couplet from Guillaume du Bartas's *La Sepmaine, ou La Creation du Monde* (1578), a much read, often translated, didactic poem, praising God and damning scientists, along with other novelties, conveys something of the coherent, single-centred, spheric universe which Copernicus conceived, and which had been demonstrated by a neat diagram in his *De Revolutionibus*

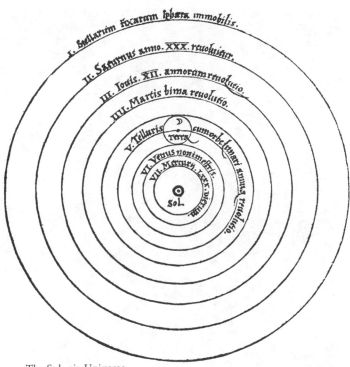

90. The Spheric Universe,
from Copernicus's *De Revolutionibus Orbium Coelestium*, 1543

Orbium Coelestium Libri Sex [90], published in 1543 and dedicated to Pope Paul III. Although Copernicus's ideas seemed at first ridiculous – only later becoming dangerous to orthodoxy – his vision was essentially of a harmonious, self-contained cosmos, bounded (as the diagram shows) by the traditional immovable sphere of the fixed stars. It was to be left to other men to break, as it were, this outer crystal wall and postulate, beyond, infinite space and even a plurality of worlds. Copernicus emphasized a less dizzy prospect and in *De Revolutionibus* praised with mystic, Paracelsian fervour the 'ruler' he had elected to be at the centre of the system:

In the midst of all sits the Sun enthroned. How could we place this luminary in any better position in this most beautiful temple from which to illuminate the whole at once? He is rightly called the Lamp, the Mind, the Ruler of the Universe . . .

91. *The Battle of Issus*, 1529. Albrecht Altdorfer

This enthusiasm – and probably never any direct influence as such from Copernicus – seems shared by artists who tried to pay their tribute to the luminous splendour of the sun, no longer a gold disc with gilded rays but a white-hot, fiery ball blazing out across the sky, even as it sets, in Altdorfer's *Battle of Issus* [91]. To convey something of the sun's luminous nature, and its apparent progress, Vasari devised a glass sun, moved on a wire, for a stage set he designed at Venice. This was for a play of Aretino's, and Aretino's enthusiastic response to a sunset seen from his window, as well as his longing for Titian to be present to paint it, has already been referred to here in Chapter 2. Vasari studied the moon carefully too, and stated that he had made a point of trying to capture (as did many other artists) in a picture the particular quality and tone of moonlight.

Comets, stars, strange lights of all kinds, whether in natural phenomena or as haloes, all found a place in paintings, displaying the skill of the artist and his ability to affect the eye, and move the mind, by increasing or diminishing areas of radiance. The unwavering high noon sunlight of the average fifteenth-century picture was exchanged for more subtle, often transient effects. The sixteenth-century French bishop and littérateur, Pontus de Tyard, included in a programme of pictures a winter landscape which might be painted as a nocturne and show accurately the position of the Northern stars, so that the effect would be both learned and agreeable. Giorgione's *Storm*, in which the distant trees glitter ominously against the inky sky, is in its aerial excitement alone a new type of picture; and in other paintings he conjures up an atmospheric mood, usually a reposeful one, by the glowing, golden sense of a calm day beginning or dying. The sun itself appears slipping over the distant hills in the *Three Philosophers* [92], the first and very early reference to which singles out the *'raggi solari'* being observed by the seated figure.

Whatever the exact meaning of this composition, it combines the magic of nature with impressive magus figures of different ages (conceivably the three kings), one of whom has actually been optimistically identified as Copernicus. The picture's 'secret' air is perhaps intentional; what is unmistakable is its depiction of man's serious response to nature (conveyed so effectively through Giorgione's own response). The trio cannot be mistaken for some picnic party; they are scholars whom an earlier period would probably have preferred to show in a

study, at their books, but here depicted actively engaged in studying Nature's books.

Altdorfer's response to Nature in general, but especially to the sky, is yet more subtle and far more varied. Marvellous as is the dramatic cosmic vista of his *Battle of Issus*, less grandiose skies in other pictures by him show equal sensitivity and response to light and air. He even reverted occasionally to the use of gold paint, as in *The Resurrection*, where a few edges of blood-red cloud are touched with it, to make a molten cauldron

92a. Detail of 92b

92b. *The Three Philosophers*. Giorgione

of stormy, victorious dawn sky. Ragged, oppressive clouds, matching a mood once again, hang over his Garden of Gethsemane, and torches gleam in the darkness as the soldiers creep up on the praying Christ.

Always there is the feeling of a shifting, never constant aerial pageant: a watery sun, soon to be muffled, or a hectic brilliance which will fade as day establishes itself. The sense of steady if unobtrusive movement in the sky, even on the hottest days, is caught with almost trembling delicacy of perception. A tissue of cloud filaments, as transparent as glass yet as mobile as water-weed, may be set floating in a radiant atmosphere which at first scarcely registers as possessing a distinct colour. Part of the marvel in Altdorfer's pictures comes from their comparatively small scale; a few inches of wooden panel have been mysteriously worked on until the result is like a burnished mirror – a magic mirror which reveals, however, new aspects of Nature rather than merely reflects the known. Into an expanse of shimmering hot sky, enlivened by some curling tendrils of drifting vapour, there may rise a pine-tree or the towers of a gorgeous, impossibly elaborate palace. The artist remains a creator and, when necessary, a conjuror.

The spectacular sky in the *Battle of Issus* is not some precise 'nature-note', but a deliberately imaginative, elemental vision, created to echo – and eclipse – the vast human forces who clash far below. Out of a whirlpool of boiling, foaming cloud, in colour ranging like the rainbow from red, through orange and yellow to indigo, the sun shoots its rays over sea and land, sinking and yet still the dominant power of the picture. A great empire is falling while the sun sets – and already a cool crescent of risen moon is visible in the quiet upper left corner of the sky. The cosmos we see both expresses and contains the magnitude of the battle, put into a perspective whereby the incident, the massed troops, the location, all shrink under the eternal aspect. What, the painter seems to ask, are even the most momentous human events when placed within the macrocosm of Nature, its mighty seas and those myriad ridges of blue arctic mountains, like endless frozen waves, which recede towards the curving horizon? In that world, man becomes the microcosm indeed; and yet the whole effect is due to one man's creative vision. The artist seems to have carried us, as Marlowe's Faustus is magically carried, into some region of upper air, 'to prove cosmography'.

Altdorfer's journey for the eye and mind is certainly one of the most astounding of the century, but ranging pictorial surveys of the world were typical. As well as being 'opened up' by the discovery of new lands, the globe was circumnavigated for the first time; Magellan set off on the journey he believed possible but which he did not live to complete. This journey too was to be the subject of topical, authoritative publication, in an accessible modern language (Pigafetta's *Le Voyage et navigation fait par les Espagnols aux isles de Molluques*, published at Paris in 1525). Geography was by no means a new study, but the novelty lay, once again, in dissemination of knowledge and a much more rapid 'popularization' of the results of recent discoveries. Improved systems of navigation, more accurate navigational charts and maps represented expert progress, often by mathematically trained men like the famous Fleming Gerard Mercator, whose name has survived in 'Mercator's Projection'. But the increasing interest in maps was also partly aesthetic. Dr Dee, who had acquired some of Mercator's globes when in the Low Countries, mentioned the demand for maps by gentlemen 'to beautifie their Halls, Parlers [*sic*], Chambers, Galeries, Studies, or Libraries with' (Preface to Billingsley's *Euclid*, 1570). In the same year the humanist Abraham Ortelius published at Antwerp his folio of world maps, a collection of known information, the *Theatrum orbis terrarum,* the first of a series of atlases which testify to his belief that every literate person should be acquainted with geography.

Ortelius was probably preaching to the converted or, at least, to a public already stimulated to take an interest in illustrations of the world, known and imaginary. It was at Antwerp early in the sixteenth century that Joachim Patenier (a Frenchman by birth) – '*der gute Landschaftsmaler*' in the words of Dürer who had met and admired him – had been active. Patenier's landscapes [93] usually have distinct human subject-matter, often of a traditional kind, but even where the figures are as prominent as in *Charon crossing the Styx*, they are very much subordinated to the wide cosmic panorama, set out in this typically sloping way which one might call 'Patenier's Projection'.

Other pictures by him seem frankly to map whole country-sides and are certainly intended to delight the eye by providing long-distance views obtainable at the time only by ascending a high tower. But no more than Altdorfer does Patenier offer a piece of accurate topography. The artist is not himself a map-maker; or at least, his map need be no precise guide to the known world. Patenier expands the possibilities of the known

93. *Charon crossing the Styx.* Joachim Patenier

into the fantasy of the *Charon*, all the more justifiably since the
subject is visionary. He uses geographical and atmospheric
truths to work for him and make convincing on one side the
softly undulating prospect of the Elysian Fields under a milky
sky and, on the other, the smoky infernal smithy of Hell, where
sinister fires flare amid the darkness. We enjoy bifocal vision –
as well as an agreeable sense of being, literally, above it all –
united by the broad channel of river which runs from the
foreground to the horizon, like a dream symbol.

Patenier's paintings were for long much sought after and
imitated. He had, in effect, devised a new category of landscape:
the fantasy panorama created with scientific, atmospheric conviction, enlivened by surprise effects, natural or unnatural,
with some abrupt outcrop of jagged crag like a great fin, or a
flaming explosion (the destruction of Sodom being a popular
occasion). Even while conveying a sense of artistic reality, he
confirmed the belief that Nature was mysterious. Despite all
the advances made by knowledge in many directions, the
century was still deeply credulous. God might once again rain
down fire from heaven; and frightening visions, portents and
dreams continued to haunt people's imaginations.

A highly scholarly, encyclopaedically learned zoologist,
Conrad Gesner, published a history of animals which, while it

dismissed Tritons and Sirens, included some other mythical marine creatures – like the merman – the existence of which the author would neither confirm nor deny. The 'Canning Jewel' [23] might, however, have seemed to Gesner not exactly good evidence. Besides, then as now, travellers' tales exercised their appeal, in addition to the tall story for its own sake; Desdemona fell in love with Othello while he told her of adventures among very Patenier-sounding landscapes, 'rough quarries, rocks, and hills whose heads touch heaven', not to mention the cannibals and the men whose heads 'do grow beneath their shoulders', the latter derived doubtless from an engraving of them in Sebastian Münster's *Cosmographia universalis* (1544). Philip II of Spain owned, among others, the Patenier landscape illustrated here and probably enjoyed it just because it was fantastic and beyond the natural, in much the same way as he appears to have enjoyed Bosch.

With Bosch the magic is so highly unnatural and the exterior world has been distorted into such freakish, surreal effects (beautifully painted though they are) that the natural philosophers, the proto-scientists and all those in pursuit of knowledge of the universe – magicians included – would have found his pictures too extraordinary. In them there is no key to the world and few suggestions of cosmic order. But in a Northern artist of the succeeding generation, Bruegel, much younger than Patenier or Bosch, fantasy and intense sensitivity to natural phenomena, as well as to humanity – to microcosm as much as to macrocosm – all united with truly Renaissance power. Too much can be made of Bruegel's satire and 'pessimism' (entirely a matter of interpretation of his art, for there is no other positive evidence). In his vividly atmospheric countryside, whether seen in stingingly cold weather or turned golden at harvest time under a glassy blue sky, mankind is always engaged in asserting its vital power. Even the clumsiest of his peasants has a Shakespearean conviction; like the grotesque and reviled Pompey Bum, he stubbornly claims one primary right, 'I am a poor fellow that would live'.

Bruegel was a friend of Ortelius, who owned some of his pictures and wrote an epitaph at his death. No peasant himself, as was once confusedly deduced from his peasant subjects, Bruegel showed in such an engraving as his *Temperance* [94] human activity as creative and highly intellectual; not only is there music, acting, and education, but men debate an experiment with weights, while in the background an angle of the moon is calculated by an astronomer bravely perched on the earth's tilted orb, itself being measured by a geographer, perhaps in reference to Ortelius. It can hardly be an accident that Bruegel emphasizes the patently active, useful aspects of Temperance, a virtue which he may well have rated higher than the less lively Patience and Hope which also appeared in the same series.

The view of life in the *Temperance* is ideal. There it is the mind which dominates, whereas in actual existence most people are dependent on, can seldom rise above, sensation. In Bruegel's seasonal paintings living is largely a matter of sensations. The truth of sensations, however squalid or grim, is what these pictures enshrine. The great vistas of landscape extend almost as far as Altdorfer's, always suggesting a plurality of country worlds, and the effect of the elements in fields and towns far beyond the foreground figures. A profoundly universal and moving effect comes from geographical range combined with the ranging activities of the inhabitants of this rustic universe. There is no place for books, no time for music except bagpipes or the tune of an itinerant fiddler. Existence is not all toil, but

94. *Allegory of Temperance*. After Pieter Bruegel

Nature dictates and largely provides such relaxation as there is: skating on a frozen lake or collapsing under a tree in a hot hayfield at a midday break for food.

Bruegel says no more perhaps than that life goes on. Yet empathy drives him to invest this scarcely novel belief with quite fresh conviction. Mankind ceases to be a blurred collective noun and is parcelled out into a myriad individualities, children's having as much reality as those of adults. A whole amusing picture of *Children's Games* confirms what is apparent in details of other pictures. Nature in Bruegel's world long ago placed men and women on an equality; as they toil in the fields or bear away baskets of fruit, the sexes cannot easily be told apart. But as bundles of sensation, uncouth, stout, coarsely clad though they usually are, each is instinct with individuality.

The trio of women who stride purposefully homeward in *The Hay Harvest* [95] are as distinctly characterized as Giorgione's three philosophers, and no less essentially dignified. From their varied headgear to the way they grasp their rakes, the three women are unobtrusively individualized; Bruegel's art half-conceals, so naturalistic does it appear, the formal device

95. Detail of *The Hay Harvest*, c. 1565. Pieter Bruegel

of showing one full face, one in profile, and the third in three-quarter face. About them is also a subtle suggestion of varied ages, of indeed the Three Ages, and one might almost claim they represented grandmother, daughter (in the middle) and mother. Nor does Bruegel's characterization stop there, for the most determined looking of them, the woman who has taken off her straw hat, is also the one who carries home the refreshment jug – very much the burdened Martha of the group, while the rather dreamy girl (even her stride appearing less vigorous than the others') is something of a Mary.

To do justice to Bruegel's creativity in this small detail alone would take Tolstoy; perhaps otherwise only in his pages does the peasant, while not losing a jot of individuality, stand for humanity with such unselfconscious pride. And as a mere grace-note of Nature, Bruegel touches in, behind this group, a patch of wild poppies blooming on the verge: straggling, fragile stems, drooping buds and the black button corolla of each flower perceived, and conveyed, with as vivid a precision as he had given to his people.

Elsewhere he fused man and Nature to achieve this unsentimentalized harmony – where man always has his place but must strive if he wants to master Nature – even in pictures that at first glance might suggest no harmony at all. The dour pervasive lack of light, the wind-ripped river and the iron ridge of bleak distant mountains which are features of *The Gloomy Day* [96] promise man no easy, agreeable climate of survival. And here, rather than in the white winter scene of the famous *Hunters in the Snow*, Bruegel really captures a new way to affect the epidermis – one is tempted to say – as well as the eye, so bitter and unmitigated is the icy weather, in which simply to lean against another human being seems to offer a moment of merciful warmth.

Yet even in this landscape, where every tree is stripped of leaves and waves buffet to destruction the few boats on the chill, rising water, men are occupied with their tasks. Trees are pollarded and sticks are gathered. A roof, damaged no doubt by the gale, is being repaired. At the right a group huddles together with a sort of tipsy vivacity, the man eating waffles, the woman and boy, in paper crown, hopeful perhaps of sharing a bite. The day depicted is probably the last before Lent, Mardi Gras, celebrated here with no carnival profusion but celebrated all the same. Down at the left in the village, where few inhabitants are visible, in as it were a minute corner of the world's

96. *The Gloomy Day*, 1565. Pieter Bruegel

macrocosm, and careless of the elements' hostility, a solitary fiddler plays outside a tavern to a dancing man and child. It is in this sense that the course of life goes on, and mankind strangely finds the will to survive by being natural. Bruegel does not blink at, still less prettify, the facts; nearby a peasant painfully heaves at the shaft of a laden cart, while against the tavern wall his companion urinates.

Bruegel's is probably the profoundest and calmest of all artistic visions of the natural world. There man becomes neither dwarf nor god – and earth is certainly no paradise. Yet his vision is always of a people-infested universe, and it is through humane, as well as human, eyes that he sees natural phenomena, themselves obedient to organic, cyclic laws. The poppies bloom at the roadside along which labourers trudge home. Trees are to be felled for firewood. Fine weather is to be utilized for fruit-picking and hay-making. Bruegel hardly pauses to ask which things, if any, are beautiful; and there is little time for contemplating them either mystically or in the scientific–artistic way of Leonardo and Dürer. His is perhaps a humble interpretation of the doctrine of making Nature work for man, but he is insistent in his reminder that in this world at least there are no miracles. Man must continually work at Nature.

Those who seriously studied Nature's laws – geographers, botanists, physicians – could find in artists not only interesting affinities, directly useful aids and sometimes personal friendship, but further, subtle tribute to the value of all such study in portrayal of themselves. The true magus seldom appeared looking like Giorgione's magi, though he might well be portrayed with the paraphernalia of his profession. If he was accompanied by a book, it would no longer be a prayer-book and might positively be identified, being perhaps one of his own works. The picture of a scholar at his desk surrounded by books and pets had been a favourite category of fifteenth-century art, but the scholar more often turned out to be a saint like St Jerome rather than an actual living person.

The many portraits done of Erasmus, the most famous example for all sixteenth-century Europe of high intellectual distinction and sober outward appearance, establish the modern sage in place of the traditional saint, and virtually establish also the iconography for portrayal. The type is charmingly initiated by Massys' *Aegidius* [97], a candid, intensely convincing image of the lively scholar, seemingly engaged in colloquy, posed so

97. *Aegidius*, 1517. Quentin Massys

as to appear unposed, unconscious of artist or spectator. The modest simplicity of the scholar's presence and his environment only increase a sense of awe at his cerebral achievements, and the value to be placed on knowledge for its own sake. Mystery can reside in what he is working on – and perhaps some chart of arcane symbols lies beside him, or the very instruments which accompany him may be themselves unfamiliar to, positively unusable by, the unlearned person. Such things have their own power and significance – replacing, it may even be, the sceptre and orb of kings, but in a different sphere no less expressive of command.

No magician, but clearly master of his particular lore, Henry VIII's astronomer, Nikolaus Kratzer, thus appears in his portrait by Holbein [98], calmly absorbed, possibly in a calculation but almost assertively encompassed by the tools of his trade. Kratzer's keen interest in the most up-to-date instruments is elsewhere testified to by a passage in one of his letters from London to Dürer at Nuremberg, requesting a drawing 'of the instrument you saw at Pirckheimer's, with which they measure

98. *Nikolaus Kratzer*, 1528. Hans Holbein

distance both far and wide'. This sentence is, too, one more tribute to the close community of intellectual interest: the humanist, the artist and the astronomer are all engaged in pursuit of knowledge, and each can admire the others' contributions. Friendship between painter and sitter explains several sixteenth-century portraits of doctors and other learned men, whose profession is usually conveyed along with their features. The painter continues to give attention to the detail which represents not so much status as the focus of the mind. Passarotti's *Apothecary* [99] seems cheerfully to have conjured up the flower sprays which do more than merely decorate the background of his portrait; Passarotti came from Bologna, as

99. *An Apothecary*, *c.* 1570. Bartolommeo Passarotti

perhaps did his sitter, and it was there that the first Chair in Botany had been founded in 1534.

The reticence of such a portrayal continues the tradition of the portraits of Aegidius and Erasmus (though adding a dash of Italianate, gentlemanly nonchalance), where scholarly integrity is expressed by an integrity of presentation. Portraits of this typical kind do not stray beyond the factual and, however fine in themselves, may often seem rather tame as likenesses of the more daring, eccentric, and persecuted 'magicians' like Paracelsus or Cardano. For those who believed in the universe as alive with secret influences and swayed by the stars, with

100. *Johannes Cuspinian, c. 1502–3*. Lucas Cranach

Nature's book always required reading, Cranach's presentation of the young Dr Cuspinian [100] might seem a profounder portrayal. Not only is the sitter exposed, as it were, to the spell of nature in the sense of open-air countryside, but there is almost certainly astrological significance in this choice of summer setting, as in the owl and other birds, and patently in the solitary star shining out over Cuspinian's head. Thus the gifted young scholar seems, like man as envisaged by Paracelsus, to be placed in two worlds, visible and invisible, elemental and celestial, under the guidance of his 'Star', itself not a physically actual body but a force which can govern, under God, wisdom or folly.

The stars might increasingly be studied from the viewpoint of scientific astronomy, by for example such an outstanding observer as Tycho Brahe, who rightly claimed his renascent role in developing 'a renewed Astronomy'. But for the majority of people they retained some presumed, if vague, sway over human affairs. A comet was a portent before it was a stellar body in a traceable orbit, controlled by physical laws. For one prince who built an observatory, as the Landgrave William of Hesse did at Cassel, there were probably ten like François I's mother, Queen Louise, who was absorbed, indeed obsessed, by astrology. Few will have bothered to keep, as did she, a sort of journal of events for presumably horoscopic purposes, but the demand for royal horoscopes continued to be great – the most obvious example of trying to plumb Nature's mysteries.

The strongly Copernican astronomer Kepler was considerably sought after for his astrological predictions, and was perhaps luckier in them than had been some other, earlier figures, like Cardano and the German magus, Heinrich Agrippa of Nettesheim. It is hard to say which was the more unfortunate of the predictions demanded from these two men about the lives of kings. Cardano, rumoured to have daringly cast the horoscope of Jesus Christ, was rash enough to prophesy a long reign for the sickly Edward VI of England, who shortly afterwards died. Agrippa, irritated by Queen Louise's insistence that he cast her son's horoscope, prognosticated in 1527 that the stars foretold death to François I within six months. The rapidity of Agrippa's fall from favour at the French court was not surprising, and his tart references to the court as Hell, and the King as Pluto, can scarcely have improved matters. Despite the prediction, 'Pluto' survived for a further twenty years, easily outliving Agrippa.

If there is some ambiguity about the activities of Agrippa and Cardano, by turns magical and scientific-cum-philosophic, the ambiguity of the century's attitude to such figures is only to be expected. Knowledge that seemed to give divine power or led to declared scepticism was bound to disturb some forms of accepted belief, social or religious, or both. The great magus or 'archemaster', as he was called, Dr John Dee, the leading English example of a scientist with occult interests, might represent a triumph of human intellect but some of his discoveries could prove more disturbing than reassuring. Leonardo da Vinci was perhaps fortunate to move in enlightened circles where no charges of witchcraft or heresy could be made against him. It was prudent of Paulina in *The Winter's Tale* to disclaim, before seeming to make the statue move, any assistance from wicked powers. Dr Dee records how the flight of the giant beetle he devised in his production of Aristophanes' *Peace* (at Cambridge in 1547) caused 'great wondring, and many vain reports spread abroad'. Cardano was arrested as a heretic (though he was never tortured and not in prison for long). Both Agrippa and Paracelsus wandered across Europe, at once attracting and alienating patrons and public. The most notorious case is that of Giordano Bruno, philosopher, astronomer and something of a magician, whose erratic career ended when he was burnt at the stake in 1600. Though lacking the help of an Inquisition, the Reformers showed themselves no better disposed to theories which seemed to challenge the Bible. Luther's 'Table Talk' has him ridiculing 'the new astronomer (Copernicus) who wants to prove that the earth goes round...'; Copernicus could be totally refuted from the Bible, since it was the sun, not the earth, which Joshua had commanded to stand still.

Only perhaps to the man of keen vision, or the visionary, was a universe with magic crackling through it – whether the white magic of natural science or the black art of the occult (or some blending of the two, as easily occurred) – entirely stable, safe and still harmonious. The traditional music of the spheres was inevitably growing faint as the existence of the spheres came under scrutiny. Copernicus had proposed displacing earth from its central procreative position in the cosmos which was a widely held belief. That the earth was the womb of the whole universe was a long-established, popular theory. As an analogy it had been mentioned by Aristotle, but dates back further. In this view, developed in differing ways by some Italian natural

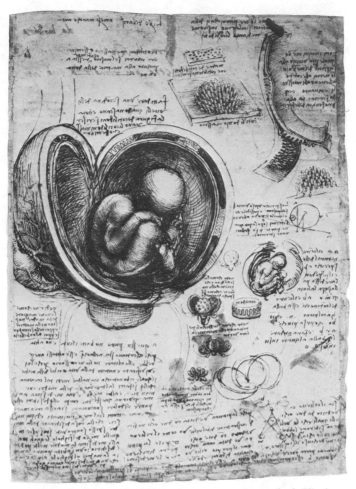

101. Study of an embryo in the womb, *c.* 1510–12. Leonardo da Vinci

philosophers and naturalists, the generative process of plants and animals may be compared to the foetus nourished in the womb – itself somewhat crudely imagined (often by pictures of what appears like a baby in a bottle) before the extraordinary studies of Leonardo [101], devastating if not disturbing as an accurate explanation of a complex process.

The generative powers of the earth, displaced or not, go on unheeding of mankind, and perhaps there was a despairing

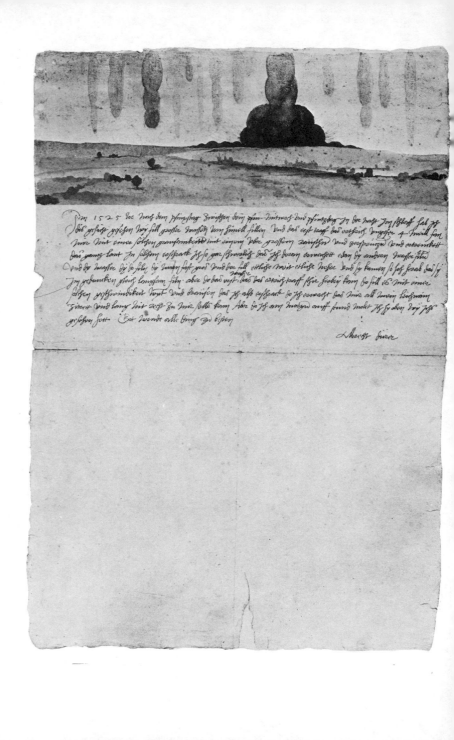

Im 1525 Jar noch dem pfingstag zwischen dem mitwoch vnd pfintztag in der nacht im schlaff hab ich
dis gesicht gesehen wi fill grosser wasser von himel filen vnd das erst traff das ertrich ungfer 4 mil von
mir mit einer solchen grausamkeit mit einem vber grossen rauschen vnd zersprützen vnd ertrenkt
das gancz lant In solchem erschrack ich so gar schwärlich das ich daruon erwachet ee dy andern wasser filen
vnd dy wasser dy do filen dy waren fast groß vnd der filen etliche weit etliche näher vnd sy kamen so hoch herab das sy
Jm gedunken gleich lonksam filen aber do das erst wasser das das ertrich traff schier herbei kam do fil es mit einer
solchen geschwindikeit wint vnd brausen das ich also erschrack do ich erwacht das mir all mein leichnam
zitert vnd lang mit nit zu mir selbs kam Aber do ich am morgen auff stund molet ich hie oben wie ichs
gesehen hett Got wende alle ding zu besten

Albrecht Dürer

102. *Vision in a dream*,
1525.
Albrecht Dürer

aspect of Leonardo's recognition that 'Nature is full of infinite causes . . .' Even more patently than Leonardo, Dürer seems always to have been haunted, and fascinated, by the freakish effects of Nature. Leonardo had drawn catastrophic deluges, and late in life Dürer dreamt a terrifying dream of the earth inundated by roaring waters pouring from heaven, a vision so frightening that he could exorcize it only by recording it in writing and by a sketch [102]. That dream was of a cosmic disaster (partly inspired on a conscious level no doubt by the Old Testament account of the Flood), but many years before he had precisely noted down such small-scale revelations of Nature's malign creativity as a monstrous eight-footed sow, four legs on its back, born in a small German village.

The astounding and truly magical effects with which Grünewald accompanied his depictions of sacred personages are studies of natural phenomena – whether of a desolate, rotting, moss-grown landscape to become the desert where two hermit–saints meet or the luminous one of the rainbow shimmering around the Virgin and Child. But they are rare or transient phenomena, made to behave strangely, as if to remind us of the limits of merely human knowledge. The dead Christ rises [103] like a flaming comet, or an exhalation of gas, his vast incandescent halo burning with an outer ring of blue fire and his insubstantial drapery trailing like a comet's tail, changing colour as it streams from the tomb. Haloes and rainbows were not in themselves new as symbols of divinity, but there is a sort of quasi-scientific precision about Grünewald's observation of light, even while he infracts nature's laws to give expression to a power greater than Nature itself. God is a mystery, and Grünewald's strange, phosphorescent beams and abrupt

103. *The Risen Christ, c.* 1515. Grünewald

hovering radiations convey spiritual mystery, avoiding the too palpable or knowable. Pontormo, working within Grünewald's lifetime, suggested the imponderable mystery of God's presence by memorably combining natural and unnatural, to achieve the surrealist symbol manifested in his *Supper at Emmaus* [104]: a triangle of face with human eye, floating within

104. *The Supper at Emmaus*, 1525. Pontormo

a glowing ball of brightness. No one can mistake the bizarreness of this spirit, replacing the reassuring, white-bearded old man who for at least two centuries had appeared as God.

Natural magicians might in reality be sober-looking, scholarly men, unlikely to be any more glamorous than today's university dons, but the concept of the magician was – as Giorgione had shown – capable of being glamorously evoked in art. There at least the sense of magic in the world could be patently expressed. Often there is a cryptic quality about the resulting work – just as in Giorgione's picture – which may well be intentional. Witches, alchemists and necromancers must hoard their knowledge to preserve their mystery, for

105. *Diogenes*. Ugo da Carpi after Parmigianino

without it they would lose their basic power over people and things. The hocus-pocus quality of many of the depictions in art doubtless derives also from the average artist's ignorance about what exactly such savants did. Anything strange or obviously irrational would serve, and the important aspect was clearly to suggest mysterious lore and – probably with more success – the mysterious nature of the universe.

In artistic terms Parmigianino's *Diogenes* [105] is certainly convincing, but it is doubtful if the figure would seem to us notably significant or meaningful had Vasari not emphasized the artist's absorption in alchemy. To what extent Parmigianino's alchemical interests can be deduced from his art remains altogether a difficult question. Claims have been made, for instance, about the presence of ovoid vases in his religious pictures – as present they undoubtedly are; it is not easy to say whether they refer to the *vas hermeticum*, a symbol of one-ness as well as of the alembic used in alchemy, egg-shaped rather than round because it symbolizes the matrix, or womb, containing the germ of everything. The rose, the stone and fire are further alchemical symbols and they also can be found in Parmigianino's work, though also in the work of other artists. The Litany of the Virgin calls her a mystical rose and a vessel of honour, a spiritual vessel, a singular vessel of devotion. That is one good reason for symbols to appear in pictures connected with her, but it is possible that on certain occasions they carry more extended meanings; the Virgin is herself a *vas honorabile* since her womb once contained the divine Germ of everything, so the correspondence is anyway close.

In drawing Diogenes Parmigianino might well sense more than one analogy between himself and the most famous drop-out philosopher. Vasari tells how from once being so handsome, elegant and gentlemanly, Parmigianino became like a savage, 'melancholy and peculiar' (*malinconico e strano*) – all because of his obsession with alchemy.

The idea that such an obsession must have been greed for gold is probably a caricature of what most alchemists sought, which was at once less material and even more elusive: a private key to Nature. Like other magus-figures of the period, and some non-alchemically inclined artists, they were often carried by their pursuits into social isolation. And just as the period tended to blend astronomy with astrology, so chemistry and alchemy were blended, despite angry declarations of the differences by some exponents. Tycho Brahe went so far as to claim that alchemy or chemistry – he did not distinguish – might be called 'terrestrial astronomy', but he also stated that he was not going to reveal his knowledge to the ordinary public. Alchemy certainly belonged in the general category of natural magic, since its physical experiments with metals and minerals, and its philosophic interpretation of such experiments, aimed to master the universe in ways inaccessible by normal human reasoning.

The artist's reasoning also is bound to be abnormal (not in any pejorative sense). None of us can claim – any more than could Renaissance men – that we would have quite expected the Battle of Issus to look as Altdorfer imagined it. As Sidney was to remark (cf. p. 99), 'Oft cruel fights well pictured forth do please'. No *Resurrection of Christ* is like Grünewald's. Parmigianino's paintings, even of the most conventional subjects such as the Virgin and Child, are intensely personal in their presentation, consciously original and still capable of appearing disconcerting. For his self-portrait he conceived the idea of painting himself in circular format as reflected in a convex mirror, and not correcting the distortions; the picture becomes a mirror. None of these things is due to some stylistic affectation of the sixteenth century but because in each case the artist has distilled, even purified, the given, traditional concept (a battle, a portrait and so on). That he should transmute the expected into the novel is part of his Renaissance role. In this sense, every artist is an alchemist.

106. *The Astrologer*, 1509. Giulio Campagnola

When the magus, magician or philosopher was depicted in natural surroundings, the artist could pay tribute to the magic influences of Nature without too much emphasis on the paraphernalia of conjuring apparatus. He thus provided more ways than one of taking seriously what he showed. Campagnola's engravings [106] may or may not have seemed to sophisticated people convincing as statements of the behaviour of magicians, but they agreeably evoked leisurely days in the Venetian countryside, with the odd semi-pet monster snuffling around, rather like St Jerome's lion in pictures of him. While the subjects are first of all evidence of the artist's *invenzione*, for which they offer excellent opportunity, they are also contributions to the climate of credulity. Even a highly intelligent person might adopt what was Gesner's prudent attitude to the 'merman'. After all, it remained true that Nature was mysterious.

Throughout Europe, a majority would certainly have affirmed a belief in witches (a belief which probably increased rather than diminished during the sixteenth century), whether or not they believed in Baldung's view of them [107]. Witchcraft was a subject to which he returned again and again, in graphic work as well as paintings. On one occasion he shows a hag-like witch casting her spell over a groom in a stable, but the two witches in the picture illustrated here are more sensual than overtly sinister. At first glance they might almost be preparing for a *Judgement of Paris*, rather than – as it may be – for the Devil, were it not for the rather depressed, goat-like familiar on which one witch sits and the upraised vessel she holds, containing presumably something nasty. With greater intensity perhaps, Baldung suggests the high site and the disturbed atmosphere – yet one more instance of sensitive response to ever-changing, aerial effects. An Essex clergyman, George Gifford, who wrote a *Discourse on the Subtill Practises of Devilles by Witches and Sorcerers* (1587) stated the common opinion that when 'there are mighty winds and thunders with terrible lightnings [that] the devil is abroad'. Baldung's sky is palely livid, and scudding stormy clouds, blending with the smoky torch, are echoed by the restless locks of the witches' flying hair.

Baldung hints strongly at diabolic mischief brewing but the beneficent magician was also contemporaneously depicted, probably never again in such a deeply lulling, incantatory mood as in Dosso Dossi's large-scale *Melissa* [108], which for so long passed ironically as of Circe. Melissa is the good enchantress of

107. *Two Witches*, 1523. Hans Baldung

Ariosto's *Orlando Furioso*, undoing all the spells cast by the evil
Alcina and bringing men back from their transmuted form of
animals and plants. Yet the key is still of enchantment pervading the whole scene. Anyone might be content to remain a
tree in this lushly beautiful countryside, while the pensive dog
seems to possess an instinctive nobility lacking in most untrans-
muted people. Exotically clad, Melissa has yet much of the

dreamy quality so typical of Dosso's figures, as she somewhat vaguely performs the necessary magic rites.

The picture, like Ariosto's poem, was executed for the Este court at Ferrara, where highly coloured extreme fantasy was enjoyed for its own sake. As a painted illustration, inspired by such poetic creation, it might be expected to stretch the artificial, fictional bubble to dangerously near bursting point, but

Dosso actually stabilizes, even reduces, the fantasy element. He takes Melissa's world more seriously perhaps than Ariosto intended, weighing down the enchantress with fringed, brocaded Renaissance fabrics and fusing her strange splendour with the splendour of the natural world which becomes a bower of harmless, timeless bliss. It is not too far-fetched to see Melissa as at once sovereign and reflection of the green-glowing Nature around her. In origin Melissa had been the name of a nymph and, suitably enough, the word in Greek means 'bee'; that it could also be applied figuratively both to poets who praised the beauties of Nature and to the priestesses at Delphi seems strictly apt when one contemplates this picture.

Almost casually, it might seem, and certainly without any learned pretensions, Dosso manages to weave one web of ever-growing, luxuriant, organic Nature, harmonious in itself and inclusive of mankind (three samples of which converse contentedly amid shrubbery in the middle distance). Nor is it just in this magical picture that he emphasizes the sheer spell of Nature. Elsewhere he creates heavy and, as it were, rustling summer foliage under heavy summer skies, or makes a huge harvest moon swim close to earth, as portent, when the Three Magi came to worship the Infant Christ, not in a stable but a woodland grove.

The magic which resides in Nature and in the animal kingdom found other sympathetic and unlearned artistic interpreters, supremely the Florentine, Piero di Cosimo. His apparent preference for animals over people, and his own rather forlorn animal nature, inevitably puzzled the worldly Vasari whose favourite form of disparagement was to say of someone that he lived 'like a beast'.

To Vasari, who had walked with kings so as to lose the common touch, solitariness was a vice in itself, but the lonely lives of sensitive artists like Piero di Cosimo and Pontormo have something in common with the loneliness suffered often by such magus figures as Cardano and Agrippa. The painter Sodoma, whose frank love of animals and boys quite astounded Vasari, had once been fashionable and rich, but ended his life poor, old and miserable in the public hospital. Other artists took sufficient interest in animals to keep exotic pets whose antics showed that there is intelligence in creatures other than man, and that a beast is not merely a synonym for beastliness.

Perhaps it was no accident that the sculptor Rustici, whom Vasari mentions as attracted by necromancy, should also have been such an animal-lover; he owned almost a menagerie, with snakes, an eagle, and a talking raven, as well as a tame porcupine which sat domestically under the table, occasionally pricking guests' legs. Even Vasari had to admit the marvellous intelligence of the baboon owned by the painter Rosso, which got up to all sorts of ingenious near-human tricks. Sodoma's house in his prosperity resembled a Noah's ark, so full was it of donkeys, apes, squirrels and doves, in addition to a pet raven which could imitate its master's voice.

The private zoo was not a new idea, though princes rather than painters had kept them, but to have animals constantly under one's own eye was likely to sharpen observation-cum-appreciation of them. Knowledge of them was likely, too, to increase one's sense of awe at Nature's achievements, and allowing animals the freedom of the house was to give them some approximation of natural freedom. Leonardo had gone further, taking action which would still seem extraordinary today in Italy, when he bought caged birds in order to set them at liberty. That all Nature should be left free and untrammelled was Piero di Cosimo's belief. He liked to go and see freaks of nature, animals and plants, Vasari records – and the empathy in his treatment of animals [109] is poignantly obvious.

109. Detail of *Forest Fire*. Piero di Cosimo

Vasari's account of Piero is an odd mixture of superiority and half-unwilling admiration, but he is careful to pay tribute to Piero's 'subtlety in investigating curious matters in nature' – almost a Baconian definition of the scientist. Like so many of the figures mentioned in this chapter, Piero di Cosimo was forced into isolation because his ideas found no response in his immediate environment. He became a sort of modern

110. *Landscape with a Fortress.* Wolf Huber

Diogenes, for where was the circle into which his serious 'primitivism' would fit? Piero's view of the natural world can be sensed in many of his pictures, yet we must be grateful to Vasari for documenting it so explicitly: 'the things of nature must be left to be looked after by nature herself' (*le cose d'essa natura bisogna lassarle custodire a lei senza farci altro*).

Perhaps Piero di Cosimo's tragedy was that he lived too early (dying in 1521) and in the wrong city. Indeed, working in a city at all was, for him, probably a mistake. Later generations or other places might have encouraged his pursuit of natural phenomena and led him to that view of Nature untamed, almost alien and entirely without man's presence, revealed by the etchings and drawings of Altdorfer and Wolf Huber [110]. In those austerely sketched scenes, Nature left to itself has sprouted with such wild abandon that the very hummocks of grass are giant pampas growths, and trees shoot weirdly upwards like tufted rockets, hung with creeper and dripping fringes of foliage. By the second half of the sixteenth century, the Brescian artist Muziano could show an exciting but not fantastic Nature of rocky gorges and stunted trees [111] in drawings which have a hallucinatory power. That the young artist had been attacked by fever, and had seen in his delirium landscapes which he felt compelled to draw, is attested early and is credible enough. There is something looming, even oppressive, in such scenery – emphasized by the high horizon – though it offers a good refuge for the solitary, the hermit-saint or the brigand.

At the same time, Muziano's drawings are a sober record of a particular type of terrain. As such they might have served to illustrate some geographical or geological work, whereas they were to be utilized largely as settings for incidents in saints' lives. Not much significance should be attached to this, since the same was true of some of the most brilliant nature studies of Dürer, and rarely, if ever, had the greatest artists actually combined on work with the greatest scientific figures. Even to claim a parallel development for artists and proto-scientists is dubious.

And yet Cortés's assertion about the universal wish to know seems to embrace not only the researches of Vesalius, the explorations of America and the activities of the natural magicians, but the artistic explorations of Altdorfer and Bruegel, as well as the restless ranging searches of Leonardo and Dürer, and the narrower yet keenly original ones of

Parmigianino and Piero di Cosimo. Although Leonardo's studies of anatomy were profounder than any other artist's, they were not unique. The painter Franciabigio executed at least one anatomical study at the specific request of a Florentine physician; Rosso disinterred corpses – according to Vasari – so as to study anatomy. A much more obscure painter, Bartolommeo Torri, from Arezzo, is mentioned by Vasari as carrying his interests so far that he kept limbs and other human members under his bed, living in the sort of squalid state which Vasari characterized as 'like a philosopher'.

It would be ludicrous to postulate that after the sixteenth century the natural world never again obsessed great artists; from Elsheimer to Turner, the evidence would be violently against such a suggestion. And there are examples of rigorous scientific study in Stubbs's investigations into the anatomy of the horse or even in van Huysum's pursuit of the exact bloom for one of his flower-pieces. But if one speaks of Nature in the widest sense as itself something of a gigantic *vas hermeticum* to which the artist and the natural magician, the astronomer and the botanist, all turned to discover some secret or germ, then the sixteenth century does perhaps represent the last age in which real affinities existed between these various students of 'great, creating Nature'. Subsequently, the scientist would become much more truly scientific, doffing for ever his semi-magic robes. Astrology and alchemy would decline, and even where they survived, their connection with astronomy and chemistry did not.

Perhaps it was exactly because on balance the century had not really disposed of magic at all that the artist could so well hold his own beside the other magus-figures; and, where so much remained to be known, his knowledge and vision could themselves be contributions to comprehension of the universe. Paracelsus constantly laid stress on what man can achieve through his imagination, which he compared to the sun with its active, kindling power. Bacon was to write of the 'wonderful operations' which properly applied natural magic should produce. As evidence of what man can achieve, the operations of artists – those, as it were, honorary natural magicians – were certainly among the most wonderful.

111. *Rocky Forest Landscape*. Girolamo Muziano

5
'A Goodly Paterne'

Nature, however fascinating to certain types of magus or artist, might yet appear somewhat disturbing to not only ordinary people but thinking people as well. Quite apart from the limits of knowledge, the discoveries made by knowledge are in themselves not necessarily reassuring. To know oneself may prove the most disturbing of all. Is man really the measure of all things?

This question was, increasingly perhaps, to be put in a 'counter-Renaissance', even pessimistic way. Yet, at the same time, Nature could also be shown to provide such a comforting environment that the question might seem hardly worth putting. Underneath Nature's most freakish behaviour there was detectable a divine harmony and pattern. Certain arts – like music and architecture – could offer particularly clear reflections of the universal order which was truly natural. All things, wrote Spenser, directly echoing Plato, have been fashioned in accordance with 'A goodly Paterne' which is perfect beauty, 'which all men adore'.

Pattern, order, harmony – all of which can include touches of the irregular, the disproportioned and the dissonant within their overall stability – inspired a great deal of High Renaissance art. Enclosed by some Palladian villa's walls, listening to, or more usually participating in, some madrigal, one might well feel part of the natural cosmic order: if no longer the measure of all things, at least with a due place in the great scheme, fixed star if not sun in the firmament.

Order in the universe, order in society, order in the arts: with such a vision there could be nothing to fear and everything to enjoy. The world is involved in one great cosmic dance claimed Sir John Davies, easily the most poetical person ever appointed Lord Chief Justice of England, whose poem significantly entitled *Orchestra* (1596) gently reminded the reader that even when we cannot see the pattern it exists:

> What if to you these sparks [the stars] disordered seem,
> As if by chance they had been scattered there?
> The gods a solemn measure do it deem
> And see a just proportion everywhere,

Breath, speech, echoes, music, the winds – these are all so many dances of the air. The sea, obedient to the moon's pavane, keeps time as it embraces the land. Thanks to the sun's now advancing, now retreating galliard, earth experiences day and night. Amid so much regulated movement only earth stands still, though Davies is up-to-date enough to remark that 'some wits enriched with learning's skill' have said it is actually heaven which stands firm and earth which moves. This, if true, seems not to disturb him or his view of the universe. The cosmic chain of dancing goes on.

Man's own place is here not dealt with, but in another poem (*Nosce Teipsum*) Davies neatly summed up that divided view of mankind, poised between what it could be and what it is, which was probably felt by many of his contemporaries. Outside Palladian walls, or when the spell of music ceases, man's place in the scheme of things violently fluctuates:

> I know my soul hath power to know all things,
> Yet she is blind and ignorant in all.
> I know I am one of nature's little kings,
> Yet to the least and vilest things am thrall.

In such lines, the High Renaissance seems to have inherited a divided, double belief, part medieval-pessimistic, part Albertian-Early Renaissance, and to be bewildered by its inheritance. All the more might goodly patterns and intimations of universal order appeal when man has become intensely aware that being born a natural king does not in itself guarantee him a long, safe or peaceful reign. This shadowed, unsettled side of existence, potentially so bright, must be recognized – not merely as the inevitable human environment out of which all art rises but as something which might be sensed the more keenly in a questioning climate. And Cardano, Agrippa, Paracelsus and Bruno – men already mentioned in the previous chapter – are just some examples of the questioners.

Pascal's '*Le silence éternel de ces espaces infinis m'effraie*' had not yet been said, but something comparable had probably been felt. In Donne's *First Anniversarie* occurs the familiar line 'And new Philosophy calls all in doubt' – though it must be remembered that this poem is intended as a lament. Still, Donne emphasizes cosmic disorder; not only is the poem's subject, Elizabeth Drury, dead, but also 'beauty's best, proportion, is dead'. The sun is lost; the element of fire extinguished; 'all coherence gone'. Shooting stars, monstrous animals, the prevalence of witches, might all join Copernican theory as evidence of a strange universe in which the shrinking microcosm, man, is vulnerable and his reasoning often powerless: 'Contracted to an inch, who was a span,' in Donne's words. Everything, Montaigne wrote, is constantly changing. The world is merely a perpetual see-saw (*le monde n'est qu'une branloire perenne*); one's own personality is not firmly fixed, and its progress is confused, unsteady, with a sort of natural drunkenness (. . . *d'une ivresse naturelle*).

New and sharper awareness of Nature, including the nature of man, was likely to produce less confidence in perfectibility and fewer claims for the essential dignity of human beings. Nature could be daunting, bizarre and as rudely rustic as a Bruegel peasant. 'Wind, rain, and thunder', Pericles cries to the stormy elements by the seashore, 'remember earthly man / Is but a substance that must yield to you'. Yet Pericles is, as it were, blown off course only briefly. Like so many of Shakespeare's heroes, he carries into every situation a sense not so much of who he is as what he is in rank, and of the privileges such rank naturally gives. In a moment of stress he may speak of being a ball in the vast tennis-court of the winds and waves, but there is none of the utter, irremediable nihilism of Webster's vision, in which all of us are 'the stars' tennis balls', for ever struck and bandied in a ghastly cosmic game, regardless of love, or hope or high birth. This is more than some dramatic convention; it seems typical of Webster that in dedicating a play to the twelfth Lord Berkeley, he should bluntly state, 'I do not altogether look up at your title' (a remark very out of character for Shakespeare).

In the poignant scene of *Pericles*, the only half-comic fishermen display a basic humanity in their treatment of a shivering, shipwrecked fellow-being ('I have a gown here; come, put it on; keep thee warm . . . Come, thou shalt go home . . . and thou shalt be welcome') who himself yet remains so deeply conscious of his high birth that he is somewhat amazed at the elements' disregard of it. 'To have bereft a prince of all his fortunes' is their notable achievement. And only temporarily, due to the accident of shipwreck, is the social order jolted sufficiently to lower Pericles to the level of fishermen. With royal complacency, he hears them compare society to sea-life – 'the great ones eat up the little ones' (a proverb Bruegel had vividly illustrated) – before resuming his role as one of nature's great ones. Shakespeare's world is rather like what is traditionally supposed about wartime England: hardship breaks down the barriers between man and man, and prince and pauper find a kinship in being human which ceases, however, with the cessation of hardship. Pericles never has to taste the puddings and flapjacks promised him by the First Fisherman; instead, a happy denouement brings him his wife again as he declares in Diana's temple at Ephesus: 'I here confess myself the king of Tyre'.

Order has reasserted itself, as order always does with Shakespeare; even the horror and pathos at the close of *King Lear* cannot obscure some proposals for the future ruling of the kingdom. In Webster, as in Marlowe, so much ambition, folly and crime has been acted out that there can scarcely be conventional assurances that mankind has any future; and their plays end in total emotional exhaustion. After seeing humanity behaving 'naturally' in *The Duchess of Malfi*, who indeed could suggest anything except its rapid replacement by some better form of being?

Nature, from one point of view, offered no guarantee of stability or coherence. It may be argued, and has been, that some products of the visual arts in the sixteenth century reflected this sense of a world with 'all coherence gone'. The rather tortured-seeming people of Pontormo's portraits, the shooting diagonals of Tintoretto's compositions, as well as some of the disturbed effects in the architecture of Michelangelo or Giulio Romano, could be brought forward as examples of underlying insecurity. Nor should we be too quick to rebut, for supposedly art-historical reasons, such possibilities. It is absurd to suppose that aggression, anxiety and instability did not exist before modern times. Particularly in the sixteenth century, an artist was very much part of the social scene, responsive to it even if he turned from it (for that too is a response), in addition to being an individual consumed with personal fears and desires – and not merely with deciding which style to adopt. Raphael may have integrated his desires and fears more successfully than Piero di Cosimo, but for all his king-like art his premature death proved him to be tragically 'in thrall'. Dürer's memorable dream (cf. pp. 196–7) may well not be typical of every artist, but at least it serves as a warning against assuming neurosis is a post-Renaissance condition, and as a useful reminder also that the interior life of a great artist should not be entirely equated with a mechanism for excogitating artistic solutions.

It is against, and amid, intimations of mortality that the artist raises the monument of his art, and perhaps his creation becomes the firmer the more deeply he senses and defies the dangers of flux. Only the very hardest and strongest of materials – marble and bronze – will serve for tombs, though altars and statues of saints were not infrequently made of wood. And in passing it may be said that at least as much as Pontormo does Bronzino, with his carved, marble-hard images in paint, seem to feel disturbing, emotional pressures – not, however, embodying but exorcizing them, in people who have become perfect patterns of art, who will not fade and cannot change [5]. Calm, total authority characterizes the Neptune of Montorsoli's marvellously sited fountain at Messina [112], where the god seems truly risen from the nearby sea to take the sadly vulnerable city under his protection.

112. Neptune Fountain, Messina, finished 1557. Montorsoli

The order which Shakespeare, along with many other artists, asserts is a bulwark against world chaos. It is significant that it should be by a musical metaphor that he conveys (in Ulysses' key speech about order in *Troilus and Cressida*) the threat of its absence:

> Take but Degree away, untune that string,
> And hark what Discord follows;

Degree is shown to govern the macrocosm, 'The heavens themselves, the planets, and this centre' and also the microcosm, 'Prerogative of age, crowns, sceptres, laurels'. Without it there would be cosmic shipwreck, no merely temporary storm but a deluge comparable to those drawn by Leonardo and dreamt of by Dürer, in which the waters, no longer obeying their natural bounds, would 'make a sop of all this solid globe'.

Under such threats to the environment, an appeal to order can be asserted in varied ways. Architecture and music are not merely 'scientific', the most obviously orderly of the arts and perhaps the most natural – since some sort of building and some sort of chanting or dancing seem deeply rooted in man; they are also the most social, offering different sorts of involvement but offering that very definitely to groups of people. By comparison it is a lonely task to appreciate a painting or a piece of sculpture. Socially, such activity may be peripheral, and that remains so even when, with the popularity of engravings, works of art travelled rapidly. Conversely, it would have been virtually impossible in the High Renaissance to avoid hearing music on most formal occasions, and many people must have felt themselves instinctive connoisseurs since they were also performers. Amateur painters are likely to have been few.

It is still hard to realize that what to us is a world-famous Renaissance picture, the *Mona Lisa* for example, had probably been seen by very few people anywhere, and outside specifically artistic circles could be little known; but any building is likely by its nature to be accessible to public view (even if its interior is not), quite apart from town-planning schemes (from a street of fine houses to the setting up of an obelisk or fountain) intended to affect the public. Alberti, in his *De re aedificatoria*, had already ranged from the construction of prisons to systems for supplying water. And although it is easy to think of the Renaissance in terms of great isolated palaces for rulers – like Nonsuch and Fontainebleau – the High Renaissance in particular saw the growth of something much more novel, the private house or villa, often on a princely scale but intended as a place in which pleasantly to live. Even one of the greatest Roman palaces [113] yet remained a family's private house.

113. *Palazzo Farnese*, Rome, begun *c.* 1513. Antonio da Sangallo and Michelangelo

The 'rules', secrets and the very patterns of up-to-date architecture were in the mid sixteenth century to be disseminated throughout Europe by a variety of illustrated books which popularized while encouraging the art of building. No comparable attempt could be made for painting or sculpture. Perhaps the nearest equivalent was the pattern-book teaching one how to write elegantly, like Vicentino's *Il modo de temperare le penne* (1523), whose very title page [114] reveals the desired standard of graceful legibility.

Architecture in any serious sense would itself have seemed remote by comparison with the ubiquity and popularity of music. In that, too, what was prized was the up-to-date new style of music, with keen response to the meaning of words set (quite apart from any urging of this for church music by the Council of Trent), subtle, complex harmonies and elaborate patterns of polyphony. New overall grasp of structure, with greater expressiveness, seemed to the period its own achievement. The music of modern composers is better, wrote Pietro

Il modo de' temperare le
Penne
Con le varie Sorti de' littere
ordinato per Ludouico Vicentino, In
Roma nel anno MDXXIII

con gratia &
Priuilegio

114. Title page of Vicentino's *Il modo de temperare le penne*, 1523

Aron in his theoretical treatise *Il Toscanello in musica* (1523), 'because they consider all parts together'. Admittedly, to Erasmus, the choral effects to be heard in church sounded 'a tumultuous bawl of diverse voices', but that is in its way a testimony to the complicated, contrapuntal webs of sound, the splendours of which were sometimes criticized as too gorgeous and sensuous – but certainly never as artless or crude. In this connection there is some parallel with attitudes to Michelangelo's *Last Judgement* fresco in the Sistine Chapel, condemned for supposed indecency yet admired for its art; Aretino stigmatized it for 'the excellence of such audacious marvels' (*la eccellenza di sì temerarie maraviglie*), a phrase leaving no doubt that he recognized the daring art involved.

Music not only seemed to be more accomplished than ever before but to be heard on, if possible, even more occasions. The church was only the most obvious location. Secular ceremonies, from a procession to a banquet, were accompanied by music – and not merely that of trumpets. The growing importance of the *intermezzo* – originally an interval of music during the performance of a play – was another aspect. The *intermezzi* at the marriage in 1539 of Cosimo de' Medici and Eleonora di Toledo were notably elaborate and indeed the whole occasion was richly celebrated in music, from the moment the bride was solemnly welcomed at Florence with a Latin motet in eight-part counterpoint until the final ballet of satyrs and bacchantes 'with various instruments all at once', which closed the evening of the nuptial feast.

Notable also were the public concerts, given often for no special occasion, provided by civic groups of musicians. Cellini's father belonged to the town band at Florence and was most eager for Cellini (rare example of a Renaissance personality who disliked music) to become a great musician and composer. In Germany and England the town bands and the waits might be hired privately or perform publicly. From 1571 onwards the London waits were required to play at the Royal Exchange 'every Sunday and holiday towards the evening' and a contemporary reference praises the listeners' sense of being 'ravished in an earthly paradise'. In a period which had revived the concept of the academy (often just regular assemblies of groups of friends) the first music academies were founded: at Verona the Accademia Filarmonica, where Mozart was to give his first concert in Italy, and the Accademia dei Concordi at

Ferrara, founded by Alfonso II d'Este, passionately fond of music like most of his family.

Most significant of all was the extension of private music-making, made finally fashionable by the involvement of rulers – no longer merely audience but active performers and even composers. The Este family at Ferrara were far from unique in their participation in concerts. Pope Leo X composed several pieces of music; Henry VIII of England was both composer and all-round performer; and the Emperor Maximilian I is said to have written the words of '*Innsbruck, ich muss dich lassen*', which his court-composer, Heinrich Isaac, set with appropriately haunting beauty. Erasmus mentions approvingly the study of various musical instruments by the young Alexander Stewart, James IV of Scotland's illegitimate son, killed with his father at Flodden. That one of the instruments he had studied should be the lute is typical, for this instrument had displaced the harp as the most popular for both amateurs and professionals. John Dowland was a famous virtuoso of the lute, as well as a composer, internationally celebrated and probably more profoundly esteemed as a performer outside England, for he was much employed abroad and could claim of his compositions that they had been 'printed in eight most famous Cities beyond the seas'. Unprofessionally but still sincerely, du Bellay was to write '*Du luth et du pinceau, j'ébatterai ma vie*' (*Les Regrets*, 32), though the words might more profoundly have been said by Sebastiano del Piombo, whom Vasari mentions as being a musician before he was a painter, and as proficient particularly on the lute.

The lute's personal, expressive and moody qualities are conveyed not only in music and poetry of the period but also in pictures [115]. As well as the concert picture, there are paintings like this where a solitary musician seems almost to dream over his instrument, listening to its voice which is really his own. In Sir Thomas Wyatt's frequent apostrophes to his lute, it becomes the poet's alter ego; however eloquently it sounds, it always speaks 'as liketh me'. It crystallizes the varied powers of music: to praise, lull, enliven, cajole, to make the performer seem less alone in the universe, even when his theme is that bereft and lonely sensation. Before Sir Philip Sidney did so, the first Earl of Essex commanded music as he lay dying in 1576. Like a scene from some Elizabethan play, where so often the sleepless, the ill or unhappy call for a song, was the Earl's

115. *A lute-player.* Cariani

summoning of his musician; what he asked for was his own song, and while the musician played he himself sang it.

In less extreme circumstances songs, whether or not accompanied, were probably the finest expression of private music-making and certainly among the most highly accomplished of all art-forms. The trio of ladies who sing and play in concert in an unknown Northern painter's small masterpiece [116] convey something of the accomplishment, along with an intelligent air of elevated relaxation. Music's charm is shown binding without any amorous overtones. As harmoniously and as seriously as three Muses, and as demurely as nuns, the three women prepare to display and interweave their skills with lute, flute and voice.

116. *Three ladies playing music.* Master of the Female Half-Lengths

Almost like a visual metaphor of musical structure is the deft arrangement and symmetry of their three heads and busts – seeming to grow out of a single trunk. At first glance they look similar to the point of sameness in costume and feature, yet each of their head-dresses, for instance, is very slightly varied, just as are their expressions. The painter's careful interest scarcely needs stressing, but is confirmed by the open music-book, which can be deciphered. A poem by Clément Marot, often set to music by his contemporaries, is the text, and the setting here is by one of the leaders of the new school of French composers, Claudin de Sermisy, who was particularly famous for this type of *chanson*.

More than two hundred such *chansons* by him were published before his death in 1562 (and, once again, publication of music is itself a new development, largely a sixteenth-century one). Claudin – mentioned among other composers by Rabelais – intended his *chansons* in many cases for amateur performance, exactly as depicted in the painting. Even the neatly evoked interior is appropriate, as well as adding to the picture's charm. This is essentially domestic music – not robust and open-air – suggestive of withdrawal to some quiet room of panelling and latticed casement, not for prayer but pleasure. Bloody or bizarre events are effortlessly kept at bay; and what seems most truly natural is to take one's part in the pervading harmony.

Like other arts, music could be judged by what was natural, which meant not the simple but rather the complex, and even – less paradoxically than might appear – the artificial (in the sense of things skilfully constructed by art). Nature, 'the greatest artist' in Alberti's words, gave the inspiration and man carried out projects which echoed Nature. Thomas Campion, musician as well as poet, wrote 'The world is made by symmetry and proportion, and is in that respect compared to music . . .' (*Observations in the Art of English Poesie*, 1602); this was no novel doctrine but a statement with which a majority of thinking people from the fifteenth century onwards would have agreed, very probably including Alberti.

In music there was no need to interpret symmetry and proportion in too precisely mathematical a way. The judgement of the ear is the standard urged – in highly professional terms – by an outstanding and still relevant theorist, Gioseffo Zarlino, in his day also a well-known composer (most of whose work is lost), who became choir-master of St Mark's at Venice in 1565. Zarlino wrote about the whole science of music, with particular attention to what constitutes true tonality. In his *Istitutioni Armoniche* (1558) he spoke of the judicious use of dissonance – '[it] causes the consonance which immediately follows it to seem more acceptable' – instancing the comparably agreeable effect on the eye of light after darkness, or the taste of sweet after bitter. This is a convenient hint that one explanation of some of the effects which may at first disconcert us in other sixteenth-century arts, in the architecture of Giulio Romano for example, is that they are deliberately planned and very much part of art's 'artificial' quality. The English composer, Thomas Morley, recommends that the setting of words signifying such emotions as cruelty should be given comparable harmony, 'somewhat harsh and hard, but yet so that it offend not' (*A Plaine and Easie Introduction to Practicall Musicke*, 1597). The overall pattern must prove pleasant, however intricate the detail or gloomy the theme.

What was valued was the maximum expressiveness to be obtained, and contained, by the form. To speak of its being valued perhaps smacks too much of theory; the expressiveness and the containing form were to be enjoyed, especially where the music was destined to be sung by amateurs at least as much as professionals. The title of Morley's book is significant: 'plain', 'easy', 'practical' are encouraging adjectives, tacitly dissolving any feeling that this art is inaccessible to the ordinary person. Instead, he is invited to join his voice to the cosmic concert. As for what he should sing, Morley was ready with material, by himself and others, in the famous collection of madrigals he edited, *The Triumphs of Oriana* (1601).

The madrigal was not precisely new but in sixteenth-century Italy and England it was wrought into the most polished – and also most popular – of all musical forms. It became virtually the century's creation and though it did not expire with the century, it was largely dead by the 1630s (Monteverdi's eighth book of madrigals, several of which are really full choral and dramatic works, was published in 1638). The madrigal was, essentially, sung chamber music, usually intended for a small group of voices, domestic rather than palatial in its dimensions, dealing often but by no means always with love, and almost visually vivid in its depiction of actions and emotions. Indeed, in an unqualified way the music became visually vivid when 'day' and 'night' were distinguished by white and black notes. Such literal word-painting (reminding one of the conceit of metaphysical poetry to print verses in the shape of wings, altars, etc.) was accompanied by a keen response to individual words of the text. Music sighed, died, laughed in a motif of rapid quavers and semi-quavers (as in an epithalamium by a supreme Italian madrigalist, Luca Marenzio) or rose at the verb to an anguished wail of pain, as in an intensely sombre madrigal by Weelkes, of which the last line is 'And *kill* my soul with double smart'.

Although the madrigal in Italy (sometimes the work of Flemish composers working there) has definite priority, it does not necessarily have superiority over the form as transplanted to England in the second half of the sixteenth century. Nicholas Yonge's publication in 1588 of a set of Italian madrigals with English words, *Musica Transalpina*, and perhaps also the publication two years later of another Italian set mainly by Marenzio, may have done much to confirm the fashion for the madrigal, but the native response was as instinctive and efflorescent as Elizabethan poetry. In England the madrigal lost nothing of its art but gained a wider public than in Italy. Yonge himself was probably a chorister at St Paul's and he is recorded to have gathered at his house nearby 'a great number of Gentlemen and Merchants of good accompt . . . for the exercize of music daily'.

All the qualities the century admired in the visual arts – Vasari's *licenzia, varietà, vaghezza* and *grazia* – are to be found in the madrigals by a whole group of English composers, many of them like Byrd, Weelkes, Morley, John Bennet and John Farmer, being contributors to *The Triumphs of Oriana* (itself with an Italian precedent, *Il Trionfo di Dori*, published at Venice in 1592). In both the formal framework is mythological-pastoral, made topical in Morley's publication by complimentary references to Queen Elizabeth, and this convention is probably the most familiar. Its artifice is inclined to strike us too readily perhaps, but any threat of insipidity is dispersed by the vigour of the madrigals themselves, which possess a Chaucerian freshness, managing to re-animate – in literally renascent manner – the stock flora and fauna of Arcadia.

Words, as well as music, deserve a tribute, for the frequently anonymous verses have their own vernal-seeming, highly sophisticated charm. Byrd's 'This sweet and merry month of May' is typical in every way, though it was written before *The Triumphs of Oriana* and appears, in fact, to be the first English madrigal published. The lyrical mood in which it opens is more courtly than rustic. Its Nature – 'And birds do sing and beasts do play' – is, generalized, a matter more of enamelled flowers, neat, tapestry trees and, as it were, clockwork creatures, all tunefully disporting, 'For pleasure of the joyful time'. The voices take turns to weave and interweave themselves around such words as 'merry', 'sing' and 'pleasure', until the air seems ringingly full of bell-like notes. Nature has been set in musical motion for a purpose and after individual voices have enunciated and decorated it, they come together in unison 'to greet Eliza with a rhyme'. The effect is almost like the advance of figures at the end of a masque or ceremonial play, to hail those in the audience who are being fêted. One might even recall the automaton devised by Leonardo da Vinci of a lion which moved towards the King of France and dropped lilies from its chest. Byrd momentarily halts his madrigal; the tapestry countryside recedes and the proffered compliment is gradually unrolled, each voice contributing, as it were, a differently coloured ribbon to the final interwoven effect:

> O beauteous Queen of second Troy,
> Take well in worth a simple toy.

The gradual unfolding and interweaving can scarcely be described, but are essential aspects of Byrd's art: 'of second Troy' being repeated and proudly echoed after the solemn, soaring invocation 'O beauteous Queen'; and the last line is wittily set with a culminating elaboration of polyphony, underlining the patent complexity of what at no point, despite its miniature scale, can be called 'a *simple* toy'.

Madrigals had other moods. Although plenty are set in the month of May and populated with shepherds, cheerful or otherwise, some are almost disturbingly serious, like Giles Farnaby's 'Construe my meaning', the religious tone of which would have made it in Italy a *madrigale spirituale*. Nothing could offer a better respite to anyone wearied by too much Fa-la-laing with nymphs, and its grave lunar beauty is in contrast to the more typical sunshine of possibly more popular madrigals. Slow in tempo, yet far from monotonous, and dying away in a last barely breathed hope 'for life everlasting', it has an introspective quality which is as remote from any glee or catch as Donne's Holy Sonnets are from Shakespeare's 'Oh, mistress mine'. What would be wrong, however, would be to claim that Farnaby's art here is in itself more serious than that of some madrigal praising *Oriana*, 'Queen of all queens renowned'.

Value was placed not on expressing oneself as such (still less on 'profound' feelings) but on the degree of art displayed. And it is indeed exactly this emphasis on art which so often makes the slightest Elizabethan lyric – like a piece of Italian or Spanish jewellery of the period – enchanting in its frank artifice. Metaphorically or actually, there is in both a good deal of enamel and pearl about the appearance of even the simplest pied daisy. The whole theme of Art versus Nature must be reserved for the next chapter, but it should be said that the authors of such lyrics, as well as the composers of madrigals, were in no sense artless warblers of 'native wood-notes wild' – any more than Dosso Dossi or Giorgione, or indeed Bruegel, were plain rustic people inhabiting the countryside they depicted. At a time when the Lake District and *Lyrical Ballads* had not been invented – still less the tenor of European thought connected with them – to be 'natural' was not necessarily to be either simple or admirable. One may recall that what Dürer admired so much about the New World artifacts was that they revealed not primitivism but 'the subtle *ingenia*' of their creators. Palladio declared that architecture imitates Nature, but his own resulting buildings and theories were highly complex. Of Palladio's Villa Barbaro at Maser, Sir Henry Wotton was aptly to say (*The Elements of Architecture*) that he knew no house 'more artificial and delicious'.

Any pattern of art aspiring to reflect perfect beauty was unlikely to be straightforward or obvious. In the sculptor Vincenzo Danti's treatise on the perfect proportions of everything, *Primo libro del trattato delle perfette proporzioni di tutte le cose* (1567), he gives as the first reason why the art of design should be considered noble that 'it is above all the other [arts] the most full of artifice' (*per essere sopra tutte l'altre artifiziosissima*). Morley positively singles out the madrigal as, after the motet, the musical form which is 'the most artificial'; for this very reason it follows that it is 'to men of understanding most delightful'.

Although music, and perhaps even architecture may, on occasion, imitate Nature in a literal way (viz. bird sounds in music or, with a good deal more straining of the medium, in architecture simulated tree-trunks and logs) their essential freedom from imitative conventions of any kind is obvious. In that sense they are profoundly artificial arts, and that was very much part of their appeal to sixteenth-century theorists, while

117. Detail of the Camera degli Amorini, Villa Imperiale.
Girolamo Genga and Dosso Dossi

at the same time their wide social basis made them accessible in
one way or another to virtually everyone. Danti's attitude is
particularly interesting, for he praises architecture as seeming
'of much greater artifice and perfection' (*di molto maggior artifizio e perfezione*) than painting or sculpture exactly because it
does not imitate. Yet, he goes on, architecture has nowadays
become too easy, and insufficiently inventive, since it has been
reduced to sets of rules: 'almost anybody who is able to draw
two lines can become an architect'. Sculpture and painting, he
claims, cannot be reduced to such rules; and of course he writes
as a sculptor himself, though one with a more than lingering
admiration for architecture, the usefulness as well as beauty of
which he is careful to mention.

When it is a matter of creating on an almost God-like scale, re-working mere Nature to shape the necessarily artificial environment for mankind, the architect has of all artists the best opportunity to impose a pervasive blue-print of perfect coherence. In the city, streets, squares, fountains, public buildings, can be arranged – like the heavens as described by Ulysses – 'in all line of order'. In the country, the challenge could be even greater in the creation of the ideal dwelling, a

118. Nymphaeum of the Villa Giulia, Rome, begun 1550. Bartolommeo Ammanati

villa which must contrive to unite the artificial with the natural – and perhaps it was the idea of such a building (and not churches or palaces) which inspired the very finest, most novel, and most typical achievements of High Renaissance architecture.

Nature was vigorously tamed, but architecture sometimes allowed to grow a little wild, playful, even rustic, to achieve the blended, balanced environment which a cultivated person could enjoy. Each world penetrated the other: the garden might seem to invade a room, as in Genga's Villa Imperiale [117] where arches of painted leaves frame *trompe l'œil* pergolas, and conversely a garden became something civilized certainly, almost urban, as it was embraced by colonnades or bisected by paths, ponds, balustrades and flights of steps, sprouting nearly as many statues as trees, the location also perhaps of some quite elaborately constructed pavilion or casino. In all such gardens, the very patches of wildness are carefully calculated by art. Reminders of what mankind can make are never far away. The Nymphaeum of Villa Giulia [118] might indeed appear by nineteenth-century Romantic standards to be dreadfully unnatural, and even Bacon, in his essay *Of Gardens*, already comments adversely on princes who 'add statues, and such things for state and magnificence, but nothing to the true pleasure of a garden'.

What constitutes the pleasure, however, must be a matter of taste; it is not open to moralizing precepts. To a fully Renaissance figure like Cardinal Bembo, Villa Imperiale represented a triumph of, in his own words, 'finely contrived conceits'. For the fourth book of his architectural treatise (1537), Serlio threw in a few designs for gardens [119] – remarking that gardens are part of the adornment of a house. The geometrically abstract severity of these patterns is such that they might serve for pavements or even for ceilings (which they immediately follow in Serlio's illustrations, the ceilings being, however, a good deal more intricate and floral). But parterres like those Serlio published were popular for a long time in at least Italian gardens: a very patent expression of the delight to be taken in ingeniously ordering Nature into something at once more controlled, formal and complex than is provided in its simple, uncultivated state. And in the grounds of the Earl of Leicester's Kenilworth were 'obelisks, spheres, and white bears all of stone', as an admiring contemporary recorded.

As a result of such ordering by man, Nature gave more pleasure. Pleasure was the key to the effect, pleasure for the mind as well as the eye, and the other senses. Artifice of all kinds was found pleasurable (since it represented an extreme of art, and art must please). The garden was only the most obvious place where art triumphed over Nature in the sense of ruthlessly imposing on raw material – and probably few people would have been found to agree with Piero di Cosimo's plaintive cry that natural things should be left in their natural state (cf. p. 209). Today, there is perhaps a tendency for the majority to side with Piero, and for the formal garden, like other displays of elaborate art, to make people feel uneasy.

At least in architecture it cannot be said that natural things have been interfered with, stunted or perverted from their organic form. Like music, architecture is entirely man-made

119. Designs for gardens, 1537. Sebastiano Serlio

and yet – as Danti had emphasized – effortlessly free of man's tendency in the other visual arts to imitate. In small or large ways, the architect has the opportunity to re-make a piece of the world. To shape the environment of just one person is to assume a significant responsibility. In his *Quattro libri* . . . (1570), Palladio speaks of the original evolution from private houses to public buildings, and how man realized that he needed 'the company of other men', and thus cities came to be built. Here too there has been evolution, for works of Palladio's own century are approaching the desirable peak of perfection. Beauty and sumptuousness in a building are highly desirable, and he singles out Sansovino's Library at Venice [120] as perhaps the most beautiful building put up since antiquity. Palladio would probably have responded to the thought behind Spenser's lines in his *Hymne in Honour of Beautie*, derived as it is from a passage in Plato's *Timaeus* (the book the philosopher is shown holding in Raphael's *School of Athens* [20]):

What time this worlds great workmaister did cast
To make al things such as we now behold,
It seemes that he before his eyes had plast
A goodly Paterne, to whose perfect mould
He fashioned them as comely as he could;

That wondrous Paterne wheresoere it bee,
Whether in earth layd up in secret store,
Or else in heaven, that no man may it see
With sinfull eyes, for feare it to deflore,
Is perfect Beautie which all men adore,

The building of something was, for the Renaissance, very much more than a selfish or vainglorious art. Positive, practical, and – hopefully – beautiful, it was also ethical. The beneficial effect of a pleasant environment had already been stressed by Alberti. When he pleaded for beauty in a building, it was as an essential, powerful quality – one capable even of disarming an enemy. The greatest French architect of the sixteenth century, Philibert de l'Orme, in his treatise *Architecture* (1567), emphasizes the practical side not only in the sense of how to construct but in the further sense of knowing what is best for 'the health and life of men'. He too involves Nature, saying that no lure of ornament or decoration should lead one away from Nature's excellent rules which are concerned with comfort and convenience. The analogy of building with self-improvement aptly came to Fulke Greville when he described Sir Philip Sidney's eagerness to make his life great and good: 'In which Architectonicall art he was . . . a Master'.

It was very much as an aspect of the wish to impart and impose the best 'rules' for architecture, public and private, that the architectural treatise became so popular. While Vincenzo Danti might deplore, and certainly exaggerate, the result whereby anyone – in his view – could now claim to be an architect, the fact is that this dissemination of up-to-date modern

120. The Library, Venice, begun 1537. Jacopo Sansovino

knowledge was typical of the sixteenth century. It assumed a comparatively wide audience for books about architecture that were practical rather than speculative, providing a variety of suggestions, plans and patterns for actual buildings which could be put up.

Although much lip-service was paid to antiquity and the 'rules', the books were frankly realistic, and again typical of their period, in offering a luxuriant amount of what can only be called original, free fantasy. They offered it in the thoroughly up-to-date way of illustrations, led by the pioneering and popular example of Sebastiano Serlio who published the first (in sequence, the fourth) book of his architectural treatise, that on the Orders, in 1537. Others followed, and by the time his seventh book appeared posthumously in 1575 the illustrated architectural treatise was an established phenomenon. That here supply and demand had coincided perfectly – coinciding everywhere and not merely in presumed Gothic-orientated Northern Europe – is shown by the number of new buildings which incorporated novel, strictly non-classical but highly inventive elements. The result was not disharmony, still less incoherence, for these elements were themselves usually subject to overall control; they might increase the rich effect of a pattern, but they did not destroy it.

What seems inclined to strike some modern architectural historians as tense, mannered, perhaps even bad-mannered, and an 'assault' on the classical grammar of architecture, is more likely to have seemed to contemporaries elegantly ingenious, commendably fanciful and an enrichment of, rather than attack on, such antique artistic grammar as they – not always deeply learned men – were aware of. Few arts at any time, incidentally, have advanced by respecting the 'rules'. In fact, the concepts of Bramante and, more patently still, the concepts and buildings of Michelangelo, broke any such rules, sensibly, in the interests of art. That Giulio Romano in designing the princely villa of the Palazzo del Te [121] should not always obey the rules does not mean that he intended to overthrow them. Still less did he design something irregular or disordered.

Vasari visited Giulio at Mantua, saw the villa and must have walked through it with him, paying more attention unfortunately to the painted decorations than to the architecture. But his admiring epithets, applied to what, after all, was a complete creation of Giulio's, suggest relaxed comprehension and total enjoyment of consciously planned virtuoso art. What he

121. Garden front of the Palazzo del Te, Mantua. Giulio Romano

emphasized were the villa's 'very fine proportions' (*bellissime proporzioni*) and how Giulio had first prepared 'a most beautiful model' (*un bellissimo modello*) for the Marquis of Mantua to judge the look of the final building. 'With wonderful art and skill' (*con mirabile arte ed ingegno*), he had devised the fresco schemes in the different rooms, and all in all the villa is seen by Vasari as a triumphant display of Giulio's genius, which was 'various, rich and prolific in its invention and artfulness' (*vario, ricco e copioso d'invenzione e d'artifizio*).

Indeed, so enthusiastic was Vasari – like other sixteenth-century visitors   that today the dusty arid site, with the barrack-yellow building, appears at first glance a considerable disappointment. Only gradually can the planned effect be recreated of advancing from low, rusticated entrance to court-yard, from courtyard to high, many-pillared atrium opening unexpectedly on to ponds, a bridge and gardens closed by a beautiful, probably semi-circular loggia.

Today there is no water and the once praised loggia is replaced by a commonplace brick exedra. Even harder to realize is that the whole site was until the last century an island, thickly planted during the Renaissance with poplars. The land was flat, and thus no exciting changes of level could be devised, as in other Renaissance villas. What could be offered instead was a series of unfolding visual sensations, concealed behind the unassuming, almost playful, screen of the façade, drawing the eye on at each point to discover the courtyard with its own façades, each inviting exploration through a porch – suites of pavilions which, if entered, would bring the visitor round eventually to the central, spacious, pillared atrium, with view of the gardens stretching into the distance. In a way not altogether fanciful, the visitor's progress seems like a gradual surrendering of known reality in exchange for the artistic reality devised by the planner; solid architecture too is increasingly left behind, until out in the garden only the lightly curving open loggia intervened between the visitor and the countryside beyond. It may well be that in its original form this loggia was supported on groups of four pillars, a deliberate echo of the pairs of four pillars which flank and support the main archway of the atrium.

Vasari was careful to state that the Palazzo del Te was built only *'a guisa di un gran palazzo'*, and as such it is really closer to the Ottoman ideal of a palace consisting of kiosks in garden settings. The graceful, playful aspects of the Renaissance can too easily be forgotten, but in a villa environment everyone relaxed. When the Emperor Charles V visited another princely Mantuan villa, that of Marmirolo (now totally destroyed), he was quickly led to see its wonderful aviary, and then found himself splashed by surprise water-jets in the grounds, before settling to a substantial picnic. Yet the creation, and the creators, of such pleasure-places were taken seriously. At the Palazzo del Te, which he also visited, the Emperor significantly praised the design of the rooms and asked for minute explanation of their décor (*'et cosi minutamente'*, a contemporary recorded). No more than Vasari does he seem to have felt aesthetically ill at ease.

Nor was the architect ministering merely to a prince's whim to have – as in any period – places of retreat and private enjoyment. What Giulio Romano did for Mantua as a city was also stressed by Vasari, mentioning how this muddy, water-logged place had been turned by his industry into something which was at once clean and healthy, as well as 'attractive and pleasant' (*tutta vaga e piacevole*). There the order imposed by the architect was in every way a patent improvement on Nature's swamps.

And although an individual building – secular or religious – may provide the most obvious example of the period's achievement, ideas of civic coherence, with the planning of complete areas and streets, were also to be developed. Sansovino's splendid creation of the Library at Venice was itself more than the creation of just that building as such. Connecting his other work in the area – the Zecca and the Loggetta of the campanile –

it made the Piazzetta an impressive approach, almost a triumphal gateway, towards St Mark's and the Clock-tower, and additionally a preparation for the huge Piazza opening unexpectedly at an angle to it. The effect was to impose an overall pattern, relating isolated buildings and monuments which had previously risen amid the clutter of small booths and scattered shops.

At Rome early in the century, under Julius II, and directed by Bramante, new streets had been executed, notably the Via Giulia [122] which is a straight line cut – the verb is almost literally apt – through medieval houses huddled near the Tiber

122. Via Giulia, Rome

123. Via Garibaldi, Genoa

(on the other bank of which an equal incision was made by the Via Lungara). In mid century the 'Strada Nuova' at Genoa was begun, a piece of public work undertaken to improve and embellish the city, most useful – it must be admitted – to those who could afford a palace along this still sumptuous street [123]. The French architect, Jacques du Cerceau the elder, drew attention to a row of arcaded shop buildings then 'recently erected' in Paris, in the second volume of his *Les plus excellents*

Bastiments de France (1579). Another, earlier work of his, the *Livre d'Architecture*, dealt not so much with town-planning as with town-houses, providing designs 'for anyone who wishes to build', in the words of the title page which adds, *'soyent de petit, moyen ou grand estat'*.

Not only is the encouragement significant, but the provision of practical patterns for the house, depending on need, wealth, rank, and so on, is typical of what the century required, and what, from Serlio onwards, it had been given. Abstract discussion, like Danti's, was all very well. But would-be patrons and builders throughout Europe wanted a quicker and less theoretical guide to the new harmonies. As quotation has shown, Danti was scornful of the resulting supply, probably having Serlio particularly in mind. Yet whatever else, the results were certainly not uniform or lacking in invention [124].

124. Square Court of the Louvre, begun 1546. Pierre Lescot

Serlio himself had pointed the way. He had provided the basic grammar of the orders, derived from antiquity, illustrated and discussed. But he had also devised architectural caprices, fanciful projects, and suites of variations on themes like the doorway or the chimney, which are entirely contemporary and in which, one may suspect, he was really at his happiest. In a disarming preface to the reader (of Book IV), Serlio offers apologies for any failures in his treatise, gives all the credit that is due to 'my preceptor', Peruzzi, emphasizes that in 'this our century' architecture flourishes as did Latin in the time of Caesar and Cicero, and speaks of his wish that everyone 'should have some knowledge of this art, which is no less pleasing (*diletteuole*) to the mind, thinking of what is to be carried out, than it is to the eyes when it has been carried out'.

If that is not frank enough, in the preface to Book VI Serlio confesses that he has been 'so free in many things' (*così licentioso in molte cose*), breaking architraves and piling up ornament, because 'most of the time most people appreciate new things'. It is true that he goes on to say that there is the authority of 'some Roman antiquities' for what he has designed, but the

125. Design for a fireplace, 1537. Sebastiano Serlio

vagueness of the remark is perhaps significant. Novelty and pleasingness clearly mattered, quite rightly, to Serlio, whose own inventions [125] are sometimes whimsical – but by no means without appeal to his period.

The tendency, revealed here, for sculpture to mingle with architecture was not merely some Northern European aberration caused by looking at the most fanciful of Serlio's plates or following the Northern European architectural books inspired by his own. Indeed, the North could produce statues for a chimneypiece, like Colyn de Nole's *Fides* [126] in the Town Hall at Kampen, more profoundly classical in their dignity than anything by Serlio. In Italy sculpture and stucco decoration

126. *Fides*,
1543-5.
Colyn de Nole

were already part – an adventurous part – of Raphael's Palazzo Branconio dell' Aquila which stood close to the Vatican. '*Vario, ricco e copioso d'invenzione*' – the terms of praise Vasari gave Giulio Romano's work at the Palazzo del Te – could be applied to Raphael's façade or equally to the display of blended sculpture and architecture in the courtyard of Alessi's Palazzo Marino at Milan [127], begun in 1558. It is easy to linger here over the rich, though controlled, fantasy of the upper storey,

127. Courtyard of Palazzo Marino, Milan, *c.* 1558. Galeazzo Alessi

but the ground floor is very consciously sober in its plain pairs of Doric columns, no less the product of '*invenzione*', and by its very sobriety and regularity adding to the burst of enjoyable exuberance overhead. And other sixteenth-century Italian palaces (like Palazzo Spada at Rome or Palazzo Anziani at Pisa as improved by Vasari himself) delight in declaring their

128. Maison Milsand, Dijon, *c.* 1561. Hugues Sambin

novelty and picturesque appeal to the eye at least as much as to the mind. Thus the façade of the Maison Milsand at Dijon [128] is no bastard but a legitimate brother of Palazzo Marino and one of a distinct family.

Serlio's wish that everyone should have some knowledge of architecture was supported by a spate of books throughout

Europe. In Italy his work was followed by Vignola's illustrated but textless *Regola delli cinque ordini d'architectura* (1562), which includes a number of his own designs, and by Palladio's *Quattro Libri* of eight years later. At Zurich in 1550 had been published Hans Blum's *Quinque Columnarum exacta descriptio atque delineatio*, based on Serlio and very much what its title proclaims. Also based on Serlio was Vredeman de Vries's *Architectura*, first published at Antwerp in 1577, and highly popular in the North. In France, the *Reigle générale d'Architecture des cinq Manières de Colonnes* (privilege to publish, 1563) by Jean Bullant, who recorded that he had visited Rome and studied its buildings, comes after du Cerceau's first publications and precedes Philibert de l'Orme's *Architecture* of 1567. The earliest English book on the subject was *The First and Chief Groundes of Architecture* (1563) by John Shute who had been sent over a decade earlier to Italy by the Duke of Northumberland, 'to confer with the doings of the skilful masters in architecture . . .'

These by no means exhaustive references confirm the prestige of Italy but also the international wish to provide goodly patterns for one's own country. The classical past, to which Serlio had always paid homage, even though not bound by it, was still a powerful force, but one perhaps of more emotional than direct inspiration. It was a challenge, to which the sixteenth century could respond in the belief it would do as well, if not better. Clément Marot was not the sole French poet of the period to state a frank preference for his own land, but his praise of the flourishing commercial and cultural centre of Lyons is also praise of the up-to-date rather than old, however respectable:

> *C'est un grand cas voir le mont Pélion,*
> *Ou d'avoir veu les ruines de Troye:*
> *Mais qui ne voit la ville de Lyon,*
> *Aucun plaisir à ses yeux il n'octroye.*

It was, incidentally, for Lyons, de l'Orme's birthplace, that Serlio (who had been taken into the service of François I) designed, though never executed, a merchant's exchange building.

In de l'Orme's writings, as in some of his few surviving works, can be sensed something of the same independence of the past, combined with patriotism, that Marot expressed.

Novel, if not indeed unique, is his graceful, fluent and yet substantial gateway to Diane de Poitiers' château of Anet [129]. Sculpture is used, though lightly and virtually in silhouette – treated as lightly as the airy, pierced balustrades and the few

129. Gateway of the Château of Anet, c. 1552. Philibert de l'Orme

unemphatic columns and pilasters. Although the result is not like anything previously built, it is far from haphazard or incoherent; in the sense of being balanced, cool and rationally planned, it is classical – though scarcely with the classicism of antiquity. It is the gateway not to a city or a palace but to a country house, crowned with the private if not especially reassuring symbolism of Diana's hounds attacking a stag (the hounds moving at the striking of the clock below).

This style is close enough to the highly individual, yet once again not merely capricious, one of the country house in Elizabethan England. However those buildings may be judged by some standard of ideal classical taste actually alien to the sixteenth century in general, they seemed to contemporaries novel, agreeable and well-proportioned – and thus, inevitably, correct. The house could be as unprecedented as Kirby Hall [130], although – as in this case – the product partly of conflicting designs from Serlio, Hans Blum and Shute's title page. The main doorway has affinities to de l'Orme's gateway at Anet –

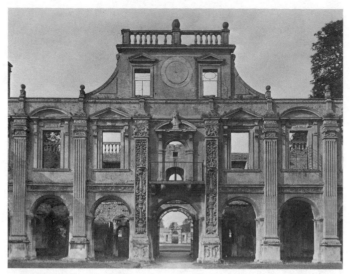

130. Kirby Hall, 1570-75

and that both are patently un-Italian does not disqualify them from being Renaissance, any more than van Eyck is disqualified by being distinct from Masaccio.

Both Kirby and Anet strive to take the 'new' language of the orders and create something bold, rich and harmonious. When Lord Burghley, himself builder of the modern-Renaissance Burghley House, visited Sir Christopher Hatton's then unfinished Holdenby House, he found approvingly not only 'a great magnificence' but 'every part answerable to other, to allure liking'. The transformations effected by the Earl of Leicester at Kenilworth made a fortified castle into a gentleman's house, one which a contemporary could praise for being 'so seemly to sight by due proportion . . .' Thus the same standard was applied as Vasari had used to praise Giulio Romano's Palazzo del Te. That in each case the building looked different is hardly surprising, but it would be rash to claim that Vasari would not have liked or understood Anet, had he seen it, and he might even have had a kind word for Kirby Hall.

What had been, as it were, catapulted into the international public domain was the idea of modern architecture as something which could pleasantly, but radically, improve the world around us. It had been given impulse, almost as a movement inaugurated, at the beginning of the century by Julius II's double decision to build a vast new St Peter's (cf. p. 42) and, on less vast but still huge scale, extend the Vatican palace. The vision behind these projects was in itself vast and daring. In neither case was the construction to be of buildings which were strictly needed; rather, it was the expression of very great magnificence, stimulated doubtless by thoughts of what rulers and builders had achieved in antiquity. It must have seemed an especially favourable omen that the Laocoön statue should have been discovered during Julius's reign; it was rapidly given a central niche in the lowest area of the Belvedere Court, the large forum-like courtyard on three levels which Bramante began for the Pope [139]. There probably lay the germ of the increasingly dramatic villa gardens of the century, delighting in shifts of level and changing vistas. Bramante's project connected the Vatican palace as such with an existing small summer-house, the Belvedere, approached – in his design – across an arcaded courtyard, up a broad staircase to another level where lateral flights of steps led from a nymphaeum to the final level, disclosing a semi-circular pilastered façade through which the actual Belvedere was reached.

That curved exedra was never built, but even in designing it (and something of its design was to be illustrated by Serlio) Bramante already expressed the century's typical interest in the possibilities of the concave façade, the curving loggia or semi-circular peristyle. That solid architecture should bend and even, as it were, move is part of art's new grace and ingenuity: the effect pleases the eye, is never entirely expected and always has about it some air of illusionism. At the Palazzo del Te Giulio Romano was to use it as the least abrupt way of terminating a garden vista (where it probably interposed itself to enhance rather than block the view beyond). Bramante himself had planned that his Tempietto at S. Pietro in Montorio should be ringed round by a circular cloister, and the small circular building would then have been set, sphere within circle, like the hub of a graceful wheel. On much larger scale, some echo of his intention there is caught in the spacious, circular, pillared courtyard in the centre of Machuca's palace for Charles V at Granada [131] – an unexpected effect, concealed behind the façade. In Vignola's Villa Giulia at Rome, built for Pope Julius III, the visitor steps from the rather heavy, rectangular

131. Courtyard of the Palace, Granada, begun 1527. Pedro Machuca

132. Courtyard of the Villa Giulia, 1550-55. Vignola

façade into the great curving space of the first courtyard [132], beyond which is discovered a repetition of the effect on a smaller scale with curved flights of steps; and gradually architecture seems dwindling and drawing back – almost literally – as one penetrates deeper down into the final secret garden. Even in an interior, a mysterious and uniquely alluring effect was to be obtained, by Palladio, in the curved colonnade behind the high altar of the Redentore [133]. Space is sensed through and beyond this screen, though its extent is at first unclear; the strong straight drive of the nave brings one into an area where curves expand on three sides, like a bubble structure softly blown from a tube. In the semi-circle of tall columns lies

133. Nave of the Redentore, Venice, 1576-7. Palladio

perhaps a last vestige of Palladio's probable original wish to
build the Redentore as a completely circular church. The
circle's symbolism of unity and perfection was obvious;
Palladio himself pronounced it (in his *Quattro libri*) to be the
most fitting pattern for a church, being uniform, equal, strong,
and demonstrating the uniformity, unity and essence of God.

Other ideas of pre-established pattern had been prompted
by less mystical considerations. Not only the whole concept of
the villa as such, but also that of its semi-circular peristyle,
could be found in the letters of the younger Pliny, where he
describes his two villas in some detail, mentioning a garden
colonnade and also that curved peristyle ('*porticus in D literae*

similitudinem circumactae') which High Renaissance architects were, in different ways, to re-create. Antiquity becomes something not to be imitated or exactly copied but to serve as inspiration. The variety of Renaissance villas is evidence that a general concept, rather than any single plan or type, was being followed. It was a concept of life almost as much as of architecture which was involved: an ordered, harmonious existence within rooms disposed for different seasons, where books as well as baths were to hand, a good kitchen no less than an elegant garden.

The Romans had distinguished between the *villa rustica*, the master's farm house on his estate, and the *villa suburbana*, a gentleman's residence often quite close to a city. But both argued an agreeable, leisurely life for the rich citizen alone, whose villa-existence is made possible only by the steady toil of

134a. *Dives and Lazarus*. Bonifazio

others. The ideal of harmony achieved in this way is essentially artificial, and that remained true of the Renaissance villa culture, whether in the princely, suburban Palazzo del Te and Villa Giulia, never meant for proper habitation, or in the more rustic villa-cum-farmhouse typical of the Veneto. Slaves or servants are necessary to support lives lived in either; and a certain irony may reside in the fact that one of the most vivid High Renaissance depictions of the optimum villa-existence [134] mingling so many pleasures of the senses, including music, should actually represent the parable of *Dives and Lazarus*. Bonifazio was in no sense of the word a revolutionary

134b. Detail of 134a

artist, but the clear contemporaneity of the rich man and his prosperous setting certainly brings home the parable's sting: '... thou in thy lifetime receivedst thy good things, and likewise Lazarus evil things: but now he is comforted and thou art tormented.'

Yet although an ordered, harmonious environment of their own was still the privilege of the few – and the vision of the world seen by Ulysses as observing 'degree, priority and place' deeply conservative – there was an aspiration towards the idea of the lived-in house which is far from being all display, while remaining very much a work of art. The Elizabethan country house is such, and one may recall the deliberately wide range of houses designed by du Cerceau. Something of the same aspiration is expressed in the writings, and the practice, of the long-lived Venetian aristocrat, Alvise Cornaro, a farmer, scholar and semi-philosopher, who wrote about architecture as a way of building comfortable, economical and well-proportioned houses – not palaces. There was nothing novel about the idea of a palace, and while it is true that the idea of the house was not new either, it was virtually new in the ways it was developed by the sixteenth century.

The challenge offered by nature was not always merely aesthetic, as is emphasized by Vasari's praise for what Giulio Romano achieved at Mantua. Elsewhere in Northern Italy land was to be reclaimed, turned agriculturally productive and made the location of farm-centres-cum-houses – with an architectural result which crystallizes all the High Renaissance urge towards a 'goodly Paterne' of existence and which for centuries went on being influential throughout the world, including America and Russia. Such are the villas – nineteen of them exist – built by Palladio.

It is he, not Bramante, not Raphael, and still less Michelangelo, who really created the sensuously attractive building, with a spell as direct as that of a great painting or piece of music, which can effortlessly be enjoyed before it is admired, without any historical argument about its 'importance'. Nor were his effects achieved by the aid of colour or sculpture. The clarity he sought is more often emphasized by pure whiteness and uncluttered lines. In following the ancients he was not particularly correct, being too profoundly original. His exuberant imagination was not, however, left uncontrolled; in the interests of harmony, proportion, lucidity, he disciplined it intellectually and severely. He left a star-trail of variety throughout the Veneto, with villas that can be almost grotesquely vigorous and rustic, like the unfinished Villa Sarego [135], whose unusual hewn and twisted giant columns might almost come from some Indian temple, and with others, like the Villa Emo [136] where the central pavilion is a concentrated essence of temple in a very different, Mediterranean, tradition, a boldly simple pediment, flanked by the plainest possible supporting blocks.

Not just without incongruity but with positively imaginative insight, Palladio again and again paid his own personal homage to antiquity (and to nature, to order and to proportion) by

135. Villa Sarego, c. 1568-9. Palladio

using temple pediments for villas. Though their settings were often isolated sites, whether on a hillside or plain, they were very much seignorial dwellings, in addition to being usually farm-centres. Grandeur and magnificence, of a logical kind, were part of Palladio's intention. The families who made their homes in the villas impressed and declared their presence on their own land at least as much as did Lord Burghley in building Burghley House.

In Palladio's hands the villa resembled a sort of secularized temple, a triumph of art with its roots in Nature, stirring

136. Villa Emo, 1550s. Palladio

associations of a dream-antiquity (a world of light-filled green landscape dotted with white colonnades and pediments) which was not so far from fact in Italy. Tilling the soil there might accidentally become an archaeological dig as well. The country-side shrine, to old or new gods, suggested continuity as much as did any pediment or row of columns which in ruined state stood as relics of the actual past. It was not merely in homage to antiquity as such that Renaissance architect and patron might unite to build as Palladio built, but as following their own ancestors. Palladio himself had been, in effect, re-baptized into

137. *The Marriage at Cana*, 1562–3. Veronese

a faith more ancient than Christianity when he received the classical name 'Palladio' from his first patron and ceased thenceforward to be called Andrea di Pietro della Gondola.

Of all architecture his was best fitted to be absorbed into pictures which would seek to present the pattern of an ideal universe, and present it on a vast scale. Not eccentric, not frightening, but stable and instinctively noble is the vision which Veronese stretched across whole walls [137], sometimes, as here, extending the rich possibilities of Palladio's architecture within rooms actually designed by Palladio. Today *The*

138. *The Musicians* (detail of 137)

Marriage at Cana is in the Louvre and the high luminous refectory of S. Giorgio Maggiore tragically lacks its focal point, planned to fill the wall area opposite the entrance. Luminosity was continued into an infinity of blue sky, against which stands out one single, gleaming, cloud-capped campanile, itself like a symbol of perfection in the Palladian city which is Cana. All the High Renaissance love of variety and richness is there: concourse of people, sumptuously dressed whether guests or servants, in an indescribable variety of poses, but all fitted into a firm overall pattern, reinforced by the levels of the architecture with its vertical procession of columns and broad horizontal of balustrade, at the centre of which sits Christ – the only full-face figure in the composition.

It needed supreme confidence in art to organize – orchestrate, one might say – this vast concept of Christ's divinity manifested miraculously, publicly and harmoniously. That music should find a central place in the picture, virtually under Christ's gaze, and that it should be a concert which is being played [138], are further visual metaphors of harmony, close indeed to the century's belief. The prominent, even dominant, figure at the left with viol poised is traditionally – possibly correctly – Veronese himself: leader perhaps in the concert and creator certainly of this great visual concert (a marriage too of human and divine, sacred and profane, art and Nature) in which a part is found for everyone.

6

'In Scorn of Nature, Art . . .'

Wishing to give the highest praise to a triptych painted by his contemporary Rogier van der Weyden, the great fifteenth-century antiquarian, Cyriac of Ancona, said that it seemed the work not of a man but of all-creating Nature herself. To be like Nature (not necessarily to be naturalistic) was the finest compliment one could then pay art and the artist. St Thomas Aquinas had pointed out that the visual arts imitate the visual aspects of created Nature, and also Nature's way of operating. For centuries before Pope, artists claimed to obey his dictum, 'First follow Nature . . .'

When Raphael was still quite young, a much older painter, Francia, addressed a generous poem to the boy he apostrophized as 'Fortunato Garxon', commending what he had already done and prophesying the result when he went on to paint yet greater work: 'nature will be conquered' (*vinta sarà natura*). Accidentally or not, this compliment is like a proclamation of new attitudes, very much to be associated with High Renaissance aesthetics. It is true that Alberti had stated that a work of art may happen to be better than Nature, but this might be achieved, he said, by selecting different parts from Nature. It is true also that, much earlier still, Dante (in the *Purgatorio*) had spoken of carved marble reliefs which put to shame Polycrates and Nature ('*Ma la natura li avrebbe scorno*'), though these happened to be the work of God. Indeed, if Nature is God's handiwork, it must be inferior to him but should at the same time be an inspiration to art. On such a scale of values art can hardly aim to do more than – at best – equal Nature.

Only three years after Bramante's death, he was put into a book, Guarna's *Simia* (1517), and imagined as arriving before St Peter at the gates of Paradise. His forthright attitude – surely characteristic, because otherwise pointless and unamusing – was one that Dante perhaps would not have thought quite fitting. First, Bramante tells St Peter, I'd improve the hard road between earth and heaven. Then I'd pull down this Paradise

and build a new one, with finer accommodation for the blessed.
If this suits you, I'll stay; if not, I'm for Pluto's place.

Seldom can the aspiring mind of the High Renaissance artist
have been more pungently conveyed. Heaven itself is now seen
as badly in need of his skill, and perhaps it is as well that Guarna
did not take Bramante on a tour of Purgatory where the God-
sculpted reliefs would probably have come in for radical
improvement. Bramante had certainly enjoyed in real life
taking on large-scale, challenging tasks [139]. But the important aspect of Guarna's imagined scene is how closely it accords
with the quite serious claims made by, and on behalf of, High
Renaissance artists. Leaving aside heaven, to knock out Nature

139. Belvedere Courtyard, Vatican, begun by Bramante

altogether in a frank competition is a new achievement, one
made coolly explicit in the motto taken for himself by Titian:
'*Natura potentior ars*' (Art is more powerful than Nature).
Raphael scarcely needed a motto to assert his conquest of
Nature, prophesied by Francia and become a commonplace by
the time it was stated by Vasari. As for Michelangelo, the superhuman scale of whose work so patently declares an intention of
surpassing Nature, his art was aptly defined by Aretino in a
letter to him, as containing 'the idea of a new Nature'; even
more pertinently, Aretino went on to mention the 'great
miracle' whereby Nature is unable to stamp on its works 'the
majesty which contains within itself the immense power of your
style and your chisel' (. . . *la maestà che tiene in se stessa l'immensa*

potenza del vostro stile e del vostro scarpello). By the time Shakespeare was writing *The Rape of Lucrece*, towards the end of the century, art's achievements were such that art could convincingly be described as acting 'In scorn of nature', so powerful, varied and ingenious are its effects in the piece of 'skilful painting' searchingly studied by Lucrece.

This sort of praise certainly does not mean that Nature was no longer a basis for artists, but the basis was now springboard rather than foundation-stone. Art's presumed greater powers had ceased to inhibit, as is apparent in Titian's motto – an almost Wildean paradox. The appeal of art becomes its very transcendence of the natural. Love of word-play made Aretino

140. Dragon pendant, sixteenth-century Spanish

suggest that Michelangelo was in danger of transcending his own art, and defeating himself. Art was set on a course which was bound to lead eventually to patent extremes of non-naturalism, teaching Nature a lesson by creating, for example, jewelled flowers – like one Cellini made for Agostino Chigi's sister-in-law.

Nor is it altogether surprising that such extremes seem to recall medieval ingenuity in the arts, for that too had been a period when artistic imagination delighted in outstripping Nature – to the notorious disapproval of St Bernard. Between objects like Abbot Suger's eagle vase (cf.p.22 of *Gothic* in this series) and such a piece of High Renaissance jewellery as the typical Spanish dragon pendant [140] there is marked affinity, not merely in richness of material (though that is undoubtedly a factor, far from Early Renaissance sobriety) but in stylish ingenuity: delighting in the artistic possibilities of setting in one example a porphyry vase, and in the other a large emerald, so that each of these objects is magically transformed into the body of a creature, non-realistic, indeed consciously fantastic, yet very much alive.

With the High Renaissance urge – for it can be called that – towards exceeding Nature goes perhaps some doubt, inevitably, about Nature's limitations. Aretino stigmatized its failure to equal Michelangelo's majesty. Nature never produced an eagle like that created for Abbot Suger, but this fact, instead of being a criticism of the work of art, may seem rather a criticism of Nature. Before the spectacle of Veronese's *Marriage at Cana* [137], we and his contemporaries could have several sensations, but never a feeling of familiarity or that this was a natural scene; it is significant that even the Palladian-style buildings exceed Palladio. The whole composition would breathe a positive 'scorn of nature', were it not that Veronese is too well-bred, too calmly assured, to express any sense of rivalry. He never attempts quite the extreme virtuoso effects of Correggio, floating great puffs of cherubim-infested cloud across vast feigned niches to support fore-shortened saints [141], but he is at one with Correggio in creating effortlessly – the adverb is important, lack of strain increasing pleasure – his own personal and perfect cosmos. In such art is implicit criticism of Nature, and in turning back from what has there been achieved to the ordinary world of experience we are bound to feel Nature's fallibility, ruefully aware of what Reynolds called 'the natural imperfection of things'.

141. *S. Hilarion*, 1526–8. Correggio

To Reynolds it seemed that art's task lay precisely in remedy-
ing that, and in saying so he once again showed himself a
sympathetic spokesman for the High Renaissance, with an
almost instinctive comprehension of its necessarily contrived,
if not 'artificial', ethos. Like many a modern art-historian,
Reynolds tended to locate the style in Rome and he tended very
much to interpret it through the art he best understood,
painting. But freed from being permanently *in statu pupillari* at
Nature's academy, the artist in media of all kinds, all over
Europe, could set about reversing the old order of things, and
start tutoring Nature. 'Art knows that Nature has not brought
the human product to full perfection,' Vincenzo Danti declared,
going on to explain that art avoids imperfection, pursuing
perfect things; many modern artists, according to him, have
therefore tried to help Nature – especially Michelangelo. 'We

painters take the same licence as poets and jesters,' Veronese said, carrying the argument further, when brought before the Inquisition about his picture of a New Testament *Supper* which seemed unsuitably elaborate, ornamental and over-populated for the subject-matter of Christ with his Apostles. There, as so often, Veronese had gone far beyond the expected or the natural. The Inquisition believed they had made a good point in asking who Veronese really thought had been at the supper, but the painter was perfectly able to distinguish between the Gospel facts ('I believe one would find Christ with his Apostles') and the requirements of his art: '. . . if in a picture there is some space to spare I enrich it with figures . . . I received the commission to decorate the picture as I saw fit'. And finally, with a ring of independence anticipatory almost of some nineteenth-century artistic personality arraigned for his art (Baudelaire, Flaubert or Whistler): 'I paint pictures as I see fit . . .' (*Io fazzo le pitture con quella consideration che è conveniente . . .*)

A commission for a work of art presented – perhaps always presents – a challenge. But this element, offering the possibility of outstripping both Nature and the earlier achievements of art, was increasingly stressed. Cellini's famous salt-cellar [142] is, or should be, a famous example of exactly that. A salt-cellar, even a costly one, was in itself no novelty. But when Cardinal Ippolito d'Este, the original commissioner, requested Cellini to make the model of a salt-cellar, he explicitly asked that it should be something quite out of the ordinary: 'he said,' (in Cellini's own account) 'he should like [me] to leave the beaten track of those who fabricate salt-cellars' (. . . *che avrebbe voluto uscir dell'ordinario di quei che avevano fatto saliere*). Not perhaps quite taking the measure of his man, the Cardinal encouraged two literary friends to propose designs for the salt-cellar; he liked both proposals so much that he decided to leave Cellini free to choose between them. Cellini's idea of freedom was very different. The salt-cellar, he declared, 'shall be of my own making and invention' (*sarà mia opera e mia invenzione*). When the Cardinal and his companions came to see the resulting model, one of the two friends sourly observed that execution of such an ambitious project would be impossible. The Cardinal decided not to risk commissioning it, leaving Cellini proph-esying violently that the trio would live to see it finally executed 'a hundred times more richly' (*più ricca l'un cento*).

Even if one prudently discounts ten per cent of this charac-teristic story as Cellini's literary enrichment years later of the

142. Salt-cellar, 1540-43. Benvenuto Cellini

bare facts, the patron's express wish and the creator's intention still remarkably accord. If there can be said to be a natural concept of a salt-cellar, it is clearly exceeded by what Cellini produced, which has a cosmic grandeur about its style, as well as its symbolism. One of the Cardinal's friends had proposed it should depict Venus and Cupid, with some suitable emblems; the other, more pertinently, suggested Amphitrite accompanied by tritons. From the latter hint, Cellini obviously evolved Neptune, balancing him as guardian of the salt by Earth with the pepper, fashioning to contain this substance a complete Ionic temple. Not only Sea and Earth, but the Seasons and Dawn and Day, Twilight and Night, are present, making up an artifact that comes to the table almost as it were some portable Michelangelo Medici tomb.

Its richness, elaboration and novelty are indeed scarcely less great, for all its miniature scale. Although its effect is of being all gold, its detail is enhanced by brilliantly coloured enamels, as gleaming as precious stones, adding to the sumptuous appearance. As an object of sheer artistic splendour it might have been too ostentatious for a *quattrocento* court like Federico da Montefeltro's, but in medieval times it could easily have joined the spectacular table-ware at some aristocratic banquet, for it is in the tradition of the highly-wrought vessel or *nef*. It was to be executed for François I, a showy prince, yet there also comes to mind an earlier patron and period in France, the fourteenth-century Duke Louis of Anjou whose vast collection of gold plate included a wonderful salt-cellar in the form of a tree.

It would certainly have been popular too in Renaissance England, and the thought of its execution here is no absurd fancy since Cellini as a young man had seriously considered coming to England with Torrigiano. Cardinal Wolsey would probably have shown more eagerness than Cardinal Ippolito d'Este. The lists of what he ordered from his goldsmith confirm a delight in the frankly luxurious, as well as Italianate artistic taste: 'A high cross made after the fashion of that of Cardinal Campeggio . . . Silver gilt spangles for his footman's coat . . . an image of our Lady in a tabernacle, and a weight of a cross of silver gilt with Mary and John, with a great foot of silver . . . the great new cross with the flying angels', not to mention rings, bracelets, chains, a whistle and a gold cup as a New Year gift for Henry VIII.

Part of Cellini's artistry lies in his salt-cellar's fitness for purpose. Amid elaboration, it retains this coherence which

143. Design for a clock, 1543. Hans Holbein

makes it more than just a charming toy that happens to be usable as a salt-cellar. Cellini thus paid attention to its manoeuvrability on the table; in the base were sunk four ivory balls, to enable it to move easily, a fact that Cellini recorded not in his *Autobiography* but, suitably, in his technical treatise, *dell' Oreficeria*. Such fitness is itself a demonstration of the artist's ingenuity; he enriches the given concept, yet without obscuring it. Holbein's closely contemporary design for a clock [143] is even more elaborate, positively triumphal, but not a mere exercise in capricious fancy. The clock was intended to be executed, to be presented by the courtier Anthony Denny to Henry VIII, once again as a New Year gift. Its elaboration has relevance therefore. The occasion required something patently out of the ordinary, and one can easily believe that Denny (who himself annotated the drawing) encouraged Holbein to *'uscir dell' ordinario'* in designing it, while not failing to emphasize that the result must also serve as a time-piece, itself a still comparatively new technical feat. The clock was due for presentation on New Year's Day 1544, by which date the artist was dead, and it succeeded perhaps in pleasing the recipient who knighted Denny later the same year.

Among other conquests of Nature, the conquest of natural materials assumes particular importance. In 1500 the medium of oil paint – to take the most obvious example – had not been mastered sufficiently to reveal anything like its full potentiality; by 1600, its possibilities might have seemed explored to the point of exhaustion. Marble and bronze too offered their challenges, so marvellously met in many of the achievements illustrated here, particularly in Chapter 3. It was left to the sculptor Puget in the seventeenth century to declare magnificently, *'Le marbre tremble devant moi'*, but one cannot help feeling that several figures of the previous century might have said it, Cellini (with the substitution of 'bronze') among them; and his own description of the casting of his bronze *Perseus* gives a clear enough idea of some of the desperate feats involved in fusing the natural imperfection of things into art.

Yet it is not only a matter of the obviously massive or apparently intractable media. Everywhere the artist sensed Nature's failure to be perfect, to possess artistic refinement, to 'finish' as exquisitely as art could [144] and to surprise in the inventive way that art can. A weapon might easily turn into a work of art, retaining its purpose but now carrying a complete miniature classical scene as ornament [145].

144. Details of crystal casket, 1532. Valeriano Belli
145. Detail of wheel-lock pistol, c. 1550. German

There is no need to think that the elaborate armour, shields and weapons of the century must essentially be 'Mannerist', for Leonardo had designed elaborately fantastic armour, and one of the very first manifestations of High Renaissance recherché refinement seems to have been a silver lyre shaped like a horse's head, which Leonardo had designed and which he took with him to Milan in the very early 1480s. Vasari approvingly characterized it as 'a curious and novel object' (*cosa bizzarra e nuova*) and though no other record of this particular instrument survives, some faint reflection of it can perhaps be seen in the novel-looking, carefully-wrought stringed instrument appearing in Filippino Lippi's *Parthenice* [146] painted no later than 1502. Rather than free fantasy, this may be another example of intended triumph by art, in bringing back the ancient form of lyre (as supposed by the period) for it is on that very account that Filippino, '*quello eccellente pittore*', is praised by a contemporary.

Vasari's epithets of 'curious and novel', combined with virtuoso triumph not merely over a medium as such but in fresh ways of handling it, characterize the High Renaissance approach to every object, touching into the rare and the extraordinary a whole range of otherwise everyday objects: from a doorknocker [147] to a lectern [148]. Raphael himself designed elaborately rich dishes for Agostino Chigi. Perino del Vaga's three designs illustrated here are not only subtly varied, as well

146. *Parthenice* (detail), before 1502. Filippino Lippi

147. *Neptune* (doorknocker). Alessandro Vittoria

148. Designs for a lectern. Perino del Vaga

as perfectly practical, but are clearly far richer than practicality requires; they turn the lectern into a work of art, one into which as much thoughtful ingenuity has gone as if it were a statue or a painting. More striking still, because positively executed and once in use on a palace door, is Vittoria's bronze Neptune knocker, with marine motifs wrought not only gracefully but into the shape necessary to serve the object's purpose.

One might pause a long time outside a doorway, marvelling at the vigorous transmutation of mere bronze into those vivid, virtually snorting sea-horses and the twisting fronds which frame the commanding figure of the god himself. Very much

149. Design for a ceremonial chair, *c*. 1527. Peter Flötner

within the same idiom, and no less deserving of praise as highly novel yet also practical (just), is Flötner's project for a ceremonial chair [149]. A great designer of furniture and metal-work, as well as a practising goldsmith, Flötner here displays an exuberance which might conventionally be called Gothic – especially since he is a Northern artist – but which is really in that vein of High Renaissance robustness, like Vittoria's, which anticipates the Baroque (and Venetian seventeenth-century furniture would provide the best parallels to Flötner's solid, sculptural boldness). Taking the simple concept of 'chair', Flötner proceeds to elaborate and animate it until four legs are transformed into winged putti, riding dolphin-like shapes whose distended mouths grasp balls – and any idea of weight or support is almost lost in this refined conjuring, which wood must be carved to convey. Foliage-like arm-rests curl upwards into the slim candclabra-cum-pillars that form the back; downwards they connect with the pair of noble, heraldic, antique beings who are the true supporters of the chair, bearers as it were of the person who takes his seat on it.

It is no chance that so much High Renaissance imagery in art is derived from, even while patently exceeding, the natural. We may reasonably guess that Leonardo's silver lyre would have been also a remarkable study of a horse's head. 'The natural' was to be interpreted again and again in terms of living creatures – man, animals, birds and reptiles, and perhaps only to a lesser degree plants. The more obviously living the form, the greater the challenge. It was a period with artistic taste for life – not for the still-life. Its art was more thickly populated with beings of every kind – actual, borrowed from antiquity or invented in the sheer joy of inventing – than any artistic style since has dared to be. There is nothing abstract about the imagery of Vittoria's doorknocker or Flötner's chair; human masks appear on the support of Perino del Vaga's lectern, as do also putti-like figures on the central design. How seminal were the painted *Ignudi* of Michelangelo's Sistine ceiling and the activated, if less energetic, painted caryatids in Raphael's Vatican Stanze. Real architectural features, from a façade to a chimneypiece, were soon to be accompanied, borne up, by solid, sculpted figures [125 and 127]. Armour was often decorated with quite strongly modelled faces, genii and creatures seeming to symbolize courage or victory – and sometimes entire battle-scenes are shown. Majolica provided the surface

150. Polychrome Dish, 1533. Francesco Xanto

for what are very often complete pictures [150]. The handle of
a cup will prove to be an arched human body or an enamelled
snake. Even the very knives and forks might terminate, like
miniature herms, in human torsos.

What perhaps began with Leonardo's lyre reaches a deliberately wilful extreme in such an object as the late sixteenth-
century Milanese rock-crystal cup [151], of which we might well
say – even while recognizing its ornithological basis – 'Bird
thou never wert'. Nature must retire defeated before the invention which equips a bird with pendant beads hanging from its
fretted wings; beyond this lies only Fabergé – or a forceful
return to directly natural inspiration. And yet, enjoyment of
its fantasy element is partly dependent on recognition of the
Nature it challenges by art. The creation is not to be just
monstrous or perverse, however strange. Even the use of glass

151. Rock-crystal cup. Saracchi Workshop

evokes something of a bird's combination of fragility with buoyant strength in flight. Art is still ready to take hints – if no longer always lessons – from Nature. When Marlowe (in *Hero and Leander*) describes the ceiling carving of a vine in Venus's marvellous temple, he makes it of 'green sea agate', not of gold or silver, as if to emphasize how in this exotic form it simulated real leaves. Few people could in reality command large-scale work in agate, but in the commoner medium of plaster virtual gardens and menageries were to be created on ceilings and walls, especially in English houses. With the vivid designation, 'your plasterer that flowereth your hall', the famous Bess of Hardwick, building at Chatsworth, begged a gifted craftsman from a fellow-builder.

Flowers and fruit form one of the many triumphs of art's ingenuity in François I's gallery at Fontainebleau where fancy

152. Galerie François I, Fontainebleau, *c.* 1533-40. Rosso

and observation everywhere entwine to surpass Nature [152]. In some ways, the effect of this room is of Michelangelo's Sistine ceiling brought down to earth, made playful and openly profane, as well as realized in a three-dimensional medium. Its affinities with the Sistine ceiling are not unimportant for those who wish to call the Galerie François I Mannerist on such grounds as that 'the forms are complex rather than clear' (Blunt, *Art and Architecture in France, 1500 to 1700*); the complex structure feigned on the Sistine ceiling must then be a very early example of large-scale Mannerism by a leading Mannerist and 'High Renaissance' as a valid stylistic label becomes doubtful. As one passes down the still beautiful room at Fontainebleau with its polished woods, its pictures and especially its graceful, white stucco statues, the climate of mythology grows excitingly palpable and Marlowe's temple of Venus again comes to mind:

> There might you see the gods in sundry shapes,
> Committing heady riots, incest, rapes:
> Jove slyly stealing from his sister's bed,
> To dally with Idalian Ganymede,
> Or for his love Europa bellowing loud,
> Or tumbling with the Rainbow in a cloud;

The walls above a certain level have undergone metamorphosis, almost disappearing under the encrustation of stucco, where amid cartouches and frames and wreaths there flourishes a race of ideal beings, slimmer, more poised and more essentially elegant than merely human ones. The concept in art of people aloof from ourselves – superior, flawless and usually untroubled – may seem here to reach an extreme, but it was already foreshadowed in the figures moving through the elevated theatre of *The School of Athens* and – even more obviously – in the *Ignudi* of the Sistine ceiling. What we admire in these differing instances is the very apartness given by art: created in it can be images of mankind so convincingly vital and yet so patently artificial that we could never mistake them for 'ordinary' people, never identify with them, never praise them as being natural. Yet, amid the fantastic ornament and the springing forms which populate the walls of the Gallery, exist floral garlands, swags and baskets of fruit, reminding one that art continues, when it wishes, and in no awe-struck way, to observe Nature as sharply as ever.

If there is an inherent ambivalence in the typical artist's attitude to Nature, this is neatly brought into the open in the art and interests of Bernard Palissy. Perhaps few products of the century are now as little admired as his bizarre ceramics [153], whose novelty has been spoilt by imitation, whose effects

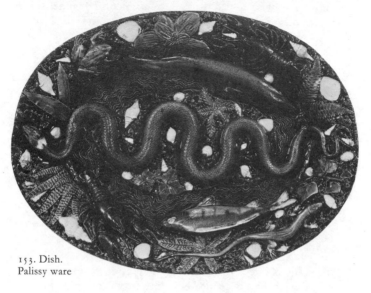

153. Dish.
Palissy ware

are often proto-Victorian in their luxuriance and to many tastes indeed actively unpleasant. But Palissy is remarkably relevant. Like so many artists of his period, he wrote an autobiography. He had too one more story to tell of trial and eventual victory in connection with a particular medium, the glazed clay of his dishes.

So bizarre has Palissy's work seemed, especially the strange, now almost entirely destroyed grottoes which he constructed in the gardens of his leading patrons, that it has quite reasonably qualified for inclusion in the style Mannerism (interpreted as abstraction from natural behaviour and appearances, fantasy, complexity of invention, high artifice, etc.). Yet it is doubtful if Palissy himself would have accepted this categorization. For one thing, he was as serious as Leonardo da Vinci in his study of Nature. Reptiles, insects and shells, the objects which ornament his artistic products, were not fantasies conjured up by him but had been scrutinized in Nature, with such attention that he can be ranked among the natural scientists of the sixteenth century, associated with Bacon, and might have found a place here in Chapter 4. He speculated about fossils, wrote about natural philosophy and religion, and was praised in at least one contemporary poem for having unlocked Nature's doors, so long closed, even while the poet ended by invoking Palissy's *'meilleure nature'*.

Palissy certainly challenged Nature. Prometheus-like, he stole its fire to put into the creatures of his art, naturalistically coloured, scrupulously recorded, but assembled with artistic, non-natural richness into positive anthologies of the fish–insect–reptile kingdoms. His plates almost drip with the result of his researches, like nets hauled up from some impossible marine source, clotted with shells, snakes, lobsters, lizards and weeds. Almost inevitably, Leonardo's Medusa-shield comes to mind: a capricious assemblage in art from so many individual studies of carefully collected newts, lizards, snakes, butterflies and so on. Perhaps if that had survived, it too would qualify as Mannerist?

Leaving Leonardo aside, Palissy's art, intentions and writings must by themselves stir much wider doubts about the extent to which Mannerism should be treated as a truly distinct style, with its own individual characteristics, rather than as a partial manifestation of High Renaissance aims from the first. The matter is too extensive for discussion here, but it may be said that among the advantages of bringing Mannerism within cover of the High Renaissance is that such artists as Raphael and Michelangelo are seen to lead less stylistically schizoid lives; and much the same becomes true of painters like Holbein whose portraits are supremely 'realistic' but whose designs for jewellery, furniture, etc. patently fantastic, i.e. 'Mannerist'. Further, no contradiction need then be felt, but rather a complementing, in the fact that around the mid point of the sixteenth century the two greatest Italian portrait-painters were Bronzino and Titian (as opposed in personal style, one might suggest, as had been Botticelli and Bellini, who are yet equally protagonists in an earlier phase of the Renaissance). Titian's effortless defeat of Nature is seen best perhaps in one of his supreme full-length portraits [154] – so much more than merely a likeness or a face. In front of this picture one easily appreciates the acuteness of Reynolds's praise of Titian: 'whatever he touched . . . by a kind of magick he invested with grandeur and importance'. That Altdorfer, so typical of the century's sensitive response to

154. *Portrait of a Man, c.* 1550. Titian

the natural world, should be active at the same time as Parmigianino and Perino del Vaga, for example, ceases to suggest a dichotomy explicable only by the tired terminology of Northern actuality versus Southern idealization (and Altdorfer's own decorative designs for wall-paintings anyway show him well capable of doing a Perino del Vaga when required). In Veronese can be found one of the last great exponents of all that Vasari meant by *maniera*, and also an epitome of the High Renaissance artist.

As for Palissy, he proves that sober, proto-scientific research about Nature, in the direct tradition of Leonardo, not merely could exist side by side with the most capricious and contrived effects of art but could positively power that art, even while providing scope for practical treatises. Thus, study of Nature leads eventually to the outwitting of Nature. Before it is exceeded, it must be known. Only when art is sure in that knowledge can it proceed to proclaim its own superiority, pushing beyond the lifelike to the invented and the artificial. And, one should add, only a public which has become sated with the homely achievements of naturalism will fully appreciate the exotic products of refinement and fantasy. Not accidentally in the history of artistic styles, extending back into classical antiquity, do periods of naturalism and realism provide a prologue to the high accomplishment of art which almost insolently proceeds (as does Hellenistic art or that of the nineteenth-century *fin-de-siècle*) to display its sheer artfulness. The poet who praised Palissy may not have been greatly gifted but he understood the artist's accomplishment, tacitly recognizing one more defeat of Nature:

> Le *lizard sur le buisson*
> N'*a point un plus nayf lustre*
> *Que les tiens en ta maison*
> D'*œuvre nouveau tout illustre.*

The most powerful, however, of all challenges involved not lizards but mankind itself; not pottery but pictures. A piece of 'skilful painting' (interestingly not a tapestry) was what Shakespeare's Lucrece sought out, trying to relieve her own emotions by studying the emotions depicted so vividly in that elaborate composition dealing with the fall of Troy. There, the miracle of art consisted in dry drops of paint simulating weeping tears and the reek of blood and the gleam of dying eyes – not so far, as it happens, from what is seen in the face of Christ in Raphael's

155. *Head of Christ* (detail of 156)

'*Lo Spasimo di Sicilia*' [155]. This is not merely a pious icon, still less a straightforward study in naturalism, but an intense effort by art to achieve an expressive image at once human and divine, beautiful yet agonized, tortured as much mentally as physically. It is less the weight of the Cross under which Christ sinks than the pain of witnessing the Virgin's pain (itself the title of the church in Sicily, S. Maria dello Spasimo, for which the picture was painted).

From the detail of Christ's distressed face one must in effect draw back, to take in the press of people surrounding him, all experiencing a series of varying, conflicting emotions aroused by this central figure, victim and victor, humanly the weakest but spiritually the most strong [156]. Art has moved far from

156. 'Lo Spasimo di Sicilia', 1517. Raphael

the typical fifteenth-century bust-length Man of Sorrows adored by the Virgin, setting the scene now in dramatic action which involves every participant. The size of the picture, one of the very largest ever designed by Raphael, increases the overwhelming effect. The private gaze of Christ and the Virgin, two kneeling figures whose glances interlock across the composition, is on a vast public stage with the triumphal stir of a Roman executional procession trying to resume its course, with flying banner, lances, bright armour and noble horses, almost trampling on the powerless mourning group of women where soft draperies and flowing hair seem to symbolize dissolving endurance. Each face and gesture is charged with some distinct sensation – from military anger at the delay to the Virgin's despairing gesticulation. Yet the final focus is on that face set lowest of all in the composition, its mouth open and its eyes distended, and its very flesh under the glistening drops of tears and blood seeming also to distend in that experience we are made to share of growing acquainted with grief.

In every way, to the sixteenth century, this picture seemed a miracle. Its popularity as a composition, engraved on completion by Agostino Veneziano, is attested by tapestries and majolica. Even its fortunes seemed miraculous, because it alone survived a shipwreck en route to Sicily: washed up at Genoa, it was immediately seized by the Genoese who were persuaded to part with it only by the Pope's personal intervention. Vasari devotes a long passage to the picture and its adventures – in contrast to his brief words about, for example, the Sistine Madonna.

Today, the latter is far more famous, and not just because Raphael's hand in the actual execution of the '*Spasimo di Sicilia*' has been questioned. Although it is meant to have an overwhelming poignancy, affecting the spectator profoundly, the '*Spasimo*' probably seldom stirs such emotion. It is not natural enough for us. The art contemporaries admired may now seem only too artificial and contrived, its pathos forced and its people too obviously posed and contrasted. Everywhere can be detected a refinement, even elegance, which suggests studied art rather than utter sorrow. For all Simon of Cyrene's vigorous gesture, there is felt to be no weight to the Cross. The hand of the Mary at the extreme right, slightly raising the Virgin's veil, might in itself illustrate genteel deportment, so gracefully are the fingers crooked.

In ways like these, the '*Spasimo di Sicilia*' seeks not only a dignity consonant with its theme but to display art's superiority over the merely natural. Any day in sixteenth-century Rome one could have seen a malefactor dragged through the streets, perhaps accompanied by a tearful mother. To such an analogy Raphael shuts his eyes. He is not illustrating but exercising his imagination over a great, familiar tragic moment in the Christian story, and to bring out its significance he aims at novel, recherché invention. The composition, derived partly from two Dürer Passion woodcuts, is itself a drastic revision of them in the interests of more elevated, more ideal effects. Dürer, for instance, thickly populated the way to Calvary with grotesquely mean faces of soldiers and onlookers, until the visual effect is like a babble of mockery and hatred. Raphael substitutes calm, silvery rhetoric, investing even the soldiers with a certain nobility – a grandeur made explicit in the commander of the guard – increased by costuming them in approximately antique style (in contrast to Dürer's touches of local contemporary fashion).

If the final result does not move us, at least we can recognize how much sheer art has gone to its achievement. Not the least part is the organization in a huge altarpiece of many large-scale figures, all involved in acting and in the central action. And then there is the richness accumulated around this action, for Raphael has fused together several incidents from the *Stations of the Cross*: Christ's meeting with his mother, his fall under the Cross, Simon of Cyrene's helping him to carry it. Although the two Dürer woodcuts were utilized, both in fact show a different, more frequently illustrated, incident, when Veronica offered Christ a handkerchief with which to wipe his face.

Copiousness, novelty, wealth of invention – Raphael displays them all. He lifts the scene onto a lofty plane, a positive stage, which is unlike any world we know; such a climate is best breathed in by the connoisseur – suitable indeed for someone like Raphael's own friend and sitter, Castiglione. Yet Raphael is also able to challenge Nature more directly still: to create within that framework the lifelike head of Christ with its uncaricatured, pathetic expression, its flecks of blood and welling tears, which would once have united the connoisseur, the simply pious and the ignorant in its praise.

'*Natura potentior ars*', all might – in their different ways – have agreed. But, it may be recalled, that motto belonged not to

157. *Assumption and Coronation of the Virgin* (the '*Assunta*'), 1518. Titian

Raphael but to Titian. And while Raphael's place as a prime creator of the High Renaissance style has been realized from his lifetime onwards – was, in effect, declared in Francia's poetic prophecy – the place of Titian has always been less clear. Sometimes it has seemed, despite his own boast, that he is more natural than artificial. Although we know about his marvellous, increasingly free handling of oil-paint, we perhaps forget to notice his particular *maniera*, as stylish and as full of artifice as Raphael's, when he wishes. Venice, too, has never at any time enjoyed the prestige of Rome, and in its very aesthetic appeal has often been slighted by the historian in search of more cerebral sensations.

Closely contemporary with the '*Spasimo di Sicilia*' was a much larger altarpiece, twice its height, Titian's so-called '*Assunta*' [157], not merely a masterpiece but a revolutionary manifesto which by itself entitles its creator to a key place in the forging of the High Renaissance style. Famous and influential as it rapidly became, it may well have disconcerted some first spectators by its novelty (yet one more instance, if so, of the often forgotten fact that there is a long tradition of stylistic changes disconcerting patrons and public). The art of Raphael's altarpiece is manifest to the point of being nowadays something of an obstacle. Ironically, the art of Titian's picture can easily be overlooked in responding to what seems so much more relaxed and 'natural', so much more glowing and thrilling. In retrospect, its novelty is forgotten. Even its subject is rarely, if ever, noticed correctly.

The picture shows a vision and a mystery – a colossal infraction of Nature – painted to convey the impact of such a vision on an epic scale. It shows us an earth of dark, giant Apostles and a radiant sky where God the Father floats with arms extended like a huge bird: extremes between which the Virgin is forever poised, severed from earth by the sweep of cherubs and cloud, and almost dancing in ecstasy, bareheaded as she soars, so solid yet so sure, to receive the reward of a heavenly crown. The composition is not just of her Assumption but also of her Coronation (the crown being borne by the prominent adult angel, under the gaze and cloak of God the Father), the final 'glorious mystery' of the Rosary, as fitting a subject for the high altarpiece of a church which is called S. Maria Gloriosa as was Raphael's for S. Maria dello Spasimo.

The challenge to Titian's imagination was vast, but he has responded to, even exceeded, the subject's implications. When one passes over the blazing expanse of heaven with its countless illuminated, half-ethereal, angel faces, the daring tilt of God the Father's silhouette which increases the sense of his floating there, the swell of the Virgin's silk mantle which billows across her body, twists behind a cherub and merges into a cloud – still there remain the varied chorus of cherubs in every conceivable playful or ardent pose and the mighty figures of the upward-staring Apostles, each of whom seems to experience the event with his own personal response. Even the human figures have taken on a mystic grandeur; the young Apostle standing full-length gracefully at the left, with hand on breast, has such unmistakable *maniera* as to bring associations beyond the century, anticipating Van Dyck [158].

And, finally, it is noticeable that Titian has banished all temporal, localizing references: no landscape and scarcely more than a symbol of the Virgin's tomb. Michelangelo could not have stripped the scene barer of everything except figures. Perhaps indeed only on the Sistine ceiling is there elsewhere in the High Renaissance such visionary fervour combined with such physical magnificence; but the sumptuous colour, the broad assurance of conception and the supreme artistic self-confidence – so well to be justified for more than fifty years *after* this picture was finished – are Titian's alone.

Looking at what he achieved here will in itself do more than any book to convey, if not 'explain', the High Renaissance. Many of its greatest painters – from Correggio to Veronese – are foreshadowed in this actual work, but more important is its frank expression of the power of artistic imagination, passing quite out of Nature but becoming only the more artistically convincing. Titian speaks therefore for Cellini no less than for Veronese, and for Grünewald too. This vision of the Virgin becomes a metaphor for artistic vision of all kinds. It is, as it were, a licence to create – so long as one can create with such tremendous conviction.

This book began by calling Sir Joshua Reynolds to testify about the High Renaissance; it has cited him frequently and cannot do better than close with some further words of his. They were not spoken specifically about the High Renaissance but they apply aptly to that period – seen, as it has been here, as an age confident it could tutor Nature, effortlessly inventive, supremely accomplished on huge or minute scale in every medium, graceful, varied, refined, and constantly asserting its right to artistic independence and freedom:

'Upon the whole, it seems to me, that the object and intention of all the Arts is to supply the natural imperfection of things, and often to gratify the mind by realising and embodying what never existed but in the imagination.'

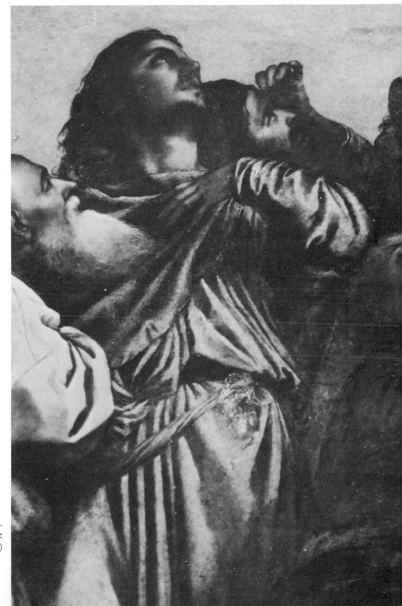

158.
An Apostle
(detail of 157)

Catalogue of Illustrations

Abbreviations used:

A.B.: *The Art Bulletin*
Blunt: A. F. Blunt, *Art and Architecture in France, 1500-1700*, Pelican History of Art, 1973 ed.
G.B.A.: *Gazette des Beaux-Arts*
J.W.C.I.: *Journal of the Warburg and Courtauld Institutes*
Pope-Hennessy: J. Pope-Hennessy, *Italian High Renaissance and Baroque Sculpture*, 1970 ed.

1. THE CARONDELET ALTARPIECE. By Fra Bartolommeo, *c.* 1511. Panel, 260 x 230 cms. *Besançon, Cathedral.* (Photograph: Giraudon.)
   Commissioned, probably in 1511, by Ferry Carondelet, archdeacon of Besançon and an imperial ambassador, when he was in Florence; a lunette with the *Coronation of the Virgin* (Stuttgart) was part of the original ensemble and was worked on by Albertinelli in collaboration. Several preparatory drawings for the main panel exist. Carondelet was also the subject of a fine portrait by Sebastiano del Piombo (Thyssen collection, Lugano).
   Lit: *Le seizième Siècle Européen* (exhibition catalogue) Paris, 1965-6, No. 30; L. Borgo, *Burlington Magazine*, cxiii, 1971, 362-71.

2. LANDSCAPE. Detail of pl. 1.

3. ANGEL'S HEAD, detail from *The Virgin of the Rocks*. By Leonardo da Vinci, *c.* 1483. Canvas, 199 x 122 cms. *Paris, Louvre.* (Photograph: Giraudon.)

4. BALDASSARE CASTIGLIONE. By Raphael, *c.* 1515. Canvas, 82 x 67 cms. *Paris, Louvre.* (Photograph: Giraudon.)
   The sitter (1478-1529), author of *Il Cortegiano*, was a friend of Raphael's. The picture's date cannot be firmly established, but it is referred to in a letter of Bembo's of 19 April 1516.
   Lit: E. Camesasca, *Tutta la Pittura di Raffaello: I Quadri*, 1962, 61-2.

5. UGOLINO MARTELLI. By Bronzino, *c.* 1535. Panel, 102 x 85 cms. *Berlin-Dahlem.* Martelli (1519-92) was a precocious scholar. The portrait's date is established approximately by the sitter's appearance. The setting is the Palazzo Martelli with the *David* (now N. G. Washington) once supposed to be by Donatello.
   Lit: A. Emiliani, *Il Bronzino*, 1960, pl. 19 (unpaginated).

6. ANDREA ODONI. By Lorenzo Lotto, 1527. Canvas, 101 x 114 cms. *Hampton Court, H.M. The Queen.* Reproduced by gracious permission of H.M. The Queen. Referred to as in the sitter's house in 1532, and mentioned as there also by Vasari.
   Lit: A. Banti and A. Boschetto, *Lorenzo Lotto*, 1953, 81 (No. 77).

7. PORTRAIT OF A WOMAN. By Frans Floris, 1558. Panel, 108 x 85 cms. *Caen, Musée des Beaux-Arts.* (Photograph: Archives.)
   Initialled and dated, and inscribed with the sitter's age, *Aetate sua XLVIII*. There exists a companion portrait, also of 1558, a *Man with a Falcon* (Brunswick).
   Lit: *Le seizième Siècle Européen* (exhibition catalogue) Paris, 1965-6, No. 141.

8. THE 'VENUS OF URBINO'. By Titian, *c.* 1538. Canvas, 119 x 165 cms. *Florence, Uffizi.*

Commissioned by Guidobaldo della Rovere, future Duke of Urbino (who was also portrayed by Titian). A letter from Guidobaldo, written from Urbino in March 1538, requires his agent not to return without what appears to be this picture, *'la donna nuda'*.

Lit: F. Valcanover, *L'opera completa di Tiziano*, 1969, No. 190; R. Pallucchini, *Tiziano*, 1969, 271–2.

9. ANGEL'S HEAD, detail from *The Marriage of S. Catherine*. By Andrea del Sarto, 1512–13. Panel, 167 x 122 cms. *Dresden, Gemäldegalerie*. (Photograph: Deutsche Fotothek.)

The date is established on stylistic grounds.

Lit: S. J. Freedberg, *Andrea del Sarto*, 1963 (catalogue raisonné volume), 34–5; J. Shearman, *Andrea del Sarto*, 1965, II, 210–11.

10. THE ADORATION OF THE SHEPHERDS ('LA NOTTE'). By Correggio, *c*. 1530. Panel, 256 x 188 cms. *Dresden, Gemäldegalerie*.

Commissioned in 1522, probably completed in 1530.

Lit: P. Bianconi, *Tutta la Pittura del Correggio*, 1953, 44; A. Bevilacqua and A. C. Quintavalle, *L'opera completa del Correggio*, 1970, No. 75.

11. STUDIES FOR AN ADORATION OF THE KINGS. By Veronese, *c*. 1573(?). Pen on paper, 28·3 x 19·8 cms. *Haarlem, Teyler's Museum*. (Photograph: Museum.)

Studies connected with the picture of the subject dated 1573 in the National Gallery, London.

Lit: H. Tietze and E. Tietze-Conrat, *The Drawings of the Venetian Painters*, 1944, 343 (No. 2070).

12. DAVID. By Michelangelo, 1501–4. Marble, 434 cms. *Florence, Accademia*. (Photograph: Brogi.)

Lit: M. Weinberger, *Michelangelo the Sculptor*, 1967, I, 77 ff.

13. S. EUSTACE. By Albrecht Dürer, *c*. 1501. Engraving, 35·7 x 26 cms. (Photograph: Trustees of the British Museum.)

The story of the saint, a pagan hunter who had a vision of the crucified Christ between the antlers of a stag, is also told of St Hubert; Dürer's own mention of his engraving refers to it as of St Eustace.

Lit: *Albrecht Dürer 1471–1971* (exhibition catalogue) Nuremberg, 1971, 254 (No. 496).

14. DAVID. Detail of pl. 12. (Photograph: Anderson.)

15. STAIRCASE OF THE BIBLIOTECA LAURENZIANA, *Florence*. (Photograph: The Mansell Collection.)

Lit: J. S. Ackerman, *The Architecture of Michelangelo*, 1961, I, 33 ff.; II, 33 ff.

16. ST PETER'S FOUNDATION MEDAL. By Cristoforo Caradosso, 1506. Bronze. (Photograph: Trustees of the British Museum.)

Lit: G. F. Hill, *A Corpus of Italian Medals of the Renaissance*, 1930, I, 171 (No. 659).

17. S. GIORGIO MAGGIORE, VENICE. By Andrea Palladio, begun 1565. (Photograph: Ackerman.)

The façade dates from early in the seventeenth century but follows Palladio's model.

Lit: J. S. Ackerman, *Palladio*, 1966, 143 ff.

18. THE MADONNA DELLA SEDIA. By Raphael, *c*. 1514–15. Panel, diameter 71 cms. *Florence, Palazzo Pitti*. (Photograph: Soprintendenza alle Gallerie.)

Undocumented and datable only on stylistic evidence. An interesting essay on the picture and its 'legend' in Gombrich cited below.

Lit: E. Camesasca, op. cit. 60; E. H. Gombrich, *Norm and Form*, 1966, 64 ff.

19. STUDIES OF THE VIRGIN AND CHILD. By Raphael. Pen and ink, 25·4 x 18·4 cms. *London, British Museum*. (Photograph: John Freeman.)

A date towards the end of Raphael's Florentine period (*c.* 1508) is suggested by the authorities cited below.

Lit: P. Pouncey and J. A. Gere, *Italian Drawings ... in the British Museum : Raphael and his Circle*, 1962, No. 19.

20. THE SCHOOL OF ATHENS. By Raphael, 1508-11. *Rome, Vatican, Stanza della Segnatura.* (Photograph: Anderson.)

Lit: E. Camesasca, op. cit. 37-40.

21. THE FIRE IN THE BORGO. By Raphael, 1514-17. *Rome, Vatican, Stanza dell' Incendio.* (Photograph: Anderson.)

The original incident was a fire in the Roman quarter of the Borgo, miraculously extinguished by Pope Leo IV in 847.

Lit: E. Camesasca, op. cit. 52; K. Oberhuber, *Vienna Jahrbuch*, 1962, 23 ff.

22. THE 'DONI TONDO'. By Michelangelo, *c.* 1505. Panel, diameter 120 cms. *Florence, Uffizi.* (Photograph: Soprintendenza alle Gallerie.)

Painted to celebrate the marriage of Angelo Doni and Maddalena Strozzi (in 1503 or early 1504), the general critical tendency has been to date the picture slightly after the event.

23. THE 'CANNING JEWEL'. Italian (?) sixteenth century. Pearl, diamond, enamel, etc. 10 x 7 cms. *London, Victoria and Albert Museum.* (Photograph: Museum.)

So-called because of being purchased by Earl Canning, in India in the mid nineteenth century and said to have been the gift of a Medici to an Indian prince. This story is unsubstantiated; the jewel may well be of German or Netherlandish origin.

24. ENAMEL DISH. By Pierre Reymond, *c.* 1560. *Luton Hoo, the late Sir Harold and Lady Zia Wernher Collection* (332). (Photograph: Museum.)

Reymond (*c.* 1513-*c.* 1584), one of a family of enamellers, specialized in grisaille ware; this example is decorated with Raphael's design of *The Judgement of Paris* engraved by Marc' Antonio and bears Reymond's initials.

25. S. EULALIA BEFORE HER JUDGE. By Bartolomé Ordóñez, *c.* 1518. Marble, 130 cms. *Barcelona, Cathedral.* (Photograph: Mas.)

The sculptor executed two reliefs of scenes from the saint's life in the trascoro of the cathedral at Barcelona; a third was executed after his design some fifty years later. He died at Carrara in 1520. The saint, the most famous virgin martyr of Spain, rebuked the local prefect for persecuting Christians.

Lit: M. E. Gómez Moreno, *Bartolomé Ordóñez*, 1956, 23-24.

26. SELF-PORTRAIT NAKED. By Albrecht Dürer, *c.* 1503. Pen and brush on paper, 29·2 x 15·4 cms. *Weimar, Schlossmuseum.* (Photograph: Museum.)

Easily the most remarkable even amid the range of Dürer's self-portraits, almost anticipatory of Egon Schiele's studies of himself.

Lit: C. White, *Dürer, The artist and his drawings*, 1971, 90.

27. NUDE STUDIES FOR 'THE BATTLE OF OSTIA'. By Raphael(?). Metal point and red chalk, 40·1 x 28·1 cms. *Vienna, Albertina.* (Photograph: Museum.)

Nowadays generally agreed to be by Raphael himself, as Dürer believed and so inscribed the drawing, dating it 1515.

Lit: K. Oberhuber, op. cit., 46-7.

28. A CONCERT. By Titian. *c.* 1512(?). Canvas, 108 x 122 cms. *Florence, Palazzo Pitti.* (Photograph: Anderson.)

Obviously early work but the exact date is not established. Previous suppositions that the picture is by, or was begun by, Giorgione are not now widely held, but Valcanover, loc. cit., postulates two hands on the picture.

Lit: F. Valcanover, *L'opera completa di Tiziano*, 1969, No. 42; Pallucchini, op. cit. 241.

29. THE RESURRECTION. Detail. By Titian, completed 1522. Panel, 278 x 122 cms. *Brescia, SS. Nazzaro e Celso.* (Photograph: Fiorentini.)
The Resurrection is the central panel of a five-part altarpiece, one panel being signed and dated 1522. It was commissioned by Altobello Averoldi, papal legate at Venice.
Lit: F. Valcanover, *L'opera completa di Tiziano*, 1969, No. 105, A–E.

30. THE STUDIO OF BANDINELLI. By Enea Vico after Bandinelli. Engraving, 31 x 48 cms. (Photograph: Trustees of the British Museum.)
Lit: N. Pevsner, *Academies Past and Present*, 1940, 40 ff.

31. AN ARTIST'S STUDIO. By Philippe Galle after Stradanus. Engraving. (Photograph: Trustees of the British Museum.)
Galle was active as a printer as well as engraver at Haarlem and then at Antwerp (where he settled probably *c.* 1557). He may have been the engraver of Bruegel's series of *Virtues* (pl. 94).

32a. THE DEAD CHRIST SUPPORTED BY NICODEMUS. By Baccio Bandinelli, completed 1559. Marble. *Florence, SS. Annunziata.* (Photograph: Alinari.)
Lit: Pope-Hennessy, 364–5.

32b. HEAD OF NICODEMUS. Detail of pl. 32a. (Photograph: Brogi.)

33. CANDELABRUM GROTESQUE. By Lucas van Leyden, 1528. Engraving, 12 x 7·6 cms. (Photograph: Trustees of the British Museum.)
Lit: F. W. H. Hollstein, *Dutch and Flemish Etchings, Engravings and Woodcuts*, Vol. x, n.d., 184.

34. MARY, QUEEN OF SCOTS. After François Clouet. Panel, 39 x 30 cms. *London, Wallace Collection.* (Photograph: Trustees of the Wallace Collection.)
Based on a drawing attributed to Clouet in the Bibliothèque Nationale, Paris.
Lit: *Wallace Collection Catalogues: Pictures and Drawings*, 1968, 67–8.

35. NYMPHS from the *Fontaine des Innocents*. By Jean Goujon, 1547–9. *Paris, Louvre.*
The Fontaine des Innocents was originally a rectangular building at a corner; most of its sculptured decoration is now in the Louvre.
Lit: Blunt, 125–7.

36. SABINA-POPPAEA. Mid sixteenth-century French School. Panel, 82·5 x 66 cms. *Geneva, Musée d'Art et d'Histoire.* (Photograph: Giraudon.)
The picture's inscribed title presumably refers to the Empress Poppaea, wife of Nero.
Lit: *L'Ecole de Fontainebleau* (exhibition cat.), Paris, 1972–3, No. 241.

37. YOUNG MAN STANDING AMID BRIARS. By Nicholas Hilliard, *c.* 1590. Miniature, 13.5 x 7 cms. *London, Victoria and Albert Museum.* (Photograph: Museum.)
Lit: E. Auerbach, *Nicholas Hilliard*, 1961, 103–9; G. Reynolds, *Nicholas Hilliard and Isaac Oliver*, 1971 ed., No. 38.

38. BUST OF THE DUKE OF ALBA. By Jacques Jonghelinck, 1571. Bronze, 116 cms. *New York, Frick Collection.* (Photograph: Museum.)
A valuable discussion of the giant related statue set up at Antwerp (destroyed) by J. Becker in *Simiolus*, v, 1971, 75 ff.
Lit: J. Pope-Hennessy, *The Frick Collection. An Illustrated Catalogue*, Vol. IV *Sculpture, German, Netherlandish, etc.*, 1970, 28–33.

39. PORTRAIT OF A MAN. By Giovanni Battista Moroni, 1554. Canvas, 185 x 115 cms. *Milan, Ambrosiana.* (Photograph: Anderson.)
The picture is dated on a piece of fallen masonry behind the sitter, whose non-chalance gives an almost amusing air to the tag from Horace, '*Impavidum ferient ruinae*' (*Odes*, III, iii, 7) inscribed on the plinth at the left.
Lit: A. Falchetti ed., *La Pinacoteca Ambrosiana*, 1969, 250–51.

40. VENUS AND ADONIS. By Titian, 1553. Canvas, 186 x 207 cms. *Madrid, Prado.*
(Photograph: Mas.)
Painted for the future Philip II of Spain and forwarded to England in 1554 at
the time of his marriage to Mary Tudor.
Lit: F. Valcanover, *L'opera completa di Tiziano*, 1969, No. 355; E. Panofsky,
Problems in Titian, mostly iconographic, 1969, 150 ff; Pallucchini, op. cit. 299-300.

41. THE FAMILY OF DARIUS BEFORE ALEXANDER. Detail. By Veronese. Canvas,
236 x 474 cms. *London, National Gallery.* (Photograph: Museum.)
Lit: C. Gould, *National Gallery Catalogues: The 16th century Venetian School,*
1959, 143-5.

42. 'THE AMBASSADORS'. Detail (perspective corrected). By Hans Holbein, 1533.
Panel, 207 x 209 cms. *London, National Gallery.* (Photograph: Museum.)
Lit: M. Levey, *National Gallery Catalogues: The German School*, 1959, 47-54.

43. HERCULES AND OMPHALE. By Lucas Cranach the Elder, 1537. Panel, 82 x
120 cms. *Brunswick, Gemäldegalerie.* (Photograph: Museum; B. P. Keiser.)
The subject was popular with Cranach and his studio. A patently humorous
touch is added by the contemporary costumes which Cranach gives to the
classical figures.
Lit: M. J. Friedländer and J. Rosenberg, *Die Gemälde von Lucas Cranach*, 1932,
70 (No. 225).

44. LUCRETIA. By Veronese, *c*. 1580. Canvas, 109 x 90 cms. *Vienna, Kunsthistorisches
Museum.* (Photograph: Fiorentini.)
Usually and reasonably dated late on stylistic grounds; the green drapery of
Lucretia, and surrounding drapery of the same colour, perhaps symbolize
fidelity.
Lit: G. Piovene and R. Marini, *L'opera completa del Veronese*, 1968, No. 213.

45. TOMB OF GIULIANO DE' MEDICI, DUKE OF NEMOURS. By Michelangelo.
Florence, S. Lorenzo. (Photograph: Soprintendenza alle Gallerie.)
The subject, brother of Pope Leo X, died in 1516; he was perhaps the commis-
sioner of Leonardo's *Mona Lisa.*
Lit: M. Weinberger, *Michelangelo the Sculptor*, 1967, 283 ff; Pope-Hennessy, 327 ff.

46. SATURN SWALLOWING A CHILD. By Caraglio after Rosso, 1526. Engraving.
(Photograph: John Freeman.)
Lit: E. Panofsky, *Studies in Iconology*, 1962 ed., 79.

47. EPITAPH FOR DR JOHANNES CUSPINIAN. Stone. *Vienna, St Stephen's.* (Photograph: Bildarchiv, Österreich Nationalbibliothek.)
Cuspinian (*see also* pl. 100) died in 1527; the designer of his monument is not
known.
Lit: E. Panofsky, *Tomb Sculpture*, 1964, 69.

48. BATTLE OF MARIGNANO. Detail of *Tomb of François I*. By Pierre Bontemps,
1551-2. *Paris, Saint-Denis.* (Photograph: Archives.)
The King died in 1547. His tomb was built by Philibert de l'Orme who gave the
sculptural portions – kneeling figures, *gisants* and bas-reliefs – to Bontemps.
Lit: M. Roy, *Artistes et monuments de la Renaissance française*, 1929, I, 157 ff.

49. DESIGN FOR LOWER PART OF THE JULIUS II TOMB. After Michelangelo. Pen.
East Berlin, State Museum. (Photograph: Museum.)
Related to Michelangelo's projects of 1505 or 1513.
Lit: L. Dussler, *Die Zeichnungen des Michelangelo*, 1959, 204.

50a. TOMB OF SANNAZARO. By Giovanni Montorsoli and Bartolommeo Ammanati.
Naples, S. Maria del Parto. (Photograph: Alinari.)
Jacopo Sannazaro (1456-1530) was the author of the *Arcadia.*
Lit: M. G. Ciardi Dupré, *Paragone*, 1961, No. 135, 7 ff.

50b. APOLLO. Detail of pl. 50a. (Photograph: Charles Davis.)
51. THE DYING SLAVE. By Michelangelo, 1513–16. Marble, height 229 cms. *Paris, Louvre*. (Photograph: Alinari.)
One of the sole pair of finished Slaves for the tomb of Julius II; the figure is more probably awakening from sleep than dying.
Lit: Pope-Hennessy, 322.
52. THE PROPHET JOEL. By Michelangelo, 1508–10. Detail from the Sistine Chapel ceiling. *Rome, Vatican*. (Photograph: Alinari.)
Lit: C. Seymour, *Michelangelo, the Sistine Chapel Ceiling*, 1972.
53. PUTTO WITH HELMET. By Conrad Meit, *c*. 1526. Detail from Tomb of Philibert of Savoy. *Bourg-en-Bresse, Church of Brou*. (Photograph: Archives.)
Philibert died in 1504; his tomb, with that of his mother, Margaret of Bourbon, and his widow, Margaret of Austria, Regent of the Netherlands, forms a complex commissioned by the latter.
Lit: E. Panofsky, *Tomb Sculpture*, 1964, 78–9.
54. THE 'HOLY HOUSE'. Designed by Bramante, *c*. 1510. *Loreto, Duomo*. (Photograph: Alinari.)
A model had been prepared to Bramante's design by 1510. Various sculptors were responsible for the existing reliefs (cf. Pope-Hennessy, loc. cit.)
Lit: A. Bruschi, *Bramante architetto*, 1969, 960 ff.; Pope-Hennessy, 347–9.
55. THE CHIGI CHAPEL. Designed by Raphael, *c*. 1513. *Rome, S. Maria del Popolo*. (Photograph: Alinari.)
Most fully discussed by Shearman, loc. cit. On the cupola of the chapel is the date 1516.
Lit: J. Shearman in *J.W.C.I.*, XXIV, 1961, 129 ff.
56. STUDY FOR THE TOMB OF THE MEDICI MAGNIFICI. By Michelangelo (?). Black chalk and brown ink on paper, 37·9 x 24·2 cms. *Paris, Louvre, Cabinet des Dessins*. (Photograph: Courtauld Institute.)
Sometimes accepted as merely from the circle of Michelangelo. Its attribution to the artist himself is proposed, along with fresh examination of the Medici tombs and chapel, by Joannides, loc. cit.
Lit: P. Joannides in *Burlington Magazine*, CXIV, 1972, 541 ff.
57. THE DOME OF THE CHIGI CHAPEL. By Raphael, *c*. 1513. *Rome, S. Maria del Popolo*. (Photograph: Alinari.)
See under ill. 55 for literature.
58. TOMB OF CASTIGLIONE. By Giulio Romano. *Mantua environs, Chiesa delle Grazie*. (Photograph: Giovetti Mantova.)
For Castiglione, see under ill. 4.
Lit: A. Venturi, *Storia dell'Arte Italiana: Architettura del Cinquecento*, I, 1938, 323–5.
59. CARACCIOLO DI VICO TOMB. Diego Ordóñez, before 1544. *Naples, S. Giovanni a Carbonara*. (Photograph: Anderson.)
Lit: M. E. Gomez-Moreno, *Bartolomé Ordóñez*, 1956, 21–3.
60a. VALENTINE BALBIANI RECLINING ON HER TOMB. Detail. By Germain Pilon, before 1583. Marble. *Paris, Louvre*. (Photograph: Giraudon.)
The subject died in 1572. Her tomb was commissioned by her husband René de Birague for his chapel in Ste Catherine du Val-des Écoliers, Paris; he died in 1583, and his own tomb was executed by Pilon at the expense of his heirs.
Lit: J. Babelon, *Germain Pilon*, 1927, 67 (for epitaph on Valentine Balbiani's dog, referred to in text); Blunt, 149–151.
60b. VALENTINE BALBIANI TOMB. Detail. (Photograph: Giraudon.)

61. ELENA SAVELLI MONUMENT. Detail. By Jacopo del Duca, *c.* 1570. Bronze and stone. *Rome, St John Lateran.* (Photograph: Anderson.)

The subject died in 1570, and the monument may be supposed to be of about that date.

Lit: A. Venturi, *Storia dell'Arte Italiana: La Scultura del Cinquecento,* II, 1936, 171 ff.

62. LEO X ENTHRONED AS CLEMENT I. By Giulio Romano, 1520-24. Fresco. *Rome, Vatican, Sala di Costantino.* (Photograph: Anderson.)

One of a series of Popes enthroned and accompanied by Virtues which flank the feigned tapestries in the room. Giulio Romano had several assistants on the frescoes and his active part can be either denied or urged strongly. The concept of the enthroned figures is well discussed by Freedberg, loc. cit.

Lit: S. J. Freedberg, *Painting of the High Renaissance in Rome and Florence,* 1961, 570 ff.

63a. S. STEPHEN. Studio of Botticelli. 1481-2. Fresco, 210 x 80 cms. *Rome, Vatican, Sistine Chapel.* (Photograph: Alinari.)

63b. S. SIXTUS II. Studio of Botticelli. 1481-2. Fresco, 210 x 80 cms. *Rome, Vatican, Sistine Chapel.* (Photograph: Alinari.)

The two Popes are typical in composition of the standing figures of the Popes in niches above the late fifteenth-century frescoes in the Chapel. This pair in particular is reasonably associated in execution with Botticelli and may in some part be autograph.

Lit: C. Bo and G. Mandel, *L'opera completa del Botticelli,* 1967, Nos. 63 F & G.

64. TOMB OF POPE PAUL III. By Guglielmo della Porta. Set up, 1575. Marble and bronze. *Rome, St Peter's.* (Photograph: Anderson.)

Commissioned in 1549 after the death of the Pope who had, however, already purchased from the sculptor a decorated marble base, etc. for his tomb.

Lit: Pope-Hennessy, 398-9.

65. DESIGNS FOR A MONUMENT TO PAUL IV. By Guglielmo della Porta, *c.* 1556-8. *Düsseldorf, Akademie.* (Photograph: Museum.)

Earlier supposed to be related to the project for Porta's tomb for Paul III, this sheet is shown by Gramberg, loc. cit., to be connected with some project for a tomb for Paul IV (Caraffa), probably *c.* 1556-8, during his lifetime therefore and conceivably intended for S. Maria sopra Minerva.

Lit: W. Gramberg, *Die Düsseldorfer Skizzenbücher des Guglielmo della Porta,* 1964, text vol., 78-9 (No. 135).

66. ALLEGORIES OF PEACE, ABUNDANCE AND JUSTICE. By Barthélemy Prieur, 1573-8. Bronze, *c.* 125 cms. each. From the monument of the heart of the Constable Anne de Montmorency. *Paris, Louvre.* (Photograph: Archives.)

Set up at the posthumous wish of Henri II in the church of the Célestins. The monument was designed by Bullant, accompanied by Prieur's Allegories. The Constable had died in 1567.

Lit: C. Day, *G.B.A.,* II, 1928, 62-74.

67. MONUMENT OF THE MARQUESS OF MARIGNANO. By Leone Leoni, completed 1563. Marble and bronze. *Milan, Duomo.*

Gian Giacomo de' Medici, Marquess of Marignano, died in 1555. The monument was commissioned in 1560 after his brother had become Pope Pius IV. Some involvement by Michelangelo in the monument's design has been both argued for and denied.

Lit: Pope-Hennessy, 401-2.

68. JACOB FUGGER TOMB. By Sebastian Loscher, 1511-18. Stone, 350 cms. *Augsburg, St Anna.*

Jacob II Fugger 'the Rich', (1459-1525). Designs for the Fugger tombs were begun in the second decade of the sixteenth century; among artists involved was almost certainly Dürer.

Lit: N. Lieb, *Die Fugger und die Kunst im Zeitalter der Spätgotik und der Früher Renaissance*, 1952, 135 ff.

69. MONUMENTS TO THE COUNTS OF WÜRTEMBURG. By Simon Schlör, begun, 1578. Stone. *Stuttgart, Stiftskirche.* (Photograph: Landesdenkmalamt Baden-Württemburg, Stuttgart.)

Schlör's original drawings for the scheme are at Budapest. The monuments were completed in 1584.

Lit: T. Demmler, *Die Grabdenkmäler des Württembergischen Fürstenhauses . . .*, 1910, 225 ff.

70. ELIZABETH OF GÖRZ. By Gilg Sesselschreiber, 1516. Bronze, 212 cms. *Innsbruck, Hofkirche.* (Photograph: Vincenz Oberhammer.)

The Empress Elizabeth, wife of Albrecht I, was the great-great-great grandmother of the Emperor Maximilian I who commissioned from 1502 onwards a series of 28 statues of his ancestors for his own tomb and as a Habsburg memorial; many were certainly executed by Sesselschreiber and his studio, and may have been designed by him.

Lit: V. Oberhammer, *Die Bronzestandbilder des Maximiliangrabmales in der Hofkirche zu Innsbruck*, 1935.

71. PROCESSIONAL CAR OF FAME FOR HENRI II'S ENTRY INTO ROUEN. 1550. Woodcut. (Photograph: John Freeman.)

From the *Entrée de Henri II à Rouen* (1551) by Robert le Hoy and Robert and Jehan du Gord.

72. ANDREA DORIA. (mutilated fragment) by Giovanni Montorsoli, *c.* 1540-45. *Genoa, Cloister of S. Matteo.* (Photograph: Alinari.)

The colossal statue, which stood in front of the Ducal Palace, was overthrown in 1797 and badly damaged.

Lit: A. Venturi, op. cit., II, 1936, 127.

73. TOMMASO RANGONE. By Jacopo Sansovino (?), completed by 1557. Bronze. *Venice, S. Giuliano.* (Photograph: Alinari.)

Rangone originally gave the commission for this statue of himself to Sansovino, but the documents show that Vittoria was involved by 1556.

Lit: R. Gallo in *Saggi e Memorie di storia dell' arte*, I, 1957, 101 ff.; Pope-Hennessy, 409-10.

74. CHARLES V RESTRAINING FURY. By Leone Leoni, commenced 1549. Bronze, 174 cms. *Madrid, Prado.* (Photograph: Mas.)

Commissioned in 1549; these two figures were cast in 1549 and 1553 respectively. The group was completed in Spain by Leoni's son, Pompeo, in 1564.

75. PHILIP II AND HIS FAMILY. By Pompeo Leoni, completed 1598. Bronze. *Escorial, S. Lorenzo, Capilla Mayor.* (Photograph: Mas.)

Bronze groups of himself with his immediate family, and of his father Charles with his, were commissioned as funerary monuments by Philip II, and are first mentioned in 1591 by Leoni as projected. By 1597 the Charles V group was cast; the Philip II group was ordered for the following year and was set up in May 1598. Philip II died at the Escorial in September of the same year.

Lit: Pope-Hennessy, 403-4.

76. 'COL TEMPO'. By Giorgione. Canvas, 68 x 59 cms. *Venice, Accademia.* (Photograph: Anderson.)

Uncontestedly recognized as by Giorgione; dates from 1506 to 1508 have been proposed. Conceivably the Giorgione listed as of his mother in the Gabriele Vendramin inventory (1569).

Lit: T. Pignatti, *Giorgione*, n.d. but 1970, 111.

77. NINE AGES OF MAN. By Jörg Breu the Younger, 1540. Engraving. (Photograph: John Freeman.)

Lit: R. van Marle, *Iconographie de l'Art Profane . . .*, 1971 ed., 11, 160.

78. TEMPERANCE. By Michel Colombe, 1499-1507. Marble, *c.* 160 cms. *Nantes, Cathedral.* (Photograph: Archives.)

One of the four Virtues sculpted by Colombe for the tomb of François II of Brittany and Marguerite de Foix.

Lit: E. Panofsky, *Tomb Sculpture*, 1964, 75-6.

79. TIME. English. Woodcut. 1509. (Photograph: Trustees of the British Museum.)

From Stephen Hawes, *The Pastime of Pleasure* (1509).

80. TOMB OF RENÉ DE CHÂLONS. Attributed to Ligier Richier, after 1544. Marble. *Bar-le-duc, St-Pierre.* (Cast of the figure).

The sculptor of this tomb is not certainly established. Richier was active largely in the service of the Dukes of Lorraine and had a style of pungent, 'neo-Gothic' realism combined with Italianate elements.

Lit: Blunt, 130-31.

81. STUDIES OF A SKELETON. By Leonardo da Vinci, *c.* 1510. Pen on paper, 28·5 x 19·5 cms. *Windsor Castle, Royal Library.* Reproduced by gracious permission of H. M. The Queen.

Lit: K. Clark and C. Pedretti, *Leonardo da Vinci Anatomical Drawings . . . Windsor*, 1969, 6-7.

82. MUSCLES OF THE HUMAN BODY. From Vesalius, *De humani corporis fabrica*, 1543. Woodcut. (Photograph: Trustees of the British Museum.)

83. DEATHBED OF HENRI II OF FRANCE, 1559. Woodcut.

From J. Tortorel and J. Perrissin, *Les grands scènes historiques du XVIᵉ siècle*, pl. vii.

84. INDIANS OF VIRGINIA FISHING. By John White, 1585-7. Watercolour. *London, British Museum* (1906-5-9-1 (6)). (Photograph: Trustees of the British Museum.)

One of a series of drawings made by White, when official artist on Sir Walter Raleigh's expedition (1585) or when Governor of the Colony in 1587.

Lit: P. Hulton, D. B. Quinn and others, *The American Drawings of John White*, 1964.

85. THE ESCORIAL. By Juan Bautista de Toledo and Francisco de Herrera, 1563-84. (Photograph: Courtauld Institute.)

The possible hermetic significance of the building, and Juan Bautista de Toledo's specific interests in the occult, are discussed by Taylor, loc. cit.

Lit: R. Taylor, 'Architecture and Magic' in *Essays in the History of Architecture presented to Rudolf Wittkower*, 1967, 81-109.

86. A DEVICE FOR RAISING A SUNKEN SHIP. From Cardano's *De Subtilitate Rerum*, 1551. Woodcut.

87. SALA DELLE PROSPETTIVE. By Baldassare Peruzzi, *c.* 1517-18. Fresco. *Rome, Farnesina.*

Lit: C. L. Frommel, *Baldassare Peruzzi als Maler und Zeichner*, 1968, 87 ff.

88. THE 'GREAT PIECE OF TURF'. By Albrecht Dürer, 1503. Watercolour. 41 x 31·5 cms. *Vienna, Albertina.* (Photograph: Museum.)

The watercolour is dated at the lower right.

Lit: C. White, *Dürer, the artist and his drawings*, 1971, No. 33.

89. THE PLANT CHRYSANTHEMUM LEUCANTHEMUM (ox-eye daisy). From Fuchs, *De historia stirpium commentarii*, 1542. (Photograph: Trustees of the British Museum.)

90. THE SPHERIC UNIVERSE. From Copernicus, *De Revolutionibus Orbium Coelestium,*
   1543. Woodcut. (Photograph: Trustees of the British Museum.)
   Lit: O. Benesch, *The Art of the Renaissance in Northern Europe,* 1965 ed., 144 ff.
91. THE BATTLE OF ISSUS. By Albrecht Altdorfer, 1529. Panel, 158·4 x 120·3 cms.
   Munich, Alte Pinakothek. (Photograph: Bayerische Staatsgemäldesammlungen.)
   One of a series of antique battle pictures painted by different artists for Duke
   William IV of Bavaria. This battle was a victory of Alexander the Great's over
   the Persians led by Darius.
   Lit: C. A. zu Salm and G. Goldberg, ed. H. Soehner, *Alte Pinakothek, München:
   Altdeutsche Malerei,* 1963, 205 ff.
92a. Detail of 92b.
92b. THE THREE PHILOSOPHERS. By Giorgione. Canvas, 123·3 x 144·5 cms. *Vienna,
   Kunsthistorisches Museum.* (Photograph: Fiorentini.)
   First recorded in 1525 by Michiel (*Notizia d'opere,* ed. T. Frimmel, 1888, 86) as
   of '*3 phylosophi nel paese . . . uno sentado che contempla gli raggi solari*'; he says it was
   begun by Giorgione, finished by Sebastiano del Piombo. Date, subject and the
   degree of intervention by Sebastiano have all been much discussed.
   Lit: T. Pignatti, *Giorgione,* n.d. but 1970, 104-5.
93. CHARON CROSSING THE STYX. By Joachim Patenier. Panel, 64 x 103 cms. *Madrid,
   Prado.* (Photograph: Mas.)
   Stylistically, late work. The picture was among those by Patenier acquired by
   Philip II.
   Lit: R. A. Koch, *Joachim Patinir,* 1968, 78 (No. 19).
94. ALLEGORY OF TEMPERANCE. After Pieter Bruegel the Elder. (Photograph:
   Trustees of the British Museum.)
   A preparatory drawing (date 1560) is in the Boymans-van Beuningen Museum,
   Rotterdam.
   Lit: R. van Bastelaer, *Les Estampes de Peter Bruegel l'ancien,* 1908, No. 138.
95. THE HAY HARVEST (JULY). Detail. By Pieter Bruegel the Elder, *c.* 1565. Canvas,
   117 x 161 cms. *Prague, National Gallery.* (Photograph: Giraudon.)
   One of Bruegel's series of paintings of the Months, of which the others are
   dated 1565. They were commissioned by Niclaes Jonghelinck, brother of the
   sculptor (cf. pl. 38).
   Lit: F. Grossmann, *Bruegel, The Paintings,* n.d. but *c.* 1955, 197-8.
96. THE GLOOMY DAY (FEBRUARY). By Pieter Bruegel the Elder, 1565. Canvas,
   118 x 163 cms. *Vienna, Kunsthistorisches Museum.* (Photograph: Museum.)
   Lit: F. Grossmann, loc. cit.
97. PORTRAIT OF AEGIDIUS. By Quentin Massys, 1517. Canvas, 73·75 x 55·25 cms.
   Private Collection.
   Lit: M. J. Friedländer, *Early Netherlandish Painting,* VII, 1971, No. 37.
98. PORTRAIT OF NIKOLAUS KRATZER. By Hans Holbein, 1528. Panel, 83 x 67 cms.
   Paris, Louvre. (Photograph: Service de Documentation Photographique.)
   The German-born sitter (1478-1550) entered the service of Henry VIII, belonged
   in the circle of Sir Thomas More and was in touch with such contemporaries
   as Dürer.
   Lit: P. Ganz, *The Paintings of Hans Holbein the Younger,* 1950, 233.
99. PORTRAIT OF AN APOTHECARY. By Bartolommeo Passarotti, *c.* 1570. Canvas,
   101 x 82·8 cms. *Rome, Galleria Spada.* (Photograph: Anderson.)
   The significance of gesture in this and other portraits by Passarotti is discussed
   by Heinz, loc. cit.
   Lit: F. Zeri, *La Galleria Spada in Roma,* 1954, 105; G. Heinz in Vienna *Jahrbuch,*
   1972, 161.

100. JOHANNES CUSPINIAN. By Lucas Cranach, *c.* 1502–3. Panel, 59 x 45 cms. *Winterthur, Reinhart Foundation.*

Originally a diptych with a portrait of the sitter's first wife Anna (also Reinhart Foundation); Cuspinian's arms are on the back of the present portrait. Cuspinian (actual name Spiessheimer) was born in 1473; died 1529 (see pl. 47).

Lit: M. J. Friedländer and J. Rosenberg, *Die Gemälde von Lucas Cranach*, 1932, 28 (6, 7).

101. STUDY OF AN EMBRYO IN THE WOMB. By Leonardo da Vinci, *c.* 1510–12. Pen and ink, 30·1 x 21·4 cms. *Windsor, Royal Library* (19102 recto). Reproduced by gracious permission of H.M. The Queen.

Notes on the subject accompany the drawing, with further small sketches.

Lit: Clark and Pedretti, op. cit., 1969, 40.

102. VISION IN A DREAM. By Albrecht Dürer, 1525. Pen and watercolour, 30 x 42·5 cms. *Vienna, Kunsthistorisches Museum.* (Photograph: Museum.)

Dürer wrote a description under the drawing, noting the occasion of his dream on the night between Wednesday and Thursday after Whitsunday (30–31 May) 1525, describing it and signing the description.

Lit: White, op. cit., No. 102.

103. THE RISEN CHRIST. By Grünewald, *c.* 1515. Panel, 269 x 143 cms. *Colmar, Unterlinden Museum.* (Photograph: Museum.)

104. THE SUPPER AT EMMAUS. By Jacopo Pontormo, 1525. Canvas, 230 x 173 cms. *Florence, Uffizi.* (Photograph: Alinari.)

Praised by Vasari for its unexaggerated naturalness. It has been suggested (G. Nicco Fasola, *Alcune revisioni sul Pontormo*, 1957, 9 ff.) that the Eye of the Trinity was possibly painted by Jacopo da Empoli, to replace too human a depiction of the Trinity by Pontormo.

Lit: L. Berti, *L'opera completa del Pontormo*, 1973, No. 85.

105. DIOGENES. By Ugo da Carpi after Parmigianino. Chiaroscuro woodcut. *London, British Museum.* (Photograph: Trustees of the British Museum.)

Lit: A. Bartsch, *Le Peintre-Graveur*, XII, vi, 100 (10).

106. THE ASTROLOGER. By Giulio Campagnola, 1509. Engraving, 9·9 x 15·2 cms. *London, British Museum.* (Photograph: Trustees of the British Museum.)

Lit: A. M. Hind, *Early Italian Engraving*, Pt II, Vol. V, 1948, 198–9.

107. TWO WITCHES. By Hans Baldung, 1523. Panel, 65 x 45 cms. *Frankfurt, Städel-Institut.* (Photograph: Busch-Hanck.)

108. MELISSA. By Dosso Dossi. Canvas, 176 x 174 cms. *Rome, Galleria Borghese.* (Photograph: Anderson.)

The dating is uncertain, but Gibbons, loc. cit. suggests around 1520. The subject has been much discussed, but seems rightly identified as Ariosto's Melissa (*Orlando furioso*, 1516).

Lit: F. Gibbons, *Dosso and Battista Dossi*, 1968, 198–200.

109. FOREST FIRE. Detail. By Piero di Cosimo. Panel, 71 x 203 cms. *Oxford, Ashmolean Museum.* (Photograph: Museum.)

Lit: M. Bacci, *Piero di Cosimo*, 1966, 74.

110. LANDSCAPE WITH A FORTRESS. By Wolf Huber. Pen and ink, 19·1 x 13 cms. *Berlin-Dahlem, State Museum, Print Room.* (Photograph: Walter Steinkopf.)

Perhaps in part an imaginary landscape; a date around 1511–13 is usually agreed.

Lit: F. Anzelewski, *Dürer and his time* (exhibition catalogue), Washington, 1967, No. 135.

111. ROCKY FOREST LANDSCAPE. By Girolamo Muziano. Pen and ink. *Florence, Uffizi.* (Photograph: Soprintendenza alle Gallerie.)

Lit: U. Procacci, *Arte Veneta*, 1954, 246.

112. NEPTUNE FOUNTAIN. By Giovanni Montorsoli, finished 1557. *Messina*. (Photograph: Alinari.)

The original fountain was largely destroyed in the earthquake of 1908 and the figure of Neptune now in position is a copy, as is the subsidiary figure of Scylla (damaged but still vigorously fine original in the Museo Nazionale, Messina). The fountain was the second of the two executed at Messina by Montorsoli; the first, that of Orion, was the commission which brought the sculptor to Messina in 1547.

Lit: Pope-Hennessy, 357-8.

113. PALAZZO FARNESE. Rome. By Antonio da Sangallo the Younger and Michelangelo, first planned *c*. 1513. (Photograph: Anderson.)

Begun by Sangallo for Cardinal Farnese (who became Pope Paul III in 1534). A competition was held by the Pope for the design of the cornice, which was won by Michelangelo who completed the whole palace after Sangallo's death in 1546. Lit: G. Giovannoni, *Andrea da Sangallo il Giovane*, 1959, I, 150 ff.; Ackerman, op. cit. I, 75 ff.; II, 67 ff.

114. TITLE PAGE OF 'IL MODO DE TEMPERARE LE PENNE'. By Ludovico Vicentino, 1523. *London, British Museum Library*. (Photograph: John Freeman.)

Published at Rome and one of the most influential of all writing books.

115. A LUTE-PLAYER. By Cariani (Giovanni Busi). Canvas, 71 x 65 cms. *Strasbourg, Musée des Beaux-Arts*. (Photograph: Giraudon.)

The date of execution is uncertain, but the Giorgionesque air of the picture is obvious. Cariani died in 1548.

Lit: *Le seizième Siècle Européen* (exhibition catalogue) Paris, 1965-6, No. 62.

116. THREES LADIES PLAYING MUSIC. By the Master of the Female Half-Lengths. Panel, 40 x 33 cms. *Schloss Rohrau, Graf Harrach Collection*. (Photograph: Museum.)

The painter is named from this and comparable pictures, usually of single figures, in the same style, and is presumed to have been active at Antwerp during the first half of the sixteenth century. The text of the music-book is a poem of Marot's, set by several composers and here in the version by Claudin de Sermisy (1490-1562). In this version it also appears in a single figure picture, by the Master, in the Robert Finck collection, Brussels.

Lit: *le Siècle de Bruegel* (exhibition catalogue), Brussels, 1963, No. 245.

117. CAMERA DEGLI AMORINI. Detail. By Girolamo Genga and Dosso Dossi. Fresco. *Pesaro, Villa Imperiale*. (Photograph: Georgina Masson, *Italian Villas and Palaces,* Thames & Hudson.)

Lit: B. Patzak, *Die Villa Imperiale in Pesaro*, 1908.

118. NYMPHAEUM OF THE VILLA GIULIA, ROME. By Bartolommeo Ammanati. See under pl. 132. (Photograph: Anderson.)

119. DESIGNS FOR GARDENS. From *Regole generali di architettura*, by Sebastiano Serlio, Book IV, 1537. Woodcut. (Photograph: Trustees of the British Museum.)

120. THE LIBRARY, (exterior), VENICE. By Jacopo Sansovino, begun 1537. (Photograph: Anderson.)

The project of a public library at Venice goes back to the donation of Cardinal Bessarion who bequeathed his library to the Republic in 1468. The final decision to construct the Library, '*secundum formam et modum modelli facti seu fiendi per dominum Jacobum Sansovinum . . .*', was taken on 6 March 1537. The progress and vicissitudes of the work occupied many years, and it was not finished until well after Sansovino's death (1570); the books had been moved into it in 1558. The concept, significance and urban setting of the Library have been much studied in recent years (notably by W. Lotz, e.g. in *Festschrift Wolfgang Schubert,* 1967, 336 ff.).

Lit: M. Tafuri, *Jacopo Sansovino e l'architettura del'500 a Venezia,* n.d. but 1970, 53 ff.

121. GARDEN FRONT OF THE PALAZZO DEL TE, MANTUA. By Giulio Romano. (Photograph: Giovetti Mantova.)

Lit: C. Paccagnini, *I. Palazzo del Te,* 1957.

122. THE VIA GIULIA, ROME.

Opened up *c.* 1508 during the pontificate of Julius II, under the direction of Bramante, as part of Julius's replanning of the city. Vasari, in his life of Bramante, explicitly uses the words '*da Bramante indirrizata*' about the new strada Giulia where Bramante built the Palazzo dei Tribunali and a new church of S. Biagio (both now destroyed).

Lit: A. Bruschi, *Bramante architetto,* 1969, 946 ff.

123. THE VIA GARIBALDI, GENOA. (Photograph: Brogi.)

Originally called the 'Strada Nuova', begun in 1550 by Bernadino Cantone da Cabio. Sites were rapidly taken in the sixteenth century by noble families for their palaces, surviving today, though later palaces have also been built.

Lit: *Genova, Strada Nuova,* ed. L. Vagnetti, 1967; E. Poleggi, *Strada Nuova,* 1968.

124. SQUARE COURT OF THE LOUVRE, PARIS. By Pierre Lescot, begun 1546.

The new palace of the Louvre was commissioned by François I, and the original plan was for a building of only two floors; the façade was heightened finally by the addition of a third floor.

Lit: Blunt, 79–82.

125. DESIGN FOR A FIREPLACE. From *Regole generali di architettura.* By Sebastiano Serlio, Book IV, 1537. Woodcut.

126. FIDES. By Colyn de Nole, 1543–5. Sandstone, height 68 cms. *Kampen, Town Hall.* Part of the elaborate fireplace decoration (with six statues of Virtues).

Lit: M. Casteels, *De beeldhouwers de Nole de Kamerijk,* 1961, 77 ff.

127. COURTYARD OF THE PALAZZO MARINO, MILAN. By Galeazzo Alessi, *c.* 1558. (Photograph: Alinari.)

Built for a Genoese merchant, Tommaso Marini, and hence the use of a Genoese architect.

128. EXTERIOR OF THE MAISON MILSAND, DIJON. By Hugues Sambin, *c.* 1561. (Photograph: Archives.)

Lit: Blunt, 146.

129. GATEWAY OF THE CHÂTEAU OF ANET. By Philibert de l'Orme, *c.* 1552. (Photograph: Archives.)

The château was commissioned in 1547 by Diane de Poitiers, mistress of the future Henri II; much of it is now destroyed.

Lit: Blunt, 88–91.

130. COURTYARD OF KIRBY HALL, NORTHAMPTONSHIRE. 1570–75. (Photograph: National Monuments Record.)

Partly altered in the 17th century and now ruined.

Lit: J. Summerson, *Architecture in Britain 1530–1830,* 1963 ed., 18–19.

131. COURTYARD OF THE PALACE, GRANADA. By Pedro Machuca, begun 1527. (Photograph: Giraudon.)

Started for Charles V as a summer palace but left unfinished for many years; the upper portion was added in 1616.

Lit: G. Kubler and M. Soria, *Art and Architecture in Spain and Portugal ... 1500–1800,* 1959, 10–11.

132. COURTYARD OF THE VILLA GIULIA, ROME. By Vignola, begun 1550. (Photograph: Anderson.)

The villa was begun by Vignola for Julius III; Ammanati was also involved in the work, as was Vasari. The Pope himself appears to have taken a hand in the plans and additionally Michelangelo was consulted. A fundamental article by Coolidge is cited below and a more recent one, with important documentation, is Falk's.

Lit: J. Coolidge in *A.B.*, 1943, 177–225; T. Falk in *Römisches Jahrbuch für Kunstgeschichte*, 1971, 101 ff.

133. NAVE OF THE REDENTORE, VENICE. By Andrea Palladio, 1576–7. (Photograph: Dearborn Massar.)

The church was founded by a decree of the Senate on delivery of Venice from the plague of 1575–6.

Lit: W. Timofiewitsch, *La Chiesa del Redentore* (Corpus Palladianum, III), 1969.

134ab. DIVES AND LAZARUS. By Bonifazio Pitati. Canvas, 205 x 437 cms. *Venice, Accademia.* (Photograph: Alinari.)

Lit: S. Moschini Marconi, *Gallerie dell' Accademia di Venezia: Opere d' Arte del Secolo XVI*, 1962, 35–6.

135. VILLA SAREGO, SANTA SOFIA. By Andrea Palladio, *c.* 1568–9. (Photograph: Dearborn Massar.)

Lit: P. Gazzola, *La Villa Sarego di Santa Sofia di Pedemonte* (Corpus Palladianum volume in preparation).

136. VILLA EMO. By Andrea Palladio, 1550s. (Photograph: Dearborn Massar.)

Lit: G. P. Bordignon Favero, *La Villa Emo di Fanzolo* (Corpus Palladianum, V), 1970.

137. THE MARRIAGE AT CANA. By Veronese, 1562–3. Canvas, 669 x 990 cms. *Paris, Louvre.* (Photograph: Alinari.)

Painted for the Refectory of the Benedictine monastery of S. Giorgio Maggiore commissioned in 1562 and completed by 1563.

Lit: G. Piovene and R. Marini, *L'opera completa del Veronese*, 1968, No. 91.

138. THE MARRIAGE AT CANA. Detail. (Photograph: Alinari.)

The tradition that this group shows Veronese, Titian and Tintoretto seems no earlier than Zanetti in the eighteenth century. It is usually accepted without question but should be treated with caution.

139. BELVEDERE COURTYARD, VATICAN, ROME. Begun by Bramante.

Begun under Julius II, possibly as early as 1503–4. The vast scheme was to link the Vatican Palace to the Belvedere (a small summerhouse); it was much altered in the sixteenth century and the intended vista interrupted by building across the courtyard.

Lit: J. Ackerman, *The Cortile del Belvedere*, 1954; Bruschi, op. cit. 865 ff.

140. DRAGON PENDANT. Spanish, sixteenth century. *London, Victoria and Albert Museum* (M.536–1910). (Photograph: Museum.)

141. S. HILARION. By Correggio. Fresco, 1526–8. *Parma, Duomo.* (Photograph: Alinari.)

One of the four spandrels, surrounding the cupola fresco of the *Assumption*.

Lit: Bianconi, op. cit., 41 ff.; Bevilacqua and Quintavalle, op. cit, No. 69B.

142. SALT-CELLAR. By Benvenuto Cellini, 1540–43. Gold and enamel, 33·5 cms. *Vienna, Kunsthistorisches Museum.* (Photograph: Museum.)

Lit: B. Cellini, *Autobiography*, 1949 ed., 249–51.

143. DESIGN FOR A CLOCK. By Hans Holbein, 1543 (?). Pen and ink, 41·6 x 21·9 cms. *London, British Museum* (1870-7-13-14). (Photograph: Trustees of the British Museum.)

Inscribed by Sir Anthony Denny, stating that the clock was intended as a New Year's gift to Henry VIII in 1544; Holbein died in 1543.

Lit: A. Woltmann, *Holbein und seine Zeit*, 1874 ed., II, 134.

144. CASKET. Details. By Valeriano Belli, 1532. Rock-crystal, silver-gilt and enamel. *Florence, Museo degli Argenti*. (Photograph: Alinari.)

Executed for Pope Clement VII. The scenes from the life of Christ concentrate on the Passion; several are signed. The casket bears the Pope's arms and the date 1532.

Lit: E. Kris, *Steinschneidekunst in der italienischen Renaissance*, 1929, I, 51 (date given as 1537, by a misprint).

145. WHEEL-LOCK PISTOL. Detail. German, *c.* 1550. Length 65 cms. *Vienna, Kunsthistorisches Museum*. (Photograph: Museum.)

The stock is decorated with a classical scene of Mucius Scaevola putting his hand in the brazier, unlike the more usual hunting and sporting scenes. The pistol was executed for Archduke Ferdinand II of Tyrol.

Lit: *Meisterwerke* (Kunsthistorisches Museum), 1968, No. 171.

146. PARTHENICE. Detail. By Filippino Lippi. Fresco. *Florence, S. Maria Novella, Strozzi Chapel*. (Photograph: Anderson.)

147. NEPTUNE DOORKNOCKER. By Alessandro Vittoria Bronze, 41 x 28 cms. *Venice, Civico Museo Correr*.

This example comes from the Palazzo Cernazei, Udine; variants of the design are known.

Lit: G. Mariacher in *Bollettino dei Musei Civici Veneziani*, 1966, No. 1, 24.

148. DESIGNS FOR A LECTERN. By Perino del Vaga. Bistre, pen and wash, 25 x 34·4 cms. *London, Courtauld Institute, Witt Collection*. (Photograph: Museum.)

Lit: *Decorative Arts of the Italian Renaissance 1400–1600* (exhibition catalogue), Detroit, 1958–9, No. 12.

149. DESIGN FOR A CEREMONIAL CHAIR. By Peter Flötner. Pen and ink, heightened with watercolour, 18·6 x 15·6 cms. *Berlin, State Museum, Print Room*. (Photograph: Walter Steinkopf.)

Other furniture and allied designs by Flötner are known. Two for organs are dated 1527 and this period approximately seems correct for the present design.

Lit: F. Anzelewski, *Dürer and his time* (exhibition catalogue), Washington, 1967, No. 80.

150. POLYCHROME DISH. By Francesco Xanto, 1533. Diameter, 46·5 cms. *London, Victoria and Albert Museum*. (Photograph: Museum.)

Decorated with the *Marriage of Alexander and Roxana* after Raphael as engraved by Marco Dente da Ravenna. The arms are those of Margherita of Montferrat, wife of Federico Gonzaga, Duke of Mantua.

Lit: B. Rackham, *Catalogue of Italian Maiolica* (V. & A. Museum), 1940, No. 63.

151. ROCK-CRYSTAL CUP. Workshop of the Saracchi. Height 31·5 cms. *Florence, Museo degli, Argenti*. (Photograph: Alinari.)

The Saracchi family was active in Milan, producing crystal *objets d'art* comparable to this, and was patronized by the Medici (in whose collection this item is recorded in 1589).

Lit: F. Rossi, *Capolavori di Oreficeria Italiana . . .*, 1956, pl. XLIX.

152. GALERIE FRANÇOIS I, Fontainebleau. By Rosso, *c.* 1533–40.

Lit: Blunt, 62–4.

153. DISH WITH WATER-SNAKE AND FISH. Palissy Ware. 49·3 x 37·1 cms. *London, Wallace Collection*. Reproduced by permission of the Trustees of the Wallace Collection.

A typical *pièce rustique*, coloured largely in blue and grey.

Lit: A. V. B. Norman, *Catalogue of Ceramics in the Wallace Collection* (forthcoming), No. C174.

154. PORTRAIT OF A MAN. By Titian, *c.* 1550. Canvas, 223 x 151 cms. *Cassel, Gemälde-galerie*. (Photograph: Museum.)

No satisfactory identification for the sitter has yet been proposed and thus no explanation of an unusually elaborate portrait. A date of *c.* 1550 is usually agreed.

Lit: Valcanover, op. cit., No. 332; Pallucchini, op. cit., 301.

155. HEAD OF CHRIST. Detail of pl. 156. (Photograph: Mas.)

156. 'LO SPASIMO DI SICILIA'. By Raphael, 1517. Canvas, 306 x 230 cms. *Madrid, Prado*. (Photograph: Anderson.)

Painted for the convent of S. Maria dello Spasimo, Palermo. For the composition's duplication in tapestry and maiolica, see Pope-Hennessy, loc. cit.

Lit: Camesasca, op. cit., 65; J. Pope-Hennessy, *Raphael*, 1970, 27.

157. ASSUMPTION AND CORONATION OF THE VIRGIN ('THE ASSUNTA'). By Titian, finished 1518. Panel, 690 x 360 cms. *Venice, S. Maria Gloriosa dei Frari*. (Photograph: Anderson.)

Commissioned for the Frari in 1516; solemnly unveiled, 20 March 1518, and probably found disconcerting, according to tradition, by the commissioners.

Lit: Valcanover, op. cit., No. 82; Pallucchini, op. cit., 253.

158. APOSTLES. Detail of pl. 157. (Photograph: Anderson.)

Books for Further Reading

Books not articles are chiefly cited in the paragraphs which follow and they have been restricted as far as possible to works available in English. The purpose is to provide some hints for following up topics touched on particularly in the text.

The vastness of the Renaissance as a subject, and its vast bibliography, may make a selective list of books the more welcome as guidance. Many of the books cited below also contain good bibliographies. On the general topic of the Renaissance, some books are mentioned at the back of the companion volume, *Early Renaissance*, 1967 and the reader should also consult the comparable paragraphs at the back of *Mannerism*, 1967 by John Shearman. Useful monographs and specific studies, including periodical literature, are sometimes cited in the notes to the illustrations in these volumes and the present one.

As background to the early part of the period there is now J. R. Hale's *Renaissance Europe 1480–1520*, 1971 (in the Fontana History series), treating aspects of the period rather than surveying it chronologically. The subsequent volume in the same series is admirably clear on a large, complex subject: G. R. Elton, *Reformation Europe 1517–1559*, 1970. For extracts from key texts of this period, there is a convenient paperback, *The Age of Reformation*, 1956 (Anvil) by R. H. Bainton. A well-illustrated survey is A. G. Dickens, *Reformation and Society in sixteenth century Europe*, 1966; and by the same author is *The Counter-Reformation*, 1971 ed. More specialized is L. Spitz, *The Religious Renaissance of the German Humanists*, 1963.

For the French cultural background, some interesting essays are collected in *French Humanism 1470–1600*, W. L. Gundersheimer (ed.), 1969 and see also A. Denieul-Cormier, *The Renaissance in France* (trans. A. and C. Fremantle) 1969. For the world of Erasmus, M. Mann Phillips, *Erasmus on his times*, paperback ed., 1967, provides a shortened version of the *Adages*; by the same author is *Erasmus and the Northern Renaissance*, 1949. See also G. Marlier, *Erasme et la peinture flamande de son temps*, 1954. An admirable synthesis of history and culture is provided by J. Buxton, *Elizabethan Taste*, 1965 ed.; see also the catalogue of the Tate Gallery exhibition *The Elizabethan Image*, 1969–70. Although obviously out-dated in some respects, L. Einstein, *The Italian Renaissance in England*, 1902, contains useful comment and even more useful appendices and bibliography. For Italy, there seem especially good recent works connected with Venice, including B. Pullan, *Rich and Poor in Renaissance Venice*, 1971; D. S. Chambers, *The Imperial Age of Venice 1380-1580*, 1970; and *Renaissance Venice*, J. R. Hale (ed.), 1973 (studies on humanism, German-Venetian artistic contacts, etc.). In general, see *The Late Italian Renaissance*, E. Cochrane (ed.), 1970, and also J. Rouchette, *La Renaissance que nous a léguée Vasari*, 1959. A very well-illustrated and substantial guide to literature of the period is the relevant volume of the *Storia della Letteratura Italiana*; IV, *Il Cinquecento*, 1966.

A valuable conspectus of European literature of the period is offered by the Pelican Guide, *The Continental Renaissance 1500-1600*, A. J. Krailsheimer (ed.), 1971, with biographies and accounts of writers and work not always easily available elsewhere.

Further, for Shakespeare and the visual arts, an apparently understudied topic, see A. H. R. Fairchild, *Shakespeare and the Arts of Design* (University of Missouri Studies, Vol. XII), 1937, and an interesting brief article by A. F. Blunt in *J.W.(C.)I.*, (Vol II), 1939, 260-62. An attractive exhibition at Manchester, *The Age of Shakespeare*, 1964, offers a succinct background survey. For art theory at Venice see M. W. Roskill, *Dolce's 'Aretino' and Venetian Art Theory of the Cinquecento*, 1968. For some brief discussion of Sannazaro, Michelangelo's poetry, etc., see L. Malagoli, *Le Contraddizioni del Rinascimento*, 1968, and for some 'drop-out' figures like Anton Francesco Doni, consult P. F. Grendler, *Critics of the Italian World (1530-1560)*, 1969. An interesting pair of themes are dealt with in A. Tenenti, *Il Senso della Morte e l'Amore della Vita nel Rinascimento*, 1957 (covers Italy and France only). For the literary aspects of praise and fame, see particularly O. B. Hardison, *The Enduring Monument: A Study of the Idea of Praise in Renaissance literary theory and practice*, 1962. Among studies of the triumphal theme in the visual arts: W. Weisbach, *Trionfi*, 1919, J. Chartrou, *Les Entrées Solennelles et Triomphales à la Renaissance*, 1928 (for France only) and also the studies collected in *Les Fêtes de la Renaissance*, J. Jacquot (ed.), 1956 (2 vols), useful on celebrations for Charles V, etc.

On the large topic of the Renaissance and science, there is a highly readable, succinct and scholarly account, much, and gratefully, drawn-on here, *The Scientific Renaissance 1450-1630*, by M. Boas, 1970 ed., and two books by W. P. D. Wightman, *Science and the Renaissance,* 1962, and *Science in a Renaissance Society*, 1972. See also A. G. R. Smith's illustrated account, *Science and Society in the Sixteenth and Seventeenth Centuries*, 1972, and also A. McLean, *Humanism and the Rise of Science in Tudor England,* 1972. For discussion and biographical accounts of some individual figures, consult: C. D. O'Malley, *Andreas Vesalius of Brussels,* 1964; C. Ore, *Cardano, The Gambling Scholar*, 1953 (and Cardano's *The Book of my Life*, trans. and ed. J. Stoner, 1931); F. A. Yates, *Giordano Bruno and the Hermetic Tradition*, 1964; W. Pagel, *Paracelsus*, 1958; C. G. Nauert Jr, *Agrippa and the Crisis of Renaissance Thought*, 1965; and see also the catalogue of the well-presented exhibition, *Copernicus and the New Astronomy*, British Museum, 1973. On the abstruse question of Parmigianino's interest in alchemy, etc., see cautiously M. Fagiolo dell' Arco, *Il Parmigianino: un saggio sull' ermetismo nel Cinquecento*, 1970. A fundamental book on its subject is D. P. Walker, *Spiritual and Demonic Magic from Ficino to Campanella*, 1958.

On geographical travel and exploration: R. R. Cawley, *Unpathed Waters*, 1940, is concerned with the influence of voyages on Elizabethan literature. As fascinating as scholarly is J. H. Elliott, *The Old World and the New, 1492-1650* (Wiles Lectures), 1970, gratefully utilized here. See also B. Penrose, *Travel and Discovery in the Renaissance, 1420-1620*, 1952.

Renaissance concepts of art's superiority to Nature are discussed usefully by J. Bialastocki in a paper in *The Renaissance and Mannerism* (Studies in Western Art, Vol. II) 1963, 19 ff.; see also E. W. Tayler, *Nature and Art in Renaissance Literature*, 1964. A variety of topics, including a valuable essay on Sabba da Castiglione, is assembled in E. Bonaffé, *Etudes sur l'Art et la Curiosité*, 1902. A much wider range of topics, as indicated, by various authors in *Art, Science and History in the Renaissance*, C. S. Singleton (ed.), 1968. The whole cultural field is surveyed in J. Delumeau, *La Civilisation de la Renaissance*, 1967. A symposium, on such topics as music, the equestrian statue and Marguerite de Valois, is commemorated by *Aspects of the Renaissance*, A. R. Lewis (ed.), 1967, and a ranging series of papers on Renaissance themes is presented in the volume for W. K. Ferguson, *Florilegium Historiale*, J. G. Rowe and W. H. Stockdale (ed.), 1971. A variety of his own papers is collected, under the sub-title *Studies in the art of the Renaissance*, by E. H. Gombrich, in *Symbolic Images*, 1972. Art as such is not dealt with here (though there are references in the catalogue of illustrations) but see the useful Sources and Documents series, particularly R. Klein and H. Zerner, *Italian Art 1500-1600*, 1966.

Index

Page numbers printed in *italics* denote illustrations